PERFECTED STEEL

TERRIBLE CRYSTAL

PERFECTED STEEL

TERRIBLE CRYSTAL

An Unconventional Source Book of
Spiritual Readings
in Poetry and Prose

The Seabury Press / New York

1981
The Seabury Press
815 Second Avenue
New York, N.Y. 10017

Library of Congress Cataloging in Publication Data
Main entry under title:

Perfected steel, terrible crystal.

1. Christian literature.   I. O'Gorman, Ned,
1929–
PN6071.R4P4   808.8′0382   80-27726
ISBN 0-8164-2330-X (pbk.)   AACR1

Acknowledgments

For permission to reprint the following works in this volume by each of the following writers grateful acknowledgment is made to the holders of copyright, publishers, or representatives named below and on the following pages (vi and vii), which constitutes an extension of the copyright page.

HENRY ADAMS, from *Mont Saint Michel and Chartres*. Originally published by Houghton Mifflin Co. Reprinted by permission of the publisher.

CHARLES BAUDELAIRE, from *The Flowers of Evil*, "Spleen LXXX", transl. by Roy Campbell. "Spleen LXVIII", transl. by Kenneth O. Hanson.

SAMUEL BECKETT, *That Time*. Copyright © 1976 by Samuel Beckett. Reprinted by permission of Grove Press, Inc.

LOUISE BOGAN, from The Blue Estuaries. Reprinted by permission of Farrar, Straus & Giroux, Inc.

DIETRICH BONHOEFFER, abridged from pp. 110-113, 116-122, of *Life Together*, transl. by John W. Doberstein. Copyright © 1954 by Harper & Row, Publishers, Inc. Reprinted by permission of the publisher.

FERNAND BRAUDEL, excerpts from pp. 1243-1244 of *The Mediterranean and the Mediterranean World in the Age of Philip II*, Volume II, transl. by Sian Reynolds. English translation copyright © 1973 by Wm. Collins Sons Ltd. and Harper & Row, Publishers, Inc. Reprinted by permission of the publishers.

JOSEPH BRODSKY, "Nunc Dimittis", pp. 165-167 in *Selected Poems*, transl. by George L. Kline. English translation copyright © 1973 by George L. Kline. Reprinted by permission of Harper & Row, Publishers, Inc. "December 24, 1971", from *A Part of Speech*, transl. by Alan Myers. Translation copyright © 1973 by Farrar Straus & Giroux, Inc. Reprinted by permission of the publisher.

HELDER CAMARA, from *Christian Readings*. Copyright © 1972 by the Catholic Book Publishing Corp. Reprinted by permission of the publisher.

ALEXANDER CARMICHAEL, *Celtic Prayers*. Copyright © 1981 by Vineyard Books, Inc. Reprinted by permission of The Seabury Press, Inc.

CARLO CARRETTO, from *Letters From the Desert*. Copyright © 1972 by Orbis Books, Maryknoll. Reprinted by permission of Orbis Books and Darton Longman & Todd, Ltd.

C. P. CAVAFY, from *Collected Poems*, transl. by Edmund Keeley and Philip Sherrard. Copyright © 1975 by the translators. Reprinted by permission of Princeton University Press and The Hogarth Press, Ltd., London.

GREGORY CORSO, from *Happy Birthday of Death*. Copyright © 1960 by New Directions. Reprinted by permission of New Directions Pub. Corp.

EMILY DICKINSON. Reprinted by permission of the publishers and the Trustees of Amherst College from *The Poems of Emily Dickinson*, edited by Thomas H. Johnson, Cambridge, Mass.: The Belknap Press of Harvard University Press. Copyright © 1951, 1955, 1979 by the President and Fellows of Harvard College.

ABBIE HUSTON EVANS. Reprinted by permission of Harcourt Brace Jovanovich, Inc.

JULIAN GREEN, from *Diary 1928-1957*. Copyright © 1964 by Harcourt Brace & World, Inc. and the Havrill Press. Reprinted by permission of Harcourt Brace Jovanovich, Inc.

GUSTAVO GUTIERREZ, from *Conscientization for Liberation*. Copyright © 1971 by the Secretariat for Latin America. Reprinted by permission.

A. D. HOPE. Courtesy of A. D. Hope.

GERARD MANLEY HOPKINS, from the fourth edition (1967) of *The Poems of Gerard Manley Hopkins*, edited by W. H. Gardner and N. H. MacKenzie, published by Oxford University Press for the Society of Jesus. Excerpts from the Journals, reprinted by permission of the Society of Jesus.

RANDALL JARRELL, from *The Complete Poems*. Copyright © 1951 by Randall Jarrell. Reprinted by permission of Farrar, Straus & Giroux, Inc.

DAVID JONES, "Religion and the Muses", and "Changes in the Coronation Service", from *Epoch and Artist*. Copyright ©1959 by David Jones. "A, a, a, Domine Deus" from *The Sleeping Lord*. Copyright © 1974 by David Jones. Reprinted by permission of Faber & Faber, Ltd., London.

JULIAN OF NORWICH, from *Revelations of Divine Love*, transl. by Clifton Wolters. Copyright © 1966 by the translator. Reprinted by permission of Penguin Books, Ltd.

VERA LACHMANN. Reprinted by permission of the author.

ROBERT LOWELL, "The Crucifix", from *Lord Weary's Castle*. Copyright © 1946 by Robert Lowell. Reprinted by permission of Harcourt Brace Jovanovich, Inc.

THOMAS MERTON, "The Roots of War", from The Catholic Worker, October 1961. Reprinted by permission of The Catholic Worker.

ALICE MORRIS, "Angel Beings". Reprinted by permission of the author.

PABLO NERUDA, from *Selected Poems*, edited by Ben Belitt. Copyright © 1961 by Ben Belitt. Reprinted by permission of Grove Press, Inc.

HENRI J. M. NOUWEN, from *The Way of the Heart*. Copyright © 1981 by Henri J. M. Nouwen. Reprinted by permission of the Seabury Press, Inc.

CHARLES PEGUY, from *God Speaks*, transl. by Julian Green. Copyright © 1954 by Pantheon Books, Inc. Reprinted by permission of Alfred A. Knopf, Inc.

J. PIAGET, from *Judgement and Reasoning in the Child*, transl. by Marjorie Warden. Copyright © 1968 by Routledge & Kegan Paul, Ltd. Reprinted by permission of Humanities Press, and Routledge & Kegan Paul, Ltd. London.

F. T. PRINCE. Courtesy of F. T. Prince.

KARL RAHNER, from *Dictionary of Theology* by Karl Rahner and Herbert Vorgrimler. Copyright © 1965, 1976, 1981 by Herder KG. Used by permission of The Crossroad Publishing Co., New York.

JOHN CROWE RANSOM, from *Selected Poems*, Third Edition Revised and Enlarged. Copyright © 1969. Reprinted by permission of Alfred A. Knopf, Inc.

PAUL RICOEUR, from *The Symbolism of Evil*. Copyright © 1967 by Paul Ricoeur. Reprinted by permission of Harper & Row, Publishers, Inc.

RAINER MARIA RILKE, "An Archaic Torso of Apollo", transl. by W. D. Snodgrass. Copyright © 1968 by W. D. Snodgrass. Reprinted by permission of Harper & Row, Publishers, Inc.

ST. JOHN PERSE, from *Anabasis*, transl. by T. S. Eliot. Copyright ©1949 by Harcourt Brace Jovanovich, Inc. Reprinted by permission of Harcourt Brace Jovanovich, Inc., and Faber & Faber, Ltd.

E. F. SCHUMACHER, *Small Is Beautiful: Economics as if People Mattered* (New York: Harper & Row, London: Blond & Briggs, 1973), pp. 277-281. Copyright © 1973 by E. F. Schumacher. Reprinted by permission of the publishers.

FREYA STARK, "Love", and "Death" from *Perseus in the Wind*. Selections from *A Peak in Darien*. Reprinted by permission of John Murray Publishers, Ltd.

READINGS FROM THE SECOND VATICAN COUNCIL, from *Christian Readings*. Copyright © 1972 by the Catholic Book Publishing Corp. Reprinted by permission of the publisher.

SIMONE WEIL, from *Waiting for God*, transl. by Emma Craufurd. Copyright © 1951 by G. P. Putnam's Sons. Reprinted by permission of the publisher.

GLENWAY WESCOTT, "The Odor of Rosemary". Reprinted by permission of the author.

RICHARD WILBUR, from *Advice to a Prophet and Other Poems*. Copyright © 1961 by Richard Wilbur. Reprinted by permission of Harcourt Brace Jovanovich, Inc.

YVOR WINTERS, "St. Teresa of Avila". Reprinted with the permission of The Ohio University Press, Athens.

WILLIAM BUTLER YEATS, "The Second Coming", from *Collected Poems*. Copyright © 1924 by Macmillan Publishing Co., Inc. renewed in 1952 by Bertha Georgie Yeats, Anne Yeats, and M. B. Yeats and Macmillan London, Ltd. Reprinted by permission of Macmillan Company.

CONTENTS

3 / ASPECTS OF ATTENTION

4 / THE CONVULSIONS OF TIME

5 / WAR

6 / WISDOM

7 / THE DESERT

8 / THE COMIC SENSE, THE TRAGIC SENSE

9 / PRAYER

10 / THINGS OF THIS WORLD

14 / RITUAL AND SIGN

15 / SOLUTIONS

16 / THE MYSTERY OF FAULT AND THE REDEEMED HEART

17 / CONVERSION

18 / THE GATHERING UP OF
ALL THE THREADS

Prelude

A, a, a, DOMINE DEUS

I said, Ah! what shall I write?
I enquired up and down.
                    (He's tricked me before
with his manifold lurking-places.)
I looked for His symbol at the door.
I have looked for a long while
                    at the textures and contours
I have run a hand over the trivial intersections.
I have journeyed among the dead forms
causation projects from pillar to pylon.
I have tired the eyes of the mind
                    regarding the colours and lights.
I have felt for His Wounds
                    in nozzles and containers.
I have wondered for the automatic devices.
I have tested the inane patterns
                    without prejudice.
I have been on my guard
                    not to condemn the unfamiliar.
For it is easy to miss Him
                    at the turn of a civilisation.

   I have watched the wheels go round in case I might see the living
creatures like the appearance of lamps, in case I might see the Living
God projected from the Machine. I have said to the perfected steel, be
my sister and for the glassy towers I thought I felt some beginnings of
His creature, but *A, a, a, Domine Deus*, my hands found the glazed
work unrefined and the terrible crystal a stage-paste...*Eia, Domine
Deus*.

—David Jones

INTRODUCTION

This collection of prose and poetry is, I fear, a rather too intimate and eccentric description of what seems to me to be the *nature of prayer*. But I could find no other way to search out the contents of this book save through identifying the experience of prayer in my own life. I sought writers who thought a little as I do, who in their wry and clumsy dance with life dance a little as I do. I think of prayer in a common fashion, a bit large-boned for some of my friends, I am sure. But for me, prayer is not just an act of piety, of praise, of petition. I think of prayer as a way to understand the world. Once I know a little about the world, then I can praise the God who made it. I find that nearly all the books I love to read are prayers—some pagan, some outright heterodox, but prayers nevertheless. They bend the stiffness of my heart a bit toward God.

I was searching as well for a text that could be of use to preachers and other people who are often at a loss to find suitable texts for sermons or instruction. It is helpful to be able to poke around in poems and novels, philosophy, history, and theology for one might just find there a word, a phrase, a passage that eases some perplexity, shatters some darkness, banishes some terrible demon, or transforms despair, even at the tip of horror, into a semblance of peace. I remember that once, at a moment of rabid grief, a priest suggested, as I trembled my spirit through the grill of the confessional, that I go home and read *The New York Times*, especially Red Smith's sports column, I did not do what he bid me to do. I was brazen enough in my faith *not* to leave the church broken and damaged in hope. (How would I have felt had he sent me rather to Peguy's great tract on hope?)

In July 1980, during a visit to Rome, the city I love most in the world, I turned a corner, and looked up into the sky, the cornice of a palazzo square against it, pots of geraniums along the edge, vines tumbling from windows. I thought then, as I usually do in Rome, of the fabric of the world, how in that city it seems to glow more radiantly than any where, where human nature is lost in a radiance of mortality so terrible and beautiful that one expects no more of heaven than what one sees in Rome. Suddenly, for no reason, I thought of Misia Sert and Mother Assumpta O.S.B. Those two women, each in her own way, knew how to live. Perhaps, I thought, I ought to plan a book that they might like to read on their separate clouds, for I am (and was) sure Divine Wisdom has a place in its geography for each of them.

Misia Sert was a woman of no exceptional genius. Her lovers and some of her friends were often little more than well-bred lounge lizards, wrecks of feeling and misguided sensuality, but in some of her friendships—those for Diaghilev and Chanel, especially, and in the court of genius that surrounded them—she did, in the corruscating energy of her life, add a decoration of sensibility and beauty to her days on earth. Mother Assumpta of the Abbey of Regina Laudis in Bethlehem, Connecticut, died in 1979, in the large austerity of her cell. She knew nothing of Misia's world. But she would not have found it uncongenial. Assumpta had an eye for the more perfect image of life in the person of Christ Jesus. She behind her grill in the cloister, I outside it, often talked of life and of love, of suffering and evil to a depth that troubled all my notions of spirituality. (Misia's life, of course, was tinged with the corruption of the belle époque, an era when grace could not often find its way into the ruckus of the *salons*.)

So, I worked to write this book for them, Misia and Assumpta, as an instruction on those parts of life that each might not know. And I wrote this book as an exercise, for me, in arriving at a definition of prayer. The great literature of my life has no exact theology. I enter its territories, travel its landscapes, peer over its boundaries, observe the inhabitants, and come away usually wiser and gentler, happier and sadder, my body and spirit suffering a sweet transformation. I do not ask more of literature—or philosophy, history, or theology—than that. I seldom read for information. When, for instance, I read the massive study of the Mediterranean by Fernand Braudel, I come away with facts that he has transformed into a cosmology. He has added a cubit to my passion for this world. It is through a passion for this world that I can see beyond it, into the palisades and rich distances of eternity.

Some of these writers are my friends: Glenway Wescott, Dame Freya Stark, Richard Wilbur, Vera Lachmann, Richard Eberhart. Some of those friends are dead: Robert Lowell, Elizabeth Bishop, David Jones. But each writer in this book—a commonplace book of a very common

man—has perceived that slant of light on the horizon, that reverbera-
tion at the center of passion, that shift in the seasons, that rending of the
fabric of history, that music within the silences of the mind, which
cannot be anything but divine in origin. Each selection is perfect in its
singular fashion. Some may loom larger in the vanity of judgment.
None fail in a radiant excellence of style. Gutierrez, his theology of
liberation, St. Francis, his humbling of the bishops, Neruda, his
sensuous, hard-boned lyricism breathing glory into artichokes, each a
prodigy of exactitude, each prophetic in his conclusions about
existence.

In assembling this anthology, I sought out the "hidden God," or,
more exactly, the hiding places of the "hidden God." By indirection we
find our way out. By the craziest paths we enter into a vista of the
sweetest symmetry. The Lord Jesus is hidden to no exclamation of joy,
to no bellow of rage, to no catastrophe of sexual bafflement, to no
bloody slaughter in the streets. I have found that the Christian sense of
the world is often found in a sense of the world that transcends the
merely Christian, that strains beyond it, by being athwart it, by even
denying it. I have not included many contemporary "Christian"
writers, because I find most of them bores. Thomas Merton is here—
but not as a spiritual writer; to me he is a prophet, minor, but perfect in
timbre. I admire Bernard Lonergan, S.J., but I think he is a little
extreme in the texture of his thought for the more common use I would
wish for this book. Rahner is here for reasons I shall presently explain.
But essentially this curious collection is prayer—a series of prayers I
would wish I might dare pray some day.

Since I am a Roman Catholic of ordinary persuasion, radical only in
fits and starts, I thought it wise to scatter, like mustard seeds, some of
the theological prose of Karl Rahner, just to keep everything more or
less tending toward the orthodox. It may seem a little weakminded, this
cautious theological seeding, but my knees do go a bit weak when I
join Misia, Assumpta, Cavafy, St. Francis, and David Jones into
communion in a heaven that has about it the bustle and savour of
a Proustian "evening," not of paradise. But the world *is* a romp and I
have chosen to think the Lord likes that notion.

I look forward to owning this book myself. My life in New York City
is, in its boisterous way, quite a lark. I have a brilliant and sassy son; I
love my work and I go rather too much to the opera. But now and then
my life—like that of most people—can be massively brutal. There is no
stillness. Dirt and violence and fear clamp down upon the skull and
remain there. On those days, when the city is an abyss, I throw a book
into my satchel and read it during those awful hours spent on subways
and buses.

I often need to be inspired, lifted up, exalted. Although this book may prove useful in many ways, I would be delighted if it became a truly inspirational book for a reader now and then. It is such a book for me.

Burning Tree Road
Greenwich Connecticut August 1980

1

POINTS
OF VIEW

ST. JOHN CHRYSOSTOM

All Flesh Is Like Grass

It is always in season but now more than ever is it seasonable to say:
Vanity of vanities and all is vanity.... Where is the gay torchlight now?
Where are the clapping hands and the dances and the assemblies and
the festivals? Where the green garlands and the curtains floating?
Where the cry of the town and the cheers of the hippodrome, and the
noisy flattering lungs of the spectators there? All that is gone: a wind
blew and on the sudden cast the leaves and showed us the tree bare and
all that was left of it from the root upwards shaking—the gale that
struck it was so fearfully strong and threatened, indeed, to tear it up
root-whole, or shatter it this way and that, even to the rending of the
grain of the timber. Where now are the friends, the make-believers,
followers of the fashion? Where are the suppers and feasts? Where the
swarm of hangers-on? The strong wine decanting all day long, the
cooks and the daintily dressed table, the attendants on greatness and all
the words and ways they have to please? They were all night and
dreaming: now it is day and they are vanished. They were spring
flowers, and, the spring being over, they all are faded together. They
were a shadow, and it has travelled on beyond. They were smoke, and it
has gone out in the air. They were bubbles, and are broken. They were
cobwebs, and are swept away. And so this spiritual refrain is left us to

sing, coming in again and again with: Vanity of vanities and all is vanity. Oh this is the verse that should be written on walls, and in clothing and at markets and at home and by waysides and on doors and over entries and above all in the conscience of each, written wherever we look that we may read it whatever we do. While this swindle of the business of life and this wearing of masks and playing of characters is taken for truth by the many, this is the verse that every day, at dinner and supper and every meeting between men, I wish that each one of you could be bringing to his neighbour's ear and hearing from his neighbour's tongue: Vanity of vanities, all is vanity.

GLENWAY WESCOTT

from *The Odor of Rosemary*

There was an English lady in the eighteenth century whose husband immortalized her in his diary by a word of praise of her sweet breath. Their name has slipped my mind, and I often hope to come upon some trace of them in a book or in a piece of literary journalism—where probably I learned about them in the first place—in order to procure his text in its entirety and to learn more, haunted by their mutual tenderness and pleasure. Unless my memory is at fault, the word of praise was "balmy."

Now and then, an instance like this suggests how one may be able to perpetuate at least a part of the life of people whom one has known well and long, observed closely and with sensitivity intensified for some reason: by recording a little uniqueness, an uninventable trait or fact. I have had that lady's sweetness in my mind for twenty-five years, two hundred years (more or less) after her death and entombment. It is a beginning of immortality.

With thoughts astray, I remember reading that somewhere on earth there is a kind of soil, lime and loam commingled, that has a human fragrance, a living and healthy and clean fragrance; no suggestion of putrefaction or of the tomb or the grave. And even as I wrote that preceding sentence—memory leading to memory, or begetting upon imagination a substitute for the forgotten matter—the name of the diarist and his wife came to me: Torrington.

Odors of course evoke not only sentiment and lust and various remembrances but fear as well, especially childish, or atavistic, irrational fear.

Some years ago my friend Will Chandlee came from Philadelphia to spend a spring afternoon with me, misty and warm, almost hot, and we walked up toward Jug Mountain on an abandoned road and came to a small stone ruin with an old seedling apple tree thrust up through it, and poison ivy cloaking it; and there three or four young rat snakes had come out of hibernation and lay on the largest stone, like a loose knot or an indecipherable monogram, gradually coming to their senses. Will picked one of them up and played with it, and afterward, on our way down out of the mountain, with a mischievous smile, narrowing his thick eyelashes, held out his rosy fingers for me to sniff.

Until that moment I don't think it had occurred to me that snakes had an odor; and the surprise of the smell of my friend's fingers verged on fright, although I hadn't been consciously afraid of snakes since my childhood in Wisconsin. And the form that the fright took was a wild over-stimulation of memory: all the reptiles that had ever impressed me in rapid succession with almost simultaneous effects, overlapping somewhat, like flash photos, like a triple or quadruple or quintuple dream: a garter snake that I stoned to death at aged six or seven, for which my mother reproved me and sent me to bed hungry; a cobra that I watched through plate glass in the Snake House in the Bronx, upright on its pedestal of tail, until it began to watch me and finally struck at me, that is, at the plate glass, bruising its round nose; and a heavy old cottonmouth encountered by Somerset Maugham and me when walking along a rice marsh in South Carolina, which tried to bar the way to us—with a good-sized stick that I had noticed on the levee and went back for, I was able to push it down the embankment—all these creatures in and out of my mind so swiftly that when the daydream ceased, there Will was still holding out his soiled, strong fingers.

One year at Stone-blossom we had a five-foot black racer, a beauty, glossy-skinned and white of chin, as though bearded, with a most beautiful swaying, dancing motion. Once or twice it came up on the front steps and twined itself into the iron railing. My housekeeper, Anna, was afraid of it, and I was afraid that she would incite her brother to destroy it. I gave her a talking-to on the subject. "Black racers are the natural enemies of copperheads," I said.

There were (perhaps still are) copperheads in our part of New Jersey. A friendly acquaintance of mine, a retired career woman, bought a stone house and barn in our hills and found a family of the venomous, thick-set, bright-brown, four-nostrilled creatures entrenched in a fallen stone wall, and it took years of vigilance with her shotgun to rid herself of them.

"We don't want copperheads," I firmly told my small, co-resident, superstitious, foreign female. "The friendly and strong black racer will protect us," I insisted.

"Well, I guess, if it's so, what you say, we'd better not do anything to it." Upon which she took her vacuum cleaner and dustmop and started upstairs, but turned, half way up, and spoke again. This time she called my reptilean protégé *he* instead of it, with emphasis. "You know, *he* caused all the trouble between the men and the women. You know that, don't you?"

Yes, I knew it, but I didn't (I don't) believe it. The widespread if not universal snake-horror is not, in my opinion, sexual or antisexual. A snake does not even resemble a penis; it resembles a stray bit of intestine. It is a living clyster or hypodermic syringe full of poison and pain. Human memory goes farther back than we realize. Reptiles were once the largest, mightiest inhabitants of this planet, and they held sway for one hundred and thirty million years. Brief, brief, the birds and the mammals, and man the briefest. If life be computed on a scale of twenty-four hours, our share has been six minutes. In characteristically human excess of cerebration and fantasy we hide from ourselves truths of this kind, except for folklore and certain intimations of our flesh and blood. Truisms are a part of our access to the time before our personal time. The prime cause of animosity is fear, and often enough, at the start, it was a wise, legitimate fear.

Hyperaesthesia I must admit to, affecting many of my sentiments and ideals and my style of writing as well as my potential of bodily pleasure and displeasure. When I was young, just by taking a deep breath, I could identify friends as they came into the room behind my back. Then unfortunately, in middle life, I smoked three or four packs of cigarettes a day, letting the birthright of my nose deteriorate a good deal.

Nevertheless, even now, the things that I enjoy the smell of are a great resource and a daydream to me. The cloud of flowers all over the country, from the first narcissus in the spring, almost poisonously sweet, to the last chrysanthemum in the fall, the flower that smells like an herb. In midsummer most of the garden herbs and herbaceous weeds. Hay, both when it is new-mown and when the sun has been working on it, readying it for the appetites of horses and cattle; and corn, when it is in tassel and in silk. A goodly number of physical fragrances, human and otherwise, in nature worship and in simple affection no less than in love and sex: for example, the fatty, smoky odor of sheep contrasting with the tart grass as they nibble it; for example, young sunburned skin with its mist of sweat.

All summer long, on Friday mornings, when I write out my weekly shopping list—we are now in our second New Jersey house, which is called Hay-meadows; my mother has died; my Anna has reached social security age and gone to live with relatives in Oregon; and I have to do my own shopping and other such chores—I think, with almost a tingle around my nostrils and along my upper lip, of a handful of lush, fragile basil that I shall help myself to in the backyard of my friend, the local Italian-American butcher, although it is only the fresh smell of basil, not the Italian taste, that I delight in. All winter long, I delight in a handful of dried vetiver roots in a chest of drawers amid my handkerchiefs. It looks like a model of some portion of the nervous system of the brain that a biology teacher might use to illustrate a lecture or a lesson; and it gives forth a soft and pale pepperiness.

Any extreme of the senses works both ways. Brahma's goose, the ancient Hindu symbol of discrimination, given a mixture of milk and water, is (or was) able to sip the milk and leave the water behind; and doubtless the same could be said of it in re agreeable and disagreeable odors. No such thing can be alleged or expected of a mere mortal. The more extraordinarily we enjoy pleasant olfactory experiences, the less apt we are to hold our breath against what sickens us and what we hate and fear.

I had a dead mouse in my dear dwelling place a month ago, between the outer and the inner wall, or perhaps between the kitchen ceiling and the floor of one of the guest bedrooms above it: worse and worse whiffs of putrefaction, which gradually quenched itself and faded away, all too gradually. It took more than a week, by which time my sensory capacity, overstimulated by this real and small misfortune, began to imagine uncertainties, unrealities. Outside the house, with the dead stink in my nostrils, I sensed that a live rat had been there, to and fro in the night, craving the garbage can; and I guessed that live squirrels were beginning to establish winter quarters amid boxes of valuable books in the attic over the garage. Back indoors, I would retreat to the opposite end of the house, beyond the range of the rottenness of the tiny body; but that didn't help much. Memory and lapse of memory joined in with the malodorous present tense. Everywhere, in queasiness and in temporary self-pity, I went on to discover other olfactory woes: sluggish plumbing, although (come to think of it) the plumber had fixed it the week before; clean clothes that I kept resmelling and finally sent back to the dry-cleaner; cow manure perhaps picked up in the pasture and dried tight on the sole of a shoe—but I couldn't find any such shoe.

This same excitability may enter into one's human relations also. One of the dozen human beings who I have loved longest and most loyally has always had, to my sense, a faint but troubling halitosis; and with the strange observation that no one else has seemed troubled or inhibited by it, I have pretended not to be. Morality (I believe) requires this of me.

On the whole I have a happy nature. Happiness (I think) obliges me to state that within my own experience, in my native part of the world at mid-point in the twentieth century, in average prosperity and good health, prior to senility, fragrance predominates over stench. Delight is all around us if we have the energy to experience it, the wit to think about it. For one thing, disgust lowers the level of sensation, whereas delight escalates it. Nothing rancid or putrid or greasy or garlicky stays in the mind as long or as precisely as various exhalations out of the mouths of flowers—such as night-flowering nicotiana white-faced in the twilight, such as white iris, purer and more mysterious than any rose—or the sweat of certain leaves when chafed, scenting the lucky thumb and forefinger that have done the chafing.

But there is a balancing factor, penalty and bad addiction, in this kind of enjoyment of life day in and day out: little by little you find yourself in the grip of a wild desire to live forever. Death is the great snake, the one and only thing that overwhelms all of us entirely in due course, in absolute parity and absolute unacceptability. And the desire to live forever is its premonitory shadow, falling on us well ahead of the fact.

When I was a small boy in Wisconsin I had a high-pitched and fairly strong boy-soprano voice; the musically trained wife of a local banker gave me some singing lessons; and once in a while I was asked to sing at funerals and was paid three dollars for doing so, standing at the head of the open coffin, not looking down. In consequence of this the great aura of roses, the moist and sluggish emanation of lilies also, seem to me sorrowful.

The sense of smell is apt to inspire or at least intensify pathos as nausea; to add to the thrust of grief into the heart as to that of fear into the mind. Late in life, when emotions of relinquishment and farewell are obligatory, nothing is more touching than the spiciness of fallen autumn leaves, rustling at the weight of one's foot, caressing one's ankles. How many autumns can you look forward to? In due course you know how many, how few; and on certain afternoons, when you have expected good weather and the weather is bad, you feel a deprivation like the chop of an axe. It may be the last chance to observe the climax of the year, missed; the bonfire colors one more time, missed; one last throatful and lungful of the perfectly chilled, perfectly fermented air, missed!

I remember my mother, a few years before her death, with very little eyesight, but with a love of sweet odors and a detestation of the opposite as keen as my own, as she took her autumn walks, pausing to hold up her head and savor the dying breath of the vegetation, then peering down to the ground at every step, picking out of the vagueness that she could see a leaf here and there, stooping and collecting leaf after leaf. And I have begun to catch myself behaving like that, though with senses still almost intact.

Hyperaesthetic! as I have said above: it weighs in the balance between my youthfulness in some respects, still, and the preliminaries of senescence and acedia. I tell myself what Marianne Moore told the fiend in Rockefeller Plaza, "Banish sloth!"—knowing full well that this disgraceful sin is bound to develop and fill a vacuum in our human nature when the sins of lust and anger have been overcome, or have worn themselves out, with their own timetable. Quite often the distress of growing old is mainly inactivity and obesity, selfishness and self-criticism.

I believe that in my case simple hedonism, desire and gratitude having to do with sensuousness and sensuality, has somewhat saved me from what Auden has called the "glare of Nothing, our pernicious foe." Worst of all, the nothing in the flesh due to bad habit; the nothing in the brain, when one's work-morality and talent have disappointed one; the nothing in the whining heart, envious and jealous. When it has come to that, one goes on living in order to smell and to taste and to hear and to see and to touch.

LOUISE BOGAN

Men Loved Wholly Beyond Wisdom

> Men loved wholly beyond wisdom
> Have the staff without the banner.
> Like a fire in a dry thicket
> Rising within women's eyes
> Is the love men must return.
> Heart, so subtle now, and trembling,
> What a marvel to be wise,
> To love never in this manner!
> To be quiet in the fern
> Like a thing gone dead and still,
> Listening to the prisoned cricket
> Shake its terrible, dissembling
> Music in the granite hill.

Girl's Song

Winter, that is a fireless room
In a locked house, was our love's home.
The days turn, and you are not here,
O changing with the little year!

Now when the scent of plants half-grown
Is more the season's than their own
And neither sun nor wind can stanch
The gold forsythia's dripping branch,—

Another maiden, still not I,
Looks from some hill upon some sky,
And, since she loves you, and she must,
Puts her young cheek against the dust.

For a Marriage

She gives most dangerous sight
To keep his life awake:
A sword sharp-edged and bright
That darkness must not break,
Not ever for her sake.

With it he sees, deep-hidden,
The sullen other blade
To every eye forbidden,
That half her life has made,
And until now obeyed.

Now he will know his part:
Tougher than bone or wood,
To clasp on that barbed heart
That once shed its own blood
In its own solitude.

Henceforth, From the Mind

Henceforth, from the mind,
For your whole joy, must spring
Such joy as you may find
In any earthly thing,

And every time and place
Will take your thought for grace.

Henceforth, from the tongue,
From shallow speech alone,
Comes joy you thought, when young,
Would wring you to the bone,
Would pierce you to the heart
And spoil its stop and start.

Henceforward, from the shell,
Wherein you heard, and wondered
At oceans like a bell
So far from ocean sundered—
A smothered sound that sleeps
Long lost within lost deeps,

Will chime you change and hours,
The shadow of increase,
Will sound you flowers
Born under troubled peace—
Henceforth, henceforth
Will echo sea and earth.

Roman Fountain

Up from the bronze, I saw
Water without a flaw
Rush to its rest in air,
Reach to its rest, and fall.

Bronze of the blackest shade,
An element man-made,
Shaping upright the bare
Clear gouts of water in air.

O, as with arm and hammer,
Still it is good to strive
To beat out the image whole,
To echo the shout and stammer
When full-gushed waters, alive,
Strike on the fountain's bowl
After the air of summer.

Several Voices Out of a Cloud

Come, drunks and drug-takers; come, perverts unnerved!
Receive the laurel, given, though late, on merit; to whom
    and wherever deserved.

Parochial punks, trimmers, nice people, joiners true-blue,
Get the hell out of the way of the laurel. It is deathless
    And it isn't for you.

Solitary Observation Brought Back from a Sojourn in Hell

At midnight tears
Run into your ears.

Cartography

As you lay in sleep
I saw the chart
Of artery and vein
Running from your heart,

Plain as the strength
Marked upon the leaf
Along the length,
Mortal and brief,

Of your gaunt hand.
I saw it clear:
The wiry brand
Of the life we bear

Mapped like the great
Rivers that rise
Beyond our fate
And distant from our eyes.

PABLO NERUDA

The Poet

That time when I moved among happenings
in the midst of my mournful devotions; that time
when I cherished a leaflet of quartz,
at gaze in a lifetime's vocation.
I ranged in the markets of avarice
where goodness is bought for a price, breathed
the insensate miasmas of envy, the inhuman
contention of masks and existences.
I endured in the bog-dweller's element; the lily
that breaks on the water in a sudden
disturbance of bubbles and blossoms, devoured me.
Whatever the foot sought, the spirit deflected,
or sheered toward the fang of the pit.
So my poems took being, in travail
retrieved from the thorn, like a penance,
wrenched by a seizure of hands, out of solitude;
or they parted for burial
their secretest flower in immodesty's garden.
Estranged to myself, like shadow on water,
that moves through a corridor's fathoms,
I sped through the exile of each man's existence,
this way and that, and so, to habitual loathing;
for I saw that their being was this: to stifle
one half of existence's fullness like fish
in an alien limit of ocean. And there,
in immensity's mire, I encountered their death;
Death grazing the barriers,
Death opening roadways and doorways.

GERARD MANLEY HOPKINS

I Wake and Feel the Fell of Dark, Not Day

I wake and feel the fell of dark, not day.
What hours, O what black hours we have spent
This night! what sights you, heart, saw; ways you went!
And more must, in yet longer light's delay.

With witness I speak this. But where I say
Hours I mean years, mean life. And my lament
Is cries countless, cries like dead letters sent
To dearest him that lives alas! away.

I am gall, I am heartburn. God's most deep decree
Bitter would have me taste: my taste was me;
Bones built in me, flesh filled, blood brimmed the curse.

Selfyeast of spirit a dull dough sours. I see
The lost are like this, and their scourge to be
As I am mine, their sweating selves, but worse.

2

JESUS AND THE THREE-PERSONED GOD

GERARD MANLEY HOPKINS

For Sunday Evening Nov. 23 1879 at Bedford Leigh

Our Lord Jesus Christ, my brethren, is our hero, a hero all the world wants. You know how books of tales are written, that put one man before the reader and shew him off handsome for the most part and brave and call him My Hero or Our Hero. Often mothers make a hero of a son; girls of a sweetheart and good wives of a husband. Soldiers make a hero of a great general, a party of its leader, a nation of any great man that brings it glory, whether king, warrior, statesman, thinker, poet, or whatever it shall be. But Christ, he is the hero. He too is the hero of a book first by the tradition in the Church that it was so and by holy writers agreeing to suit those words to him/ Thou art beautiful in mould above the sons of men: we have even accounts of him written in early times. They tell us that he was moderately tall, well built and slender in frame, his features straight and beautiful, his hair inclining to auburn, parted in the midst, curling and clustering about the ears and neck as the leaves of a filbert, so they speak, upon the nut. He wore also a forked beard and this as well as the locks upon his head were never touched by razor or shears; neither, his health being perfect, could a hair ever fall to the ground. The account I have been quoting (it is from memory, for I cannot now lay my hand upon it) we do not indeed for certain know to be correct, but it has been current in the Church and many generations have drawn our Lord accordingly either in their own minds or in his images. Another proof of his beauty may be drawn from the words *proficiebat sapientia et aetate et gratia apud Deum et homines* (Luc. ii 52)/ he went forward in wisdom and bodily frame and favour with God and men; that is/ he pleased both God and men daily more and more by his growth of mind and body. But he could not have pleased by growth of body unless the body was strong, healthy, and beautiful that grew. But the best proof of all is this, that his body was the special work of the Holy Ghost. He was not born in nature's course, no man was his father; had he been born as others are he must have inherited some defect of figure or of constitution, from which no man born as fallen men are born is wholly free unless God interfere to keep him so. But his body was framed directly from heaven by the power of the Holy Ghost, of whom it would be unworthy to leave any the least botch or failing in his work. So the first Adam was moulded by God himself and Eve built up by God too out of Adam's rib and they could not but be pieces, both, of faultless workmanship: the same then and much more must Christ have been. His constitution too was tempered perfectly, he had neither disease nor the seeds of any: weariness he felt when he was wearied, hunger when he fasted, thirst when he had long gone without drink, but to the touch of sickness he was a stranger. I leave it to you, brethren, then to picture him, in whom the fulness of the godhead dwelt bodily, in his bearing how majestic, how strong and yet how lovely and lissome in his limbs, in his look how earnest, grave but kind. In his Passion all this strength was spent, this lissomness crippled, this beauty wrecked, this majesty beaten down. But now it is more than all restored, and for myself I make no secret I look forward with eager desire to seeing the matchless beauty of Christ's body in the heavenly light.

I come to his mind. He was the greatest genius that ever lived. You know what genius is, brethren—beauty and perfection in the mind. For perfection in the bodily frame distinguishes a man among other men his fellows: so may the mind be distinguished for its beauty above other minds and that is genius. Then when this genius is duly taught and trained, that is wisdom; for without training genius is imperfect and again wisdom is imperfect without genius. But Christ, we read, advanced in wisdom and in favour with God and men: now this wisdom, in which he excelled all men, had to be founded on an unrivalled genius. Christ then was the greatest genius that ever lived. You must not say, Christ needed no such thing as genius; his wisdom came from heaven, for he was God. To say so is to speak like the heretic Apollinaris, who said that Christ had indeed a human body but no soul, he needed no mind and soul, for his godhead, the Word of God, that stood for mind and soul in him. No, but Christ was perfect man and must have mind as well as body and that mind was, no question, of the rarest excellence and beauty; it was genius. As Christ lived and breathed and moved in a true and not a phantom human body and in that laboured, suffered, was crucified, died, and was buried; as he merited by acts of his human will; so he reasoned and planned and invented by acts of his own human genius, genius made perfect by wisdom of its own, not the divine wisdom only.

A witness to his genius we have in those men who being sent to arrest him came back empty handed, spellbound by his eloquence, saying/ Never man spoke like this man.

A better proof we have in his own words, his sermon on the mount, his parables, and all his sayings recorded in the Gospel. My brethren, we are so accustomed to them that they do not strike us as they do a stranger that hears them first, else we too should say/Never man, etc. No stories or parables are like Christ's, so bright, so pithy, so touching; no proverbs or sayings are such jewellery: they stand off from other men's thoughts like stars, like lilies in the sun; nowhere in literature is there anything to match the Sermon on the Mount: if there is let men bring it forward. Time does not allow me to call your minds to proofs or instances. Besides Christ's sayings in the Gospels a dozen or so more have been kept by tradition and are to be found in the works of the Fathers and early writers and one even in the Scripture itself: It is more blessed, etc. When these sayings are gathered together, though one cannot feel sure of every one, yet reading all in one view they make me say/These must be Christ's, never man etc. One is: Never rejoice but when you look upon your brother in love. Another is: My mystery is for me and for the children of my house.

HENRY VAUGHAN

The Night

Through that pure virgin shrine,
That sacred veil drawn o'er Thy glorious noon,
That men might look and live, as glowworms shine,
    And face the moon,
Wise Nicodemus saw such light
As made him know his God by night.

Most blest believer he!
Who in that land of darkness and blind eyes
Thy long-expected healing wings could see,
    When Thou didst rise!
And, what can never more be done,
Did at midnight speak with the Sun!

O who will tell me where
He found Thee at that dead and silent hour?
What hallowed solitary ground did bear
    So rare a flower,
Within whose sacred leaves did lie
The fulness of the Deity?

No mercy-seat of gold,
No dead and dusty cherub, nor carved stone,
But His own living works did my Lord hold
    And lodge alone;
Where trees and herbs did watch and peep
And wonder, while the Jews did sleep.

Dear night! this world's defeat;
The stop to busy fools; care's check and curb;
The day of spirits; my soul's calm retreat
    Which none disturb!
Christ's progress, and His prayer time;
The hours to which high heaven doth chime;

God's silent, searching flight;
When my Lord's head is filled with dew, and all
His locks are wet with the clear drops of night;
    His still, soft call;
His knocking time; the soul's dumb watch,
When spirits their fair kindred catch.

Were all my loud, evil days
Calm and unhaunted as is thy dark tent,
Whose peace but by some angel's wing or voice
    Is seldom rent,
Then I in heaven all the long year
Would keep, and never wander here.

But living where the sun
Doth all things wake, and where all mix and tire
Themselves and others, I consent and run
    To every mire,

And by this world's ill-guiding light,
Err more than I can do by night.

There is in God, some say,
A deep but dazzling darkness, as men here
Say it is late and dusky, because they
    See not all clear.
O for that night! where I in Him
Might live invisible and dim!

CARLO CARRETTO

from *Letters from the Desert*

THE FRIENDLY NIGHT

When I first came to the Sahara I was afraid of the night.

For some, night means more work, for others dissipation, for still others insomnia, boredom.

For me now it's quite different. Night is first of all rest, real rest. At sunset a great serenity sets in, as though nature were obeying a sudden sign from God.

The wind which has howled all day ceases, the heat dies down, the atmosphere becomes clear and limpid, and great peace spreads everywhere, as though man and the elements wanted to refresh themselves after the great battle with the day and its sun.

Yes, the night here is different. It has not lost its purity, its mystery. It has remained as God made it, his creation, bringer of good and life.

With your work finished and the caravan halted, you stretch out on the sand with a blanket under your head and breathe in the gentle breeze which has replaced the dry, fiery daytime wind.

Then you leave the camp and go down to the dunes for prayer. Time passes undisturbed. No obligations harass you, no noise disturbs you, no worry awaits you: time is all yours. So you satiate yourself with prayer and silence, while the stars light up in the sky.

Those who have never seen them cannot believe what the stars are like in the desert; the complete absence of artificial light, the vastness of the horizon only seem to increase their number and brightness. It is certainly an unforgettable experience. Only the camp fire with the tea water boiling on top and the bread for supper baking underneath, glows with a mellow light against the sparkling heaven.

The first nights spent here made me send off for books on astronomy and maps of the sky; and for months afterwards I spent my free time learning a little of what was passing over my head up there in the universe.

It was all good material for my prayer of adoration. Kneeling on the sand I sank my eyes for hours and hours in those wonders, writing down my discoveries in an exercise book like a child.

I understood, for example, that finding one's way in the desert is much easier by night than by day, that the points of reference are numerous and certain. In the years which I spent in the open desert I never once got lost, thanks to the stars.

Many times, when searching for a Tuareg camp or a lost weather station, I lost my way because the sun was too high in the sky. But I waited for night and found the road again, guided by the stars.

The Saharan night is not only a wonderful time for repose; it also provides a restful dwelling place for the soul. After the day—with all that light—the soul closes up like a house without windows to have their shutters unhinged by the wind or burnt by the sun.

I shall never forget the nights under the Saharan stars. I felt as if I were wrapped around by the blanket of the friendly night, a blanket embroidered with stars.

Yes, a friendly night, a benevolent darkness with restful shadows. In them the movement of my soul is not hindered. On the contrary, it can spread out, be fulfilled, grow and be joyful.

I feel at home, safe, fearless, desirous only of staying like this for hours; my only worry that of the shortness of the night so avid am I to read within and outside myself the symbols of divine language.

The friendly night is an image of faith, that gift of God defined, "The guarantee of the blessings we hope for and proof of the existence of the realities that at present remain unseen" (Hebrew 11:1).

I have never found a better metaphor for my relationship with the Eternal: a point lost in infinite space, wrapped round by the night under the subdued light of the stars.

I am this point lost in space: the darkness, like an irreplaceable friend, is faith. The stars, God's witness.

When my faith was weak, all this would have seemed incomprehensible to me. I was afraid as a child is of the night. But now I have conquered it, and it is mine. I experience joy in night, navigating upon it as upon the sea. The night is no longer my enemy, nor does it make me afraid. On the contrary, its darkness and divine transcendence are a source of delight.

Sometimes I even close my eyes to see more darkness. I know the stars are there in their place, as a witness to me of heaven. And I can see why darkness is so necessary.

The darkness is necessary, the darkness of faith is necessary, for God's light is too great. It wounds.

I understand more and more that faith is not a mysterious and cruel trick of a god who hides himself without telling me why, but a necessary veil. My discovery of him takes place gradually, respecting the growth of divine life in me.

"No man may see God and live," says the Scripture, in the sense that to see him face to face is possible only for those who have passed beyond death.

On earth such is the light, the infinity of the mystery and the inadequacy of human nature, that I must penetrate it little by little. First through symbols, then through experience, and finally in the contemplation which I can achieve on this earth if I remain faithful to God's love.

But it will be only a beginning, getting the eyes of my soul accustomed to so much light: the process will go on endlessly and the mystery will remain as long as we are dominated by God's infinity.

What is our life on earth, if not discovering, becoming conscious of, penetrating, contemplating, accepting, loving this mystery of God's, the unique reality which surrounds us, and in which we are immersed like meteorites in space? "In God we live and move and have our being" (Acts 17:28).

There aren't many mysteries, but there is one upon which everything depends, and it is so immense that it fills the whole space.

Human discoveries do not help us to penetrate this mystery. Future millennia will illuminate no further what Isaiah said and what God himself declared to Moses before the burning bush, "I am who I am" (Exodus 3:4).

Perhaps the sky was less dark for Abraham and the men with the tents than for modern man; perhaps faith was simpler for medieval poets than present-day technicians. But the situation is the same, and the nature of our relationship with God does not change.

The more man grows in maturity, the more he is required to have faith, devoid of sentiment. But the road will remain the same until the last has been born on this earth.

"This is the victory over the world—our faith" (John 5:4).

God asks faith of man and this is the true, authentic submission of the creature to the Creator, an act of humility, of love.

Trust in God; giving praise to the All-Powerful; satisfying our thirst for knowledge in the infinite sea of his Fatherhood; accepting his mysterious plan; entering school to listen to his word; knowing how to wait on him. This is an act of adoration worthy of man on this earth.

But if through pride we do not wish to set out on the path of faith, and we turn our backs on divine reality and close our eyes before the witness of the stars, where does it get us? Will our consciousness of the mystery increase? Shall we find more light somewhere else?

Without speaking of God, of the Incarnation of the Word and of the Eucharist, what do we know of the physical world itself which surrounds us? Or what, indeed, happens after death? What of the suffering of the creatures or the purpose of creation?

What we know is little more than nothing; and what little we know is all relative unless we go to first causes.

We should be overcome when each discovery we make seems to proclaim, 'Have you only just got there?' The advice of Jesus remains true, "If you do not become little children, you will not enter..."

What I have tried to say about faith is valid for everyone. No one can escape this reality. It is a gift of God but it needs effort on our part if it is to bear fruit.

God gives us the boat and the oars, but then tells us, "It's up to you to row." Making 'positive acts of faith' is like training this faculty; it is developed by training, as the muscles are developed by gymnastics.

David developed his faith by accepting to fight against Goliath. Gideon exercised himself in faith not only by asking a favorable sign from the Lord through the test of the fleece, but by going into battle with few soldiers against a stronger enemy.

Abraham became a giant in faith by making the supreme act of obedience which demanded of him the sacrifice of his son.

In Paul's letter to the Hebrews we read:

> It was for faith that our ancestors were commended.... Many submitted to torture, refusing release so that they would rise again to a better life. Some had to bear being pilloried and flogged, or even being chained up in prison. They were stoned or sawn in half, or beheaded; they were homeless and dressed in the skins of sheep and goats; they were penniless and were given nothing but ill-treatment. They were too good for the world and they went out to live in deserts and mountains and in caves and ravines (Hebrews 11:2).

But of all the men and women who lived by faith, two reached towering heights.

They lived at the watershed between the Old and New Testaments and were called by God to such a unique and magnificent vocation that heaven was made to wait in suspense for their reply: Mary and Joseph.

Mary became the mother of the Word; she gave flesh and blood to the Son of God; and Joseph must veil the mystery, placing himself at her side so that everyone might believe that Jesus was his son.

For these two creatures the night of faith was not only dark, but also painful.

One day Joseph, engaged to Mary, realises that she is to give birth to a child which he knows is not his.

Think of the task of convincing one's betrothed that the mystery of that birth is due to nothing less than the power of God.

No reasoning could give Joseph peace and serenity. Only faith.

And it is precisely this faith which sustained him, placing him next to the mother of God to accompany her in her destiny and take a full part in her mission.

It won't be easy to follow the example of such a man destined to suffer, the spouse of a woman who is to be called the Mother of Sorrows.

The Baby is born.

A few angels came, it is true, to chase away a little of that darkness, but at once the sky closed on a yet greater darkness. The children of the entire village are slain on account of their Baby, and Joseph and Mary, fleeing, hear the cry and lament of the women of Bethlehem.

Why? Why is the All-Powerful silent? Why doesn't he kill Herod? But this is the point: it is necessary to live by faith. Flee into Egypt, become exiles and refugees, let cruelty and injustice triumph. And so it will be until the end of time.

God didn't soften the path of those whom he put beside his Son. He asked of them a faith so pure and uncompromising that only two souls could live up to his demand.

What an adventure, to live for thirty years in a house where God lived in the flesh of an earthly man; to eat with him, listen to him speak, see him sleep, see the sweat on his brow, and on his hands the calluses of weariness and work.

And all this quite simply, as something normal and everyday; so normal that absolutely nobody will unveil the mystery or realise that the carpenter's son is the Son of God, the Word made flesh, the new Adam, heaven and earth.

My God, what great faith!

Mary and Joseph, you it is who are masters of faith, perfect examples to inspire us, correct our course and support our weakness.

Just as you were beside Jesus, you are still beside us to accompany us to eternal life, to teach us to be small and poor in our work, humble and hidden in life, courageous in trial, faithful in prayer, ardent in love.

And when the hour of our death comes and dawn rises over our friendly night, our eyes, as they scan the sky, may pick out the same star that was in your sky when Jesus came upon earth.

GEORGE HERBERT

Redemption

Having been tenant long to a rich lord,
    Not thriving, I resolvéd to be bold,
    And make a suit unto him, to afford
A new small-rented lease, and cancel the old.

In heaven at his manor I him sought;
    They told me there that he was lately gone
    About some land, which he had dearly bought
Long since on earth, to take possession.

I straight returned, and knowing his great birth,
    Sought him accordingly in great resorts;
    In cities, theaters, gardens, parks, and courts;
At length I heard a ragged noise and mirth
    Of thieves and murderers; there I him espied,
    Who straight, *Your suit is granted,* said, and died.

The Collar

I struck the board and cried, "No more;
    I will abroad!
What? shall I ever sigh and pine?
My lines and life are free, free as the road,
    Loose as the wind, as large as store.
        Shall I be still in suit?
Have I no harvest but a thorn
To let me blood, and not restore
What I have lost with cordial fruit?
        Sure there was wine
Before my sighs did dry it; there was corn
    Before my tears did drown it.
Is the year only lost to me?
    Have I no bays to crown it,
No flowers, no garlands gay? All blasted?
        All wasted?
Not so, my heart; but there is fruit,
    And thou hast hands.
Recover all thy sigh-blown age
On double pleasures: leave thy cold dispute

Of what is fit and not. Forsake thy cage,
  Thy rope of sands,
Which petty thoughts have made, and made to thee
 Good cable, to enforce and draw,
  And be thy law,
 While thou didst wink and wouldst not see.
   Away! take heed;
   I will abroad.
Call in thy death's-head there; tie up thy fears.
  He that forbears
  To suit and serve his need,
   Deserves his load."
But as I raved and grew more fierce and wild
  At every word,
Methought I heard one calling, *Child!*
  And I replied, *My Lord.*

JOHN CLARE

Lord, Hear My Prayer

A PARAPHRASE OF THE 102ND PSALM

Lord, hear my prayer when trouble glooms,
Let sorrow find a way,
And when the day of trouble comes,
Turn not thy face way:
My bones like hearthstones burn away,
My life like vapory smoke decays.

My heart is smitten like the grass,
That withered lies and dead,
And I, so lost to what I was,
Forget to eat my bread.
My voice is groaning all the day,
My bones prick through this skin of clay.

The wilderness's pelican,
the desert's lonely owl—
I am their like, a desert man
In ways as lone and foul.
As sparrows on the cottage top
I wait till I with fainting drop.

I hear my enemies reproach,
All silently I mourn;
They on my private peace encroach.
Against me they are sworn.
Ashes as bread my trouble shares,
And mix my food with weeping cares.

Yet not for them is sorrow's toil,
I fear no mortal's frowns—
But thou hast held me up awhile
And thou hast cast me down.
My days like shadows waste from view,
I mourn like withered grass in dew.

But thou, Lord, shalt endure for ever,
All generations through;
Thou shalt to Zion be the giver
Of joy and mercy too.
Her very stones are in thy trust,
Thy servants reverence her dust.

Heathens shall hear and fear thy name,
All kings of earth thy glory know
When thou shalt build up Zion's fame
And live in glory there below.
He'll not despise their prayers, though mute,
But still regard the destitute.

JOSEPH BRODSKY

December 24, 1971

[FOR V.S.]

When it's Christmas we're all of us magi.
At the grocers' all slipping and pushing.
Where a tin of halvah, coffee-flavored,
is the cause of a human assault-wave
by a crowd heavy-laden with parcels:
each one his own king, his own camel.

Nylon bags, carrier bags, paper cones,
caps and neckties all twisted up sideways.
Reek of vodka and resin and cod,
orange mandarins, cinnamon, apples.

Floods of faces, no sign of a pathway
toward Bethlehem, shut off by blizzard.

And the bearers of moderate gifts
leap on buses and jam all the doorways,
disappear into courtyards that gape,
though they know that there's nothing inside there:
not a beast, not a crib, nor yet her,
round whose head gleams a nimbus of gold.

Emptiness. But the mere thought of that
brings forth lights as if out of nowhere.
Herod reigns but the stronger he is,
the more sure, the more certain the wonder.
In the constancy of this relation
is the basic mechanics of Christmas.

That's what they celebrate everywhere,
for its coming push tables together.
No demand for a star for a while,
but a sort of good will touched with grace
can be seen in all men from afar,
and the shepherds have kindled their fires.

Snow is falling: not smoking but sounding
chimney pots on the roof, every face like a stain.
Herod drinks. Every wife hides her child.
He who comes is a mystery: features
are not known beforehand, men's hearts may
not be quick to distinguish the stranger.

But when drafts through the doorway disperse
the thick mist of the hours of darkness
and a shape in a shawl stands revealed,
both a newborn and Spirit that's Holy
in your self you discover; you stare
skyward, and it's right there:
a star.

JULIAN GREEN

From His Diary

DECEMBER 17. Someone I am very fond of told me that he had great
difficulty in going to sleep, because anguish grips him the moment he

turns out the light. It is the anguish of solitude, the fear of dying in the night. A short time before, he spoke to me about the extraordinary effect produced on him by the cantata *Schlage doch, gewünschte Stunde*, which immediately carried him away to another world filled with unclouded serenity. I told him that this was the real world, and the one that frightens and makes us suffer is a world of terrible delusions; it must be quitted at all costs, but what keeps us there are covetous desires of all kinds, which are our tyrants. Our real master is Jesus. He alone will free us from the terrors of this life. The first step is to leave pleasure behind; the rest follows of itself.

CHARLES DE FOUCAULD

The Poor and the Lowly Are Those Christ Calls First

For his parents, Jesus chose two poor working people; for his first adorers he chose poor shepherds. Jesus does not reject the rich. He died for them, he calls all of them, and he loves them. But he refuses to share their riches and he calls the poor first.

How divinely good you are, my God! If you had first called the rich, the poor would not have dared to come near you. They would have thought it was their duty to remain at a distance because of their poverty. They would have looked at you from afar, letting you be surrounded by wealth.

But, by first calling the shepherds, you have called everybody to you: the poor, for you want to show thereby, until the end of time, that they are those who have been called first, the favorites, the privileged; the rich, for, on the one hand, they are not timid and, on the other hand, it depends on them to become as poor as the shepherds. Instantaneously, if they wish, if they have the desire of being like you, if they fear that their wealth might keep them away from you, they can become perfectly poor.

How good you are! How excellent the means you have chosen to call at the same time around you all your children without any exception! And what a balm you have put into the heart of the poor, the lowly, those whom the world despises, until the end of time, by showing them from your very birth that they are your privileged ones, your favorites, the first called, those who are always called around you, for you have desired to be one of them and to have them around you from your cradle and throughout your life.

God has not attached salvation to knowledge, understanding, riches, long experience, or great talents, which have not been received by all.

No, indeed! He has attached it to that which comes into the hands of all, of absolutely all, of the young and the old, of any age and any class, of any intelligence and any fortune. He has attached it to what all can give him, if there be a little goodwill.

A little goodwill is all that is necessary to gain the heaven which Jesus attaches to humility, to the fact that we make ourselves little, that we take the last place, that we obey, which he attaches elsewhere to poverty of spirit, to purity of heart, to the love of justice, to the spirit of peace.

Let us have hope because by the mercy of God salvation is close to us, it is in our hands. It can be obtained just by a little goodwill.

EMILY DICKINSON

A Word made Flesh is seldom
And tremblingly partook
Nor then perhaps reported
But have I not mistook
Each one of us has tasted
With ecstasies of stealth
The very food debated
To our specific strength—

A Word that breathes distinctly
Has not the power to die
Cohesive as the Spirit
It may expire if He—
"Made Flesh and dwelt among us"
Could condescension be
Like this consent of Language
This loved Philology.

ROBERT SOUTHWELL

The Burning Babe

As I in hoary winter's night stood shivering in the snow,
Surprised I was with sudden heat which made my heart to glow;
And lifting up a fearful eye to view what fire was near,
A pretty babe all burning bright did in the air appear;
Who, scorchéd with excessive heat, such floods of tears did shed

As though his floods should quench his flames which with his tears
were fed.
"Alas," quoth he, "but newly born in fiery heats I fry,
Yet none approach to warm their hearts or feel my fire but I!
My faultless breast the furnace is, the fuel wounding thorns,
Love is the fire, and sighs the smoke, the ashes shame and scorns;
The fuel justice layeth on, and mercy blows the coals,
The metal in this furnace wrought are men's defiléd souls,
For which, as now on fire I am to work them to their good,
So will I melt into a bath to wash them in my blood."
With this he vanished out of sight and swiftly shrunk away,
And straight I called unto mind that it was Christmas day.

A GOD AND YET A MAN?

A god and yet a man?
A maid and yet a mother?
Wit wonders what wit can
Conceive this or the other.

A god and can he die?
A dead man, can he live?
What wit can well reply?
What reason reason give?

God, truth itself, doth teach it.
Man's wit sinks too far under
By reason's power to reach it.
Believe and leave to wonder.

—Anonymous

ROBERT LOWELL

The Crucifix

How dry time screaks in its fat axle-grease,
As spare November strikes us through the ice
And the Leviathan breaks water in the rice
Fields, at the poles, at the hot gates to Greece;
It's time: the old unmastered lion roars
And ramps like a mad dog outside the doors,

Snapping at gobbets in my thumbless hand.
The seaways lurch through Sodom's knees of sand
Tomorrow. We are sinking. "Run, rat, run,"
The prophets thunder, and I run upon
My father, Adam. Adam, if our land
Become the desolation of a hand
That shakes the Temple back to clay, how can
War ever change my old into new man?
Get out from under my feet, old man. Let me pass;
On Ninth Street, through the Hallowe'en's soaped glass,
I picked at an old bone on two crossed sticks
And found, to *Via et Vita et Veritas*
A stray dog's signpost is a crucifix.

KARL RAHNER

Jesus Christ

The Life of Jesus. The historical existence of Jesus, his life, death, and
resurrection and his affirmations about himself are established with
certainty by the four Gospels, the letters of the Apostles, non-Christian
witnesses (Flavius Josephus, Tacitus, Suetonius, Pliny the Younger,
the Talmud) and early Christianity.

Jesus was born a Jew before the year 4 B.C. at Bethlehem in Palestine.
His mother was Mary. Herod the Edomite ruled Palestine at that time
under Roman suzerainty: the Jewish nation, divided as to religion, had
lost its political independence; and the Graeco-Roman civilization of
the Roman Empire had laid the foundations for the future historical
unity of Europe (and hence of the world). After a youth spent in
obscurity at Nazareth Jesus comes forward about the year 27 as an
itinerant religious teacher in Palestine. He announces that in himself,
the Son of the Father, the definitive reign of God is victoriously and
irreversibly at hand which redeems lost and sinful men if they
uncompromisingly believe in him and are converted. This is the
central point of his message and mission, which initially is directed to
all Israel as the chosen people of God. Within the framework of his
summons to the radical conversion of faith he demands a morality
which must be the gift of God's grace, which while quite realistic about
the concrete moral achievement human beings are capable of (as
compared with unlimited truthfulness, purity, humility, self-denial
and love of our neighbour) breaks through all ethical and religious
formalism and establishes a personal relationship between a man and

the living God. Jesus teaches that though God is infinitely exalted he can be loved; that morality is what it should be only when it rises above itself—when the human being who has received the message of God's love in faith loves God with his whole heart. Jesus makes this possible for man by making the Kingdom of God a matter of concrete experience, taking up the cause of the "weak," anticipating the Kingdom at table with the "unclean" and in healing the sick, and appearing with the disadvantaged and with sinners, so as to become a brother to man, like him in all but sin. This message is addressed to each individual, because in each individual Jesus sees a person absolutely distinct and valid before God, freely deciding his eternal destiny in this one life that is his. Jesus confirms his doctrine by his own life. He accepts its narrowness and rigour without complaint. With a pure heart and as a matter of course he humbly loves every human being who encounters him. He remains inflexibly devoted to his task, unflinching in face of contradiction and threats, perfectly obedient to his Father's will which governs his life in every detail, in loving adoration of this Father whom he always has before him, whether at solitary prayer, in daily life or in the abandonment of death. Jesus' life testifies more eloquently than any words to his joy in God, the merciful and loving Father.

His message and demands meet with growing resistance from his people in the person of their officials and religious leaders who see in Jesus' independent attitude to the Law an attack on God himself. Jesus avoids the summoning of a "holy remnant" of the good and those ready for conversion to form a messianic community apart. He makes his message universally applicable to the heathen and to all men and women, and consciously attends his violent death under the Roman rulers, which he looks on as the consequence of his mission. After fully two years' activity he dies on the 14th or 15th Nisan (about April 7th), probably in the year 30. Because of his claim to be *the* Son of God and the Saviour he is executed on a cross at Jerusalem, having been betrayed by his friends and condemned by both religious and secular authority. On the third day his tomb, which has been sealed and guarded by his enemies, is empty. But he shows himself physically alive, though transfigured, to his disciples—on one occasion to more than five hundred of them at once. He leaves behind him a community he has founded, which believes in him as the Lord and Redeemer by the power of his Holy Spirit. This community, the Church, placed under the authoritative government of the Apostolic College with Peter at its head, is united by its confession of Jesus, its common faith in his truth preached by the Apostles in obedience to his command; by baptism, the sacrament of faith through which, confessing the Trinity, one enters his Church; by common celebration of the Last Supper, in which through *anamnesis* his death on the cross is made present and his Body and Blood are received; by expectation of his return, which will fully reveal God's dominion, already become an indestructible reality in the world through Jesus' life and liberating work, death and resurrection.

JESUS' WOUNDS SO WIDE

> Jesus' wounds so wide
> Be wells of life to the good,
> Namely the stround of his side
> That ran full breme on the rood.
>
> If thee list to drink,
> To flee from the fiends of hell,
> Bow thou down to the brink
> And meekly taste of the well.

—Anonymous

ANGELUS SILESIUS

Three Poems

ALL WEAL IN ONE

In One is all my peace, in One my weal is done,
Though many things be lost to me, I run to One.

THE SPIRITUAL PEAK

I am a peak in God, and upward must I pace
Upon myself, that God may show His tender face.

LET THE SOMETHING FALL

Man, if you love some thing, you love no thing at all,
God is not this or that, so let the Something fall.

3

ASPECTS
OF
ATTENTION

ST. FRANCIS OF ASSISI TO CARDINAL HUGOLINO AND HIS BROTHERS

When Saint Francis was at the General Chapter held at Sancta Maria de Portiuncula . . . and five thousand brothers were present, a number of them who were schoolmen went to Cardinal Hugolino who was there, and said to him: "My lord, we want you to persuade Brother Francis to follow the council of the learned brothers, and sometimes let himself be guided by them." And they suggested the rule of Saint Benedict or Augustine or Bernard who require their congregations to live so and so, by regulation. When the Cardinal had repeated all this to Saint Francis by way of counsel, Saint Francis, making no ⌐ ⌐swer, took him by the hand and led him to the brothers assembled in Chapter, and in the fervour and virtue of the Holy Ghost, spoke thus to the brothers:

"My brothers, my brothers, God has called me by the way of simplicity and humility, and has shown me in verity this path for me and those who want to believe and follow me; so I want you to talk of no Rule to me, neither Saint Benedict nor Saint Augustine nor Saint Bernard, nor any way or form of Life whatever except that which God has mercifully pointed out and granted to me. And God said that he wanted me to be a pauper [poverello] and an idiot—a great fool—in this world, and would not lead us by any other path of science than this. But by your science and syllogisms God will confound you, and I trust in God's warders, the devils, that through them God shall punish you, and you will yet come back to your proper station with shame, whether you will or no."

C. P. CAVAFY

The God Abandons Antony

At midnight, when suddenly you hear
an invisible procession going by
with exquisite music, voices,
don't mourn your luck that's failing now,
work gone wrong, your plans
all proving deceptive—don't mourn them uselessly:
as one long prepared, and full of courage,
say goodbye to her, to Alexandria who is leaving.
Above all, don't fool yourself, don't say
it was a dream, your ears deceived you:
don't degrade yourself with empty hopes like these.
As one long prepared, and full of courage,
as is right for you who were given this kind of city,
go firmly to the window
and listen with deep emotion,
but not with the whining, the pleas of a coward;
listen—your final pleasure—to the voices,
to the exquisite music of that strange procession,
and say goodbye to her, to the Alexandria you are losing.

An Old Man

At the noisy end of the café, head bent
over the table, an old man sits alone,
a newspaper in front of him.

And in the miserable banality of old age
he thinks how little he enjoyed the years
when he had strength, and wit, and looks.

He knows he's very old now: sees it, feels it.
Yet it seems he was young just yesterday.
The time's gone by so quickly, gone by so quickly.

And he thinks how Discretion fooled him,
how he always believed, so stupidly,
that cheat who said: "Tomorrow. You have plenty of time."

He remembers impulses bridled, the joy
he sacrificed. Every chance he lost
now mocks his brainless prudence.

But so much thinking, so much remembering
makes the old man dizzy. He falls asleep,
his head resting on the café table.

F. T. PRINCE

Soldiers Bathing

The sea at evening moves across the sand.
Under a reddening sky I watch the freedom of a band
Of soldiers who belong to me. Stripped bare
For bathing in the sea, they shout and run in the warm air;
Their flesh, worn by the trade of war, revives
And my mind towards the meaning of it strives.

All's pathos now. The body that was gross,
Rank, ravening, disgusting in the act or in repose,
All fever, filth and sweat, its bestial strength
And bestial decay, by pain and labor grows at length
Fragile and luminous. Poor bare forked animal,
Conscious of his desires and needs and flesh that rise and fall,
Stands in the soft air, tasting after toil
The sweetness of his nakedness: letting the sea-waves coil
Their frothy tongues about his feet, forgets
His hatred of the war, its terrible pressure that begets
That machinery of death and slavery,
Each being a slave and making slaves of others; finds that he
Remembers his proud freedom in a game,
Mocking himself; and comically mimics fear and shame.

He plays with death and animality.
And, reading in the shadows of his pallid flesh, I see
The idea of Michelangelo's cartoon
Of soldiers bathing, breaking off before they were half done
At some sortie of the enemy, an episode
Of the Pisan wars with Florence. I remember how he showed
Their muscular limbs that clamber from the water

And heads that turn across the shoulder, eager for the slaughter,
Forgetful of their bodies that are bare
And hot to buckle on and use the weapons lying there.
—And I think too of the theme another found
When, shadowing men's bodies on a sinister red ground—
Was it Ucello or Pollaiulo?—

Painted a naked battle: warriors, straddled, hacked the foe,
Dug their bare toes into the soil and slew
The brother-naked man who lay between their feet and drew
His lips back from his teeth in a grimace.

They were Italians who knew war's sorrow and disgrace
And showed the thing suspended, stripped. A theme
Born out of the experience of that horrible extreme
Of war beneath a sky where the air flows
With *Lachrimae Christi.* For that rage, that bitterness, those blows
That hatred of the slain, what could it be
But indirectly or directly a commentary
On the Crucifixion? and the picture burns
With indignation and pity and despair by turns
Because it is the obverse of the scene
Where Christ hangs murdered, stripped, upon the Cross.
   I mean,
That is the explanation of its rage.

And we too have our bitterness and pity that engage
Blood, spirit in this war. But night begins,
Night of the mind: who nowadays is conscious of our sins?
Though every human deed concerns our blood,
And even we must know what nobody has understood,
That some great love is over all we do
And that is what has driven us to fury, for so few
Can suffer all the terror of that love:
The terror of that love has set us spinning in this groove
Greasy with our blood.
               These dry themselves and dress,
Resume their shirts, forget the fright and shame of nakedness.
Because to love is terrible we prefer
The freedom of our crimes; yet, as I drink the dusky air,
I feel a strange delight that fills me full,
Strange gratitude, as if evil itself were beautiful,
And kiss the wound in thought, while in the west
I watch a streak of red that might have issued from Christ's breast.

GABRIELA MISTRAL

Sleep Close to Me

Fold of my flesh
I carried in my womb,
tender trembling flesh
sleep close to me!

The partridge sleeps in the wheat
listening to its heartbeat.
Let not my breath disturb you
sleep close to me!

Little tender grass
afraid to live,
don't move from my arms;
sleep close to me!

I have lost everything,
and tremble until I sleep.
Don't move from my breast;
sleep close to me!

4

THE CONVULSIONS
OF
TIME

PABLO NERUDA

The United Fruit Co.

When the trumpets had sounded and all
was in readiness on the face of the earth,
Jehovah divided his universe:
Anaconda, Ford Motors,
Coca-Cola Inc., and similar entities:
the most succulent item of all,
The United Fruit Company Incorporated
reserved for itself: the heartland
and coasts of my country,
the delectable waist of America.
They rechristened their properties:
the "Banana Republics"—
and over the languishing dead,
the uneasy repose of the heroes
who harried that greatness,
their flags and their freedoms,
they established an *opéra bouffe:*
they ravished all enterprise,

awarded the laurels like Caesars,
unleashed all the covetous, and contrived
the tyrannical Reign of the Flies—
Trujillo the fly, and Tacho the fly,
the flies called Carias, Martinez,
Ubico—all of them flies, flies
dank with the blood of their marmalade
vassalage, flies buzzing drunkenly
on the populous middens:
the fly-circus fly and the scholarly
kind, case-hardened in tyranny.
Then in the bloody domain of the flies
The United Fruit Company Incorporated
unloaded with a booty of coffee and fruits
brimming its cargo boats, gliding
like trays with the spoils
of our drowning dominions.

And all the while, somewhere, in the sugary
hells of our seaports,
smothered by gases, an Indian
fell in the morning:
a body spun off, an anonymous
chattel, some numeral tumbling,
a branch with its death running out of it
in the vat of the carrion, fruit laden and foul.

**FROM THE DOCUMENTS OF
THE SECOND VATICAN COUNCIL**

The Work of the Lay Apostle

The Second Vatican Council promulgated a number of documents reflecting its basic pastoral orientation toward Church renewal. One of these was the Decree on the Apostolate of the Laity, which seeks to delineate the nature, character, and variety of the lay apostolate, as well as to state its basic principles and offer pastoral directives for its more effective exercise. It stresses the fact that the laity are the People of God, co-responsible with bishops, priests, and religious for Christ's mission on earth; as such, their work is essential in an age when there is an ever-widening gap between the modern world and the message of the gospel. The following selection succinctly summarizes the work of the lay apostle.

Christ's redemptive work, while essentially concerned with the salvation of men, includes also the renewal of the whole temporal order. Hence, the mission of the Church is not only to bring the message and grace of Christ to men but also to penetrate and perfect the temporal order with the spirit of the gospel. . . .

The mission of the Church pertains to the salvation of men, which is to be achieved by belief in Christ and by his grace. The apostolate of the Church and of all its members is primarily designed to manifest Christ's message by words and deeds and to communicate his grace to the world. This is done mainly through the ministry of the Word and the sacraments, entrusted in a special way to the clergy, wherein the laity also have their very important roles to fulfill if they are to be "fellow workers for the truth" (3 Jn 8). It is especially on this level that the apostolate of the laity and the pastoral ministry are mutually complementary.

There are innumerable opportunities open to the laity for the exercise of their apostolate of evangelization and sanctification. The very testimony of their Christian life and good works done in a supernatural spirit have the power to draw men to belief and to God; for the Lord says, "Even so let your light shine before men in order that they may see your good works and give glory to your Father who is in heaven" (Mt 5:16).

However, an apostolate of this kind does not consist only in the witness of one's way of life; a true apostle looks for opportunities to announce Christ by words addressed either to non-believers with a view to leading them to faith, or to the faithful with a view to instructing, strengthening, and encouraging them to a more fervent life. "For the charity of Christ impels us" (2 Cor 5:14). The words of the Apostle should echo in all hearts, "Woe to me if I do not preach the gospel" (1 Cor 9:16).

Since, in our own times, new problems are arising and very serious errors are circulating which tend to undermine the foundations of religion, the moral order, and human society itself, this sacred synod earnestly exhorts laymen—each according to his own gifts of intelligence and learning—to be more diligent in doing what they can to explain, defend, and properly apply Christian principles to the problems of our era in accordance with the mind of the Church. . . .

The laity must take up the renewal of the temporal order as their own special obligation. Led by the light of the gospel and the mind of the Church and motivated by Christian charity, they must act directly and in a definite way in the temporal sphere. As citizens they must cooperate with other citizens with their own particular skill and on their own responsibility. Everywhere and in all things they must seek the justice of God's kingdom.

The temporal order must be renewed in such a way that, without detriment to its own proper laws, it may be brought into conformity with the higher principles of the Christian life and adapted to the shifting circumstances of time, place, and peoples. Preeminent among the works of this type of apostolate is that of Christian social action which the sacred synod desires to see extended to the whole temporal sphere, including culture.

HELDER CAMARA

The Eucharist and Social Justice

When the Christian community participates in the celebration of the Eucharist, at the offertory it sees in the hands of the celebrant "the bread which earth has given and human hands have made." From this it can draw a lesson for living according to social justice as is required of men. How is it possible, as we see the bread, not to connect it with money and recall that there are millions upon millions—two thirds of mankind—who lack bread?

Throughout the Eucharistic celebration we hear it said that we are brothers and sisters. We journey toward one and the same Father. We seemingly gather around one same table. We eat the same Bread of Life. Nevertheless, after Mass, every one goes to his own family, his own cares, his own problems, and those who momentarily had been called brothers are treated as strangers, when they are not dealt with as adversaries and enemies.

The eucharistic presence, in Communion, is not of long duration, but it intensifies our unity with Christ which began at our baptism. Keeping in mind our unity with Christ, how can we help being grieved when we consider the frightful consequences of selfishness on individuals, in the bosom of the family, on the level of fundamental communities, and on the national, continental, or international plane? How can we remain indifferent when we discover the growth of injustice and as a result of it the growth of radicalism and hatred?

As we partake of the food of the Eucharist we become ever more profoundly plunged into Christ and at the same time ever more bound to all mankind, which means that our presence among men should be the presence of Christ. When we look at things through the eyes of Christ, is it possible not to realize that in our day it is not enough to give alms and ask others to be generous toward those who are hungry? Today the supreme alms is fostering justice, it is working for the establishment of social justice.

In our century "the poor" are not only individual persons and groups but whole countries and continents. The reason for this poverty, which leads to wretchedness and even to a subhuman existence for millions of men, for "sons of God," is the most grievous injustice practiced in the international politics of commerce.

We need to find in the Bread of Life the strength to accept changes in mentality, to shake up our lives, and to be converted. This would be relatively easy if it were only a matter of explaining even complex and difficult arguments. But what is much harder is to labor for fundamental reforms or, to speak more precisely, for changes in structures....

At the beginnings of the Church the pagans were amazed as they saw the way those who received the Bread of Life loved one another, not theoretically and in words, but practically and in deeds. The world is once more in need of our testimony. We must feel, see, discover that the Eucharist makes us live in justice and love, and these are the only ways that lead to true peace.

GUSTAVO GUTIERREZ

A Latin American Perception of a Theology of Liberation

To get at the theological meaning of liberation, we first have to define our terms. That will make up the first part of this article. It will permit us to emphasize that in these pages we are particularly sensitive to the critical function of theology regarding the Church's presence and activity in the world. The principal fact about that presence today, especially in underdeveloped countries, is the participation by Christians in the struggle to construct a just and fraternal society in which men can live in dignity and be masters of their own destinies. We think that the word "development" does not well express those profound aspirations. "Liberation" seems more exact and richer in overtones; besides, it opens up a more fertile field for theological reflection.

The situation of Latin America, the only continent of underdeveloped and oppressed peoples who are in a majority Christians, is particularly interesting for us. An effort to describe and interpret the Church's ways of being present there will enable us to pose the fundamental question upon which we can then turn our theological reflection. That will make up the second part of this article.

This will permit us to see that asking the theological meaning of liberation is really asking the meaning of Christianity itself and the Church's mission. There used to be a time when the Church answered problems by calmly appealing to its doctrinal and vital reserves. Today, however, the gravity and scope of the process we call liberation is such that Christian belief and the Church itself are called radically in question. They are asked what right they have to address the mighty human task now before us. A few paragraphs will allow us to outline that problem, or rather to state, without attempting to answer them, the new questions. To approach this subject properly, we should explain precisely what we mean by "theology" and by "liberation."

THEOLOGY

Through the Church's history, theology has carried out various functions. Two stand out in particular. In the first centuries, what we today call theology was closely allied to the spiritual life. Primarily it dealt with a meditation on the Bible, geared toward spiritual progress. From the twelfth century on, theology began to be a science. The Aristotelian categories made it possible to speak of theology as a "subordinate science." This notion of science is ambiguous and does not satisfy the modern mind. But the essential in the work of St. Thomas is that theology is the fruit of the meeting between faith and reason. Perhaps we do better, then, to speak of a rational knowledge. In résumé, theology is necessarily spiritual and rational knowledge. These two elements are permanent and indispensable functions of all theological reflection.

Another function of theology has slowly developed and been accepted in recent years: theology as a critical reflection on the Church's pastoral action.

The renewed stress on charity as center of the Christian life has brought us to see faith more biblically, as a commitment to God and neighbor. In this perspective the understanding of faith is likewise seen to be the understanding of a commitment, an attitude, a posture toward life, in the light of the revealed Word.

At the same time, the very life of the Church has become a *locus theologicus.* This was clear in the so-called "new theology," and has frequently been emphasized since then. God's word, which assembles us, is incarnated in the community of faith totally devoted to the service of all men.

Something similar happened with what has been called since Pope John and Vatican II a theology of the signs of the times. Let us not forget that the signs of the times are not only a call to intellectual analysis. They are, above all, a demand for action, for commitment, for service of others. "Scrutinizing" the signs of the times takes in both elements.

All these factors have brought us to rediscover and make explicit theology's function as a critical reflection on the Church's presence and activity in the world, in the light of revelation. By its preaching of the gospel message, by its sacraments, by the charity of its members, the Church announces and accepts the gift of the kingdom of God into the heart of human history. The Church is effective charity, it is action, it is commitment to the service of men.

Theology is reflection, a critical attitude. First comes the commitment to charity, to service. Theology comes "later." It is second. The Church's pastoral action is not arrived at as a conclusion from theological premises. Theology does not lead to pastoral activity, but is rather a reflection on it. Theology should find the Spirit present in it, inspiring the actions of the Christian community. The life of the Church will be for it a *locus theologicus*.

Reflecting on the Church's presence and activity in the world means being open to the world, listening to the questions asked in it, being attentive to the successive stages of its historical growth. This task is indispensable. Reflection in the light of faith should always accompany the Church's pastoral efforts. Theology, by relativizing all its undertakings, keeps the Church from settling down into what is only provisory. Theology, by harking back to the sources of revelation, will guide action, setting it into a broader context, thus contributing to keep it from falling into activism and immediatism.

As reflection on the Church's activity, theology is a progressive and, in a certain sense, variable understanding. If the commitment of the Christian community takes on different forms down through history, the understanding that accompanies that commitment will constantly take a fresh look at it—and may then take surprising initiatives.

Theology, therefore, as a critical reflection on the Church's presence and action in the world, in the light of faith, not only complements the other two functions of theology (wisdom and rational knowledge) but even presupposes them.

DEVELOPMENT OR LIBERATION?

Today's world is going through a profound sociocultural transformation. Modern man has also become fully aware of the economic basis for that transformation. In the poor countries, where the immense majority of the world's population lives, the struggle for social change is being made with great urgency and is starting to become violent.

The term "development" does not seem to express well the yearning of contemporary men for more human living conditions. A basic problem is: the notion of development is not univocal; a considerable number of definitions are given. Instead of looking at them one by one, let us see the perspectives they start from.

First, development can be taken in a purely economic sense, as synonymous with *economic growth*. In that case, a country's development will be measured, e.g., by comparing its GNP or its per capita income with those of some country assumed to have achieved a high level of development. This yardstick can be improved on and made more sophisticated, but the basic presumption will be that development is primarily an increase of wealth. Those who speak this way, explicitly at least, are few today. Such a yardstick is used rather to contrast with other, more integral norms. One may still ask, however, if all the norms do not retain something of the capitalist concept of development.

The inadequacies of the purely economic yardstick have popularized another, more important and frequent today, which looks on development as a *global social process*, with economic, social, political, and cultural aspects. This strategy of development, keeping in view all these aspects, permits a people to make global progress and also avoid certain dangerous pitfalls.

Seeing development as a global social process involves, of necessity, ethical values, and that implies ultimately a concept of what man is. A detailed explication of such a *humanist perspective* in development takes time and extends, without contradicting it, the point of view just presented. Fr. L. J. Lebret strove constantly in that direction. For him, developmental economics is "the discipline covering the passage from a less human to a more human phase." The same notion is contained in that other definition of development: "having more in order to be more." This humanistic view places the notion of development in a broader context: a historical vision, in which humanity takes charge of its own destiny. But that involves a change of perspective, which we prefer to call "liberation." That is what we shall try to explain in the following paragraphs.

In recent decades the term "development" has been used to express the aspirations of the poor nations. Of late, however, the term has seemed weak. In fact, today the term conveys a pejorative connotation, especially in Latin America.

There has been much discussion recently of development, of aid to the poor countries; there has even been an effort to weave a mystique around those words. Attempts to produce development in the 1950's aroused hopes. But because they did not hit the roots of the evil, they failed, and have led to deception, confusion, and frustration.

One of the most important causes of this situation is the fact that development, in its strictly economic, modernizing sense, was advanced by international agencies backed by the groups that control the world economy. The changes proposed avoided sedulously, therefore, attacking the powerful international economic interests and those of their natural allies: the national oligarchies. What is more, in many cases the alleged changes were only new and concealed ways to increase the power of the mighty economic groups.

Here is where conflict enters the picture. Development should attack the causes of our plight, and among the central ones is the economic, social, political, and cultural dependence of some people on others. The word "liberation," therefore, is more accurate and conveys better the human side of the problem.

Once we call the poor countries oppressed and dominated, the word "liberation" is appropriate. But there is also another, much more global and profound view of humanity's historical advance. Man begins to see himself as a creative subject; he seizes more and more the reins of his own destiny, directing it toward a society where he will be free of every kind of slavery. Looking on history as the process of *man's emancipation* places the question of development in a broader context, a deeper and even a more radical one. This approach expresses better the aspiration of the poor peoples, who consider themselves primarily as oppressed. Thus the term "development" seems rather antiseptic, inaccurately applying to a tragic, tense reality. What is at stake, then, is a dynamic and historical concept of man as looking toward his future, doing things today to shape his tomorrow.

This topic and this language are beginning to appear in certain actions of the magisterium. One isolated text of *The Development of Peoples*, e.g., speaks of "building a world where every man, regardless of race, religion, or nationality, can live a fully human life, free of the servitude that comes from other men and from the incompletely mastered world about him." The notion is more forcibly expressed in the *Message of Fifteen Bishops of the Third World,* published in reply to *The Development of Peoples.* The topic of liberation comes up frequently, almost as the leitmotif of the document, in another text of greater importance because of its doctrinal authority: in the Medellín *Conclusions.*

Liberation, therefore, seems to express better both the hopes of oppressed peoples and the fullness of a view in which man is seen not as a passive element, but as agent of history. More profoundly, to see history as a process of man's liberation places the issue of desired social changes in a dynamic context. It also permits us to understand better the age we live in. Finally, the term "development" clouds up somewhat the theological issues latent in the process. To speak of liberation, on the other hand, is to hint at the biblical sources that illuminate man's presence and actions in history: the liberation from sin by Christ our Redeemer and the bringing of new life.

In résumé, then, there are three levels of meaning to the term "liberation": the political liberation of oppressed peoples and social classes; man's liberation in the course of history; and liberation from sin as condition of a life of communion of all men with the Lord.

We have seen that one of theology's functions is to be a critical reflection on the Church's pastoral activity. The flow of history reveals unsuspected aspects of revelation, and the role of Christians in that history constitutes, we have said, a real *locus theologicus*. In this regard it may help to recall, on broad lines, the option or choice that important sectors of the Church are making in the only continent with a majority of its people Christian. Crucial and difficult problems connected with liberation face the Latin American Church.

THE PROCESS OF LIBERATION IN LATIN AMERICA

After many years of genuine ignorance of what was going on, and after a brief moment of induced and artificial optimism, Latin America is now acquiring at least a partial, but more global and structural understanding of its situation. The most important change in the understanding of Latin America's reality lies in the fact that it is not a mere description, prescinding from the deep causes; rather, it gives particular attention to those causes and examines them in a historical perspective.

The decade of the 1950's was marked in Latin America by a great optimism for the possibilities of achieving economic development. The hope was based on a favorable historical moment and was theoretically expressed in a number of masterly economic studies. The developmental models popular in those years were the ones proposed by international agencies.

For them, however, to develop meant imitating the processes followed by the more developed societies. The ideal imitated was the "modern society" or the "industrialized society." This approach was supposed to solve all the problems the underdeveloped countries were experiencing because they were "traditional societies." Thus underdeveloped countries were thought of as in some "prior stage" to that of the developed ones and as having to go through, more or less, the same historical experience they did in their progress to becoming modern societies. The result was some timid and, as later seen, misdirected efforts at change, which merely consolidated the existing economic system.

In the 1960's a new attitude emerged. The developmental model has not produced the promised fruits. A pessimistic diagnosis has now replaced the former optimistic one. Today we see clearly that the proposed model was an improper one. It was an abstract model, an ahistorical one, which kept us from seeing the complexity of the problem, the inevitably contradictory aspects of the proposed solution. The process of underdevelopment should be studied in historical perspective, i.e., contrasting it with the development of the great capitalist countries in whose sphere Latin America is situated.

Underdevelopment, as a global social fact, can be seen as the historical subproduct of the development of other countries. The dynamics of capitalistic economics lead simultaneously to the creation of greater wealth for fewer, and of greater poverty for more. Our national oligarchies, teamed up in complicity with these centers of power, perpetuate, for their own benefit and through various subterfuges, a situation of domination within each country. And the inequality between developed and underdeveloped countries is worse if we turn to the cultural point of view. The poor, dominated countries keep getting farther and farther behind. If things go on this way, we will soon be able to speak of two human groups, two kinds of men.

All these studies lead us to conclude that Latin America cannot develop within the capitalistic system.

Labeling Latin America an oppressed and dominated continent brings us naturally to speak of liberation and to start acting accordingly. Indeed, this is a word that reveals a new conviction of Latin Americans.

The failure of the efforts at reform has accentuated this attitude. Today the most "conscientized" groups agree that there will be a true development for Latin America only through liberation from the domination by capitalist countries. That implies, of course, a showdown with their natural allies: our national oligarchies. Latin America will never get out of its plight except by a profound transformation, a social revolution that will radically change the conditions it lives in at present. Today, a more or less Marxist inspiration prevails among those groups and individuals who are raising the banner of the continent's liberation. And for many in our continent, this liberation will have to pass, sooner or later, through paths of violence. Indeed, we recognize that the armed struggle began some years ago. It is hard to weigh its possibilities in terms of political effectiveness. The reverses it has suffered have obligated it to rethink its program, but it would be naive to think that the armed struggle is over.

We must remember, however, that in this process of liberation there is, explicitly or implicitly, an added thrust. Achieving the liberation of the continent means more than just overcoming economic, social, and political dependence. It also means seeing that humanity is marching toward a society in which man will be free of every servitude and master of his own destiny.

THE CHURCH IN THE LIBERATION PROCESS

The Latin American Church has lived, and still does, largely in a ghetto state. Thus the Church has had to seek support from the established powers and the economically powerful groups, in order to carry out its task and, at times, face its enemies. But for some time now, we have been witnessing a mighty effort to end that ghetto situation and shake off the ambiguous protection offered by the upholders of the unjust order our continent lives in.

The pastoral goal of setting up a "new Christianity" has brought about a political commitment by many Christians to create a more just society. The lay apostolic movements, in particular those of youth, have given their best leaders in years gone by to the political parties of Social Christian inspiration. Today, however, the apostolic youth movements have gone more radical in their political stance. In most Latin American countries the militants no longer gravitate toward the Social Christian parties, or if they do, they become their more radical wing. The increasingly more revolutionary political postures of Christian groups frequently lead the lay apostolic movements into conflict with the hierarchy, open the question of where they fit into the Church, and cause serious conscience problems for them. In many cases the laymen's interest in social revolution is gradually displacing their interest in the kingdom.

Clearer notions about the continent's tragic plight, sharp breaks provoked by the political polarization, the trend toward more active participation in the Church's life as urged by the Council and Medellin—all of these have made the clergy (including religious) one of the most dynamic and restless segments of the Latin American Church. In many countries groups of priests have organized to channel and accentuate the growing restlessness. They call for radical changes in the Church's presence and activity. These activities, and other factors, have in a number of cases led to frictions with local bishops and nuncios. It seems probable that, unless radical changes take place, these conflicts will multiply and get even worse in coming years. Many priests, as well, feel bound in conscience to engage actively in the field of politics. And it happens frequently today in Latin America that priests are labeled "subversives." Many of them are watched or sought by the police. Others are in jail, are exiled, or are even assassinated by anticommunist terrorists.

These new and serious problems facing the Latin American Church cause conflicts, and many bishops are ill prepared to cope with them. Yet there is a gradual awakening to the social overtones of the Church's presence and a rediscovery of their prophetic role. Bishops in the more impoverished and exploited areas have most vehemently denounced the injustices they witness. But as soon as they point out the profound causes behind these evils, they collide with the great economic and political blocs of their countries. Inevitably they are accused of intruding into matters that do not pertain to them and called Marxists. Often it is Catholic conservatives who most readily make those charges.

These activities have led to manifestoes expressing them and developing theologico-pastoral bases for them. In the past two years we have seen a flurry of public statements: from lay movements, groups of priests and bishops, and entire episcopates. A constant refrain in these statements is the admission of the Church's solidarity with Latin America's plight. The Church refuses to disregard that plight, seeking instead to accept its responsibility to correct the injustices. The poverty, injustice, and exploitation of man by fellow man in Latin America is often called "institutionalized violence." Theologically, that phenomenon is called a "situation of sin." The reality so described is more and more obviously the result of a *situation of dependence*, i.e., the centers where decisions are made are located outside our continent —a fact that keeps our countries in a condition of neocolonialism.

In all these statements, from a variety of sources inside the Latin American Church, the term "development" is gradually being displaced by the term "liberation." The word and the idea behind it express the desire to get rid of the condition of dependence, but even more than that they underline the desire of the oppressed peoples to seize the reins of their own destiny and shake free from the present servitude, as a symbol of the freedom from sin provided by Christ. This liberation will only be achieved by a thorough change of structures. The term "social revolution" is heard more and more—and ever more openly.

PROBLEMS

This situation questions, among other things, the Church of Latin America in respect to her actual community, in the meaning of her mission, in her social status, in her fidelity to the gospel. Thus new problems are planted and unsuspected perspectives are opened.

1) Active participation in the process of liberation is far from being a fact in all of the Latin American Christian community. The bulk of the Church remains tied in various ways (conscious or unconscious) to the established order. The worst of it is that among the Christians of Latin America not only are there different political options within the framework of a free exchange of ideas; rather, the polarization of the options and the hardening of the situation have put some Christians among the oppressed and others among the persecutors, some among the tortured and others among those who torture. From this results a

serious and radical confrontation. In the liberation process the Latin American Church is found strongly divided. In these conditions, life in the center of the Christian community becomes particularly difficult and conflictive. Participation in the Eucharistic celebration, for example, in its present-day form is seen by many as an act that lacks support in the real human community; it takes on fictitious appearances.

It will be impossible in the future not to face the problems which emerge from such a division between Christians. The lyric call for the union of all Christians, without taking into account the deep causes of the present situation and the real conditions for construction of society together, is nothing but an evasion. We are on the way to a new conception of unity and communion in the Church. This does not involve a fact acquired once and for all, but something always in process, something achieved with valor and liberty of spirit, with the price, at times, of painful severances.

2) In the Latin American world, where the Christian community should live and rejoice, its eschatological hope is that of social revolution, where violence is present in different ways. Its mission is before it. The choices which (with the limits already indicated) the Church is making are confronting her more and more with the dilemma which she presently is living on the continent: reform or revolution. Faced with this polarization, can the ecclesiastical authority stay on the level of generalized declarations? But can it go further without leaving that which is normally considered as its specific mission?

For the Latin American Church to be *in* in the world without being *of* the world means concretely and more clearly to be in the system but not of the system. It is evident, in effect, that only a break with the unjust present order and a frank commitment to a new society will make believable to the men of Latin America the message of love of which the Christian community is carrier. This demand should lead to a profound revision of the way it preaches the Word. The so-called "political theology" which assigns to the Church a socio-critical function with a basis in its eschatological hope is an interesting line of thought, especially in Latin America, where the exercising of that function (in practice already initiated) has enormous repercussions.

3) Another problem, closely related to the previous, is hotly debated: Should the Church use its social weight in favor of a social transformation in Latin America? There are those who are scandalized at hearing of a Church dedicated to necessary and urgent changes. They fear that after having been tied to one ruling order, the Church will simply commit herself to another. They also fear that this effort may terminate

in a noisy failure: the Latin American espiscopate does not have a unanimous position and does not have the necessary means to orient all Christians to one line of social advancement.

One cannot deny the reality of this risk. But the social influence of the Church is a fact; and to do nothing in favor of the oppressed of Latin America is to act against them. On the other hand, the best way for the Church to break her ties with the present order (and thus lose that ambiguous social prestige) is to denounce the fundamental injustices on which it is based. To discern what action is appropriate for the Latin American Church, it is necessary to keep in mind her historical and social co-ordinates. Not to do this is to move on the level of an abstract and "historic" theology—perhaps more subtly, a theology which is more careful not to repeat past errors than to see the originality of the present situation and to commit itself to the future.

4) The Latin American Christian community finds itself on a poor continent. But the image which she herself offers, taken globally, is not that of a poor Church. This is accurately reflected by the final document of Medellin, and whoever is interested can verify the image by consulting the middle-class Latin American. In the projection of this image, without doubt, prejudices and generalizations intervene, but no one can deny its basic validity. We often confuse what is "necessary" with a comfortable installation in this world, the liberty to preach the gospel with the protection of the powerful groups, the instruments of service with the means of power.

Our next step must be to go back to the question raised earlier and suggest certain answers that we find in modern-day theological reflection—or better, suggest certain tasks. Continuing the method we hinted at in the first part of this essay, we will keep as our backdrop in this discussion the praxis of the Christian community, especially in Latin America. The point to remember is this: the scope and importance of the process of liberation are such that to ask its meaning is to ask the meaning of Christianity itself, and the mission of the Church in the world. These are the root questions explicitly or implicitly behind the involvement of Christians in the fight against injustice. Only this approach will allow us to see with new eyes what liberation means in the light of faith.

THE FAITH AND THE NEW MAN

What ultimately brings Christians to participate in liberating oppressed peoples is the conviction that the gospel message is radically incompatible with an unjust, alienated society. They see clearly that they cannot be authentic Christians unless they act. But what they are to do to achieve this just world calls for great effort and imagination.

Theology, as a critical reflection in the light of faith on the presence of Christians in this world, ought to help us find our answer. It ought to verify the faith, hope, and charity contained in our zeal. But it ought also correct possible deviations and omissions in our Christian living that the demands of political action, however nobly inspired, may make us fall into. This too is a task for critical reflection.

In addition to the struggle against misery, injustice, and exploitation, what we seek is the *creation of a new man*. This aspiration questions and challenges our Christian faith. What that faith can say about itself enables us to see its relation with the yearning of men who fight to emancipate other men and themselves. What does that struggle, that creation, mean in the light of faith? What does this decision mean for man? What is the meaning of newness in history, or turning toward the future? Three questions, and three roads for theological reflection to follow. But primarily, three tasks.

LIBERATION AND SALVATION

What is the connection between salvation and the process of man's emancipation in the course of history? To answer this without staying in generalities would take a more searching study into what we mean by salvation than we can here afford. It is one of modern-day theology's lacunae. We do not seem to have drawn all the conclusions latent in the rediscovery of the truth of universal salvation. This is a bigger question than merely asking if one can be saved outside the visible Church. To talk of the presence of grace, accepted or rejected, in all men implies also forming a Christian judgment on the very roots of human actions. It makes it impossible to talk about a profane world; for human existence is ultimately nothing but a yes or no to the Lord.

There are not, then, two histories, one profane and one sacred, juxtaposed or interrelated, but a single human progress, irreversibly exalted by Christ, the Lord of history. His redemptive work embraces every dimension of human existence. Two great biblical themes illustrate this view: the relation between creation and salvation, and the eschatological promises.

In the Bible, *creation* is presented not as a stage previous to the work of salvation, but as the first salvific action: "God chose us before the creation of the world" (Eph 1:3). It is part of the process of salvation, of God's self-communication. The religious experience of Israel is essentially history, but that history is merely a prolongation of the creative act. Hence the Psalms sing of God simultaneously as Creator and Saviour (cf. Ps 135, 136, 74, 93, 95). God, who made a cosmos out of chaos, is the same who acts in salvation history. The work of Christ is seen as a re-creation and narrated for us in a context of creation (Jn 1).

Creation and salvation thus have a Christological meaning: in Him everything was created and saved (cf. Col 1:15-20).

So when we say that man realizes himself by continuing the act of creation through work, we are saying that he thereby places himself in the interior of salvation history. Mastering the earth, as Genesis bids him do, is a work of salvation, meant to produce its plenitude. To work, to transform this world, is to save. The Bible reveals the profound meaning of that effort. Building the temporal city is not a mere step in "humanizing," in "pre-evangelizing," as theologians used to say a few years back. Rather, it means participating fully in the salvific process that affects the whole man.

A second great biblical theme brings us to similar conclusions. This is the theme of *eschatological promises*, i.e., the events that herald and accompany the eschatological era. This is not a once-mentioned theme; rather, like the first one, it occurs repeatedly all through the Bible. It is vividly present in the history of Israel and hence deserves a place in the present progress of the people of God.

The prophets spoke of a kingdom of peace. But peace supposes the establishment of justice (Is 32:17), defense of the rights of the poor, punishment of the oppressor, a life without fear of being enslaved. A poorly understood spirituality has often led us to forget the human message, the power to change unjust social structures, that the eschatological promises contain—which does not mean, of course, that they contain nothing but social implications. The end of misery and exploitation will indicate that the kingdom has come; it will be here, according to Isaiah, when nobody "builds so that another may dwell, or plants so that another may eat," and when each one "enjoys the work of his hands" (65:22). To fight for a just world where there will be no oppression or slavery or forced work will be a sign of the coming of the kingdom. Kingdom and social injustice are incompatible. In Christ "all God's promises have their fulfillment" (2 Cor 1:20; cf. also Is 29:18-19, Mt 11:5, Lv 25:10; Lk 4:16-21).

The lesson to be drawn from these two biblical themes is clear: *salvation embraces the whole man*. The struggle for a just society fits fully and rightfully into salvation history. That conclusion is emphasized in *The Development of Peoples* (21), where it is said that "integral development" (viz., salvation) of man extends, without discontinuity, from the possession of what he needs to communion with the Lord, the fullness of the salvific work.

Christ thus appears as the Saviour who, by liberating us from sin, liberates us from the very root of social injustice. The entire dynamism of human history, the struggle against all that depersonalizes man— social inequalities, misery, exploitation—have their origin, are sub·

limated, and reach their plenitude in the salvific work of Christ. The following two points confirm and qualify the conclusions of these paragraphs.

MEETING GOD IN HISTORY

The purpose of Christians who participate in the process of liberation is, then, to *create a new man.* We have sought to answer the first question: What is the meaning of that struggle, that creation, in the light of faith? Perhaps we can now ask: What is the meaning of that decision for man?

In his political commitment, modern man is especially sensitive to basic human needs and tries to be of service to those suffering oppression and injustice. It is not enough to assert that love of God is inseparable from love of neighbor. We must also affirm that love of God is necessarily expressed through love of neighbor. Charity cannot exist in the abstract, outside our human scope for loving. Charity exists only incarnated in human love, raising it to its fulfillment. Loving neighbor is a necessary application of loving God; in fact, it is loving God.

"The Lord is the goal of human history." So says the *Constitution on the Church in the Modern World* (45). We meet the Lord when we meet men. Siding with man is siding with the God of our Christian faith, with the God-man, with Christ. Today, someone has said, our neighbor is not only some individual man, but also whole peoples, especially those suffering misery and oppression.

ESCHATOLOGY AND POLITICS

Dedication to bringing about a just society and a new man supposes trust in the future. It is an act that is open to whatever comes. What is the meaning of this *newness,* seen in the light of faith?

Modern man's tendency to live in function of the morrow, to be turned toward the future, intrigued by what still has to happen, has often been pointed out. This characteristic of our day no doubt contributed to the rediscovery of the eschatological values contained in revelation. The Bible, but particularly the Old Testament, offers eschatology as the motor force of salvation history. It thus appears not as one of many elements in Christianity, but as the very key to understanding it. The story of Exodus describes very well the Christian community's situation in history.

The new emphasis on eschatological values has brought about a renewal of the theology of hope. Christian life is essentially forward-looking. What distinguishes the Christian, Moltmann writes, "is not faith, nor charity, but hope." The Christian is, before all else, he who must answer for the hope that is in him (1 Pt 3:15).

The eschatological vision becomes operative, and hope becomes creative, when they meet the social realities in today's world, thus producing what is termed "political theology." Metz suggests that this is a needed corrective for a theology that, under the influence of existentialism and personalism, had grown too individualistic. Political theology seeks to focus on the social dimensions of the biblical message. The Bible tells us not only of a *vocation* to communion with God but of a *convocation*. That fact ought to have an impact on the political behavior of Christians.

This conclusion is particularly appropriate in Latin America, where the Christian community is accepting more and more delicate and even radical political involvements. But some questions arise. Will political theology stop at analyzing the meaning of those involvements? Or will it go further and inspire a new political doctrine for the Church? In the latter case, how can we avoid a return to the familiar old problem of Christendom? Shall theology become a new "ideology"? The challenge will be to find a way between a Christian politics and an abstention. Very likely no solution can be found by hit-and-miss methods. Yet it is hard to work out in advance (as we used to believe we could) the precise norms that should govern the Church's conduct, which will probably have to be decided by the needs of the moment, with the lights the Church has at its disposition, and with a mighty effort to be true to the gospel. There are certain chapters of theology that can only be written afterwards.

In any event, if we can recapture a historical vision focusing on the future and animated by hope that Christ will bring about the fullness we wait for, we shall see in a fresh light the *new man* we are trying to create by our activity in the present. In we hope in Christ, we will believe in the historical adventure—which opens a vast field of possibilities to the Christian's action.

THE CHURCH'S MISSION

The Church as the visible community of faith is frequently challenged and questioned today. What we have seen about the meaning of Christianity situates in a new way the Church's mission in the world. Two points can help us here: the first concerns the meaning of the Church's mission; the second, an inescapable condition for carrying it out.

HUMANITY'S ESCHATOLOGICAL AWARENESS

The unqualified assertion of the universal possibility of salvation changes radically our way of conceiving the Church's mission in the world. This shift in perspective implies a "decentralizing" of the Church, which is no longer the exclusive place for salvation, and now turns toward a new, radical service of mankind.

If, as we saw above, the construction of a just society fits squarely into salvation history, then the Church must play a role in that establishment of a new order. Political theology makes the Church an "institution of social criticism." This is a critique undertaken in function of its eschatological message, which will perform a liberating mission by pointing out the provisory nature of every historical situation and every human achievement.

The Church's role, however, is not only to exercise a social critique, which would run the risk of being something excessively intellectual. The Church will stimulate and radicalize the dedication of Christians to history about them. The Christian community, which professes a truth "that keeps working itself out," is called on to participate actively in constructing a just order. Here is a fact that theology dare not neglect, lest it incur the reproach, so often merited, that Christians undervalue all involvement in the world.

Thus we can justify the Church's "earthly" mission. But this eschatological perspective also permits us to grasp in a clear and dynamic way the antitheses: temporal vs. spiritual, and Church vs. world. The Church, indeed, is the world itself living in history, as it proceeds toward the future promised by the Lord. As Teilhard de Chardin noted, the Church is the "reflexively Christified" part of humanity. That is what the Church celebrates in the Eucharist; so we can see the indissoluble bond between it and the efforts to create a just society (Mt 5:23–24).

In Latin America the Church must realize that it exists in a continent undergoing revolution, where violence is present in different ways. The "world" in which the Christian community is called on to live and celebrate its eschatological hope is one in social revolution. Its mission must be achieved keeping that in account. The Church has no alternative. Only a total break with the unjust order to which it is bound in a thousand conscious or unconscious ways, and a forthright commitment to a new society, will make men in Latin America believe the message of love it bears. The Church's critico-political function becomes doubly important in Latin America, where the ecclesial institution carries so much prestige. In consideration, then, of the Church's mission, concrete circumstances should affect not only pastoral attitudes but theological thought itself.

POVERTY—IN SOLIDARITY AND IN PROTEST

For several years we have been hearing a growing call in the Church for an authentic witness of poverty. It is important, however, to grasp very precisely the point of this witness and to avoid sentimentalism (there has been trivial talk of the "eminent dignity of the poor in the Church"), as well as the fanciful project of making poverty into an ideal (which would be ironic indeed for those who undergo real misery).

In the Bible poverty, as deprivation of the basic needs for living, is considered an evil, something that degrades man and offends God; the words it uses in referring to the poor show this (cf. Is 10:2, Amos 2:6-7; 5:1-6; 2:1). On the other hand, spiritual poverty is not merely an interior indifference to the goods of this world, but an attitude of openness to God, of spiritual simplicity (Wis 2:3; Is 66:2; Ps 25, 34, 37, 149; Prv 22:4; 15:33; 18:2; Mt 5:3).

Christian poverty makes no sense, then, except as a promise to be one with those suffering misery, in order to point out the evil that it represents. No one should "idealize" poverty, but rather hold it aloft as an evil, cry out against it, and strive to eliminate it. Through such a spirit of solidarity we can alert the poor to the injustice of their situation. When Christ assumed the condition of poverty, He did so not to idealize it, but to show love and solidarity with men and to redeem them from sin. Christian poverty, an expression of love, makes us one with those who are poor and protests against their poverty.

Yet we must watch the use of that word. The term "poor" can seem vague and churchy, sentimental, even antiseptic. The "poor" man to-day is the one who is oppressed, who is kept marginal to society, the proletariat or subproletariat struggling to get his most elemental rights. The solidarity and protest we are talking about have a real political overtone in today's world.

Making oneself one with the poor today can entail personal risk, even of one's life. That is what many Christians—and non-Christians —who are dedicated to the revolutionary cause are finding out. Thus new forms of living poverty, different from the usual "giving up the goods of this world," are being found.

Only by repudiating poverty and making itself poor in protest against it can the Church preach "spiritual poverty," i.e., an openness of man and the history he lives in to the future promised by God. Only in that way can it fulfill honestly, and with a good chance of being heard, the critico-social function that political theology assigns. For the Church of today, this is the test of the authenticity of its mission.

We will have to rethink, too, the wisdom of having the churches of wealthy countries help the churches of poor countries. Financial aid can be self-defeating as witness of the poverty they should show, unless it is properly envisaged. Besides, it could lull them into settling for reformist solutions and superficial social changes that in the long run will only prolong the misery and injustice. Such aid can also salve the conscience of Christians in the countries that control the world economy.

A final word. If theological reflection does not help us to vitalize the Church's action in the world, and to make our commitment to charity deeper and more radical, it will amount to very little. We will have to watch out that we do not fall into an intellectual self-satisfaction, a sort of triumphalism of clever "new" visions of Christianity. Adapting Pascal, we can say that all the political theology of hope, of liberation, of revolution, is not worth as much as one act of faith, hope, and charity leading to an active effort to liberate man from all that dehumanizes him and keeps him from living according to the Lord's will.

KARL RAHNER

from *The World and Its People*

QUIETISM

A heterodox, or at least an undesirable, trend in mystical theology in the Romance countries during the seventeenth century (principal representatives M. de Molinos, Madame de Guyon, Fénelon; opposed by Bossuet; there were similar tendencies in the Eastern Church in twelfth-century Hesychasm, and in the West the Béguines of the thirteenth century). Quietism holds that perfection is selfless love of God in the sense of purely passive inwardness and resignation, from which all activity and all concern for one's own salvation has been eliminated. Hence active asceticism, vocal prayer, prayer of petition, and non-mystical meditation are more or less rejected. Pietism is an analogous movement in Protestantism. Both Pietism and Quietism are reactions against dry academic theology and a voluntaristic asceticism on the Stoic model which stultifies man's deeper powers instead of freeing and orientating them to God. Quietism was condemned by Innocent XI in 1687 and Innocent XII in 1699.

5

WAR

RUDYARD KIPLING

Epitaphs of the War

1914-18

"Equality of Sacrifice"

A. "I was a Have." B. "I was a 'have-not.'"
   (Together.) "What hast thou given which I gave not?"

A Servant

We were together since the war began.
He was my servant—and the better man.

A Son

My son was killed while laughing at some jest. I would I knew
What it was, and it might serve me in a time when jests are few.

An Only Son

I have slain none except my mother. She
(Blessing her slayer) died of grief for me.

Ex-clerk

Pity not! The army gave
Freedom to a timid slave:
In which freedom did he find
Strength of body, will, and mind:

By which strength he came to prove
Mirth, companionship, and love:
For which love to death he went:
In which death he lies content.

The Wonder

Body and spirit I surrendered whole
To harsh instructors—and received a soul . . .
If mortal man could change me through and through
From all I was—what may the God not do?

Hindu Sepoy in France

This man in his own country prayed we know not to what powers.
We pray them to reward him for his bravery in ours.

The Coward

I could not look on death, which being known,
Men led me to him, blindfold and alone.

Shock

My name, my speech, my self I had forgot.
My wife and children came—I knew them not.
I died. My mother followed. At her call
And on her bosom I remembered all.

A Grave Near Cairo

Gods of the Nile, should this stout fellow here
Get out—get out! He knows not shame nor fear.

Pelicans in the Wilderness

(A GRAVE NEAR HALFA)

The blown sand heaps on me, that none may learn
    Where I am laid for whom my children grieve. . . .
O wings that beat at dawning, ye return
    Out of the desert to your young at eve!

Two Canadian Memorials

1

We giving all gained all.
    Neither lament us nor praise.
Only in all things recall,
    It is fear, not death that slays.

2
From little towns in a far land we came,
  To save our honor and a world aflame.
By little towns in a far land we sleep;
  And trust that world we won for you to keep.

The Favor

Death favored me from the first, well knowing I could not endure
  To wait on him day by day. He quitted my betters and came
Whistling over the fields, and, when he had made all sure,
  "Thy line is at end," he said, "but at least I have saved its name."

The Beginner

On the first hour of my first day
  In the front trench I fell.
(Children in boxes at a play
  Stand up to watch it well.)

R.A.F. (Aged Eighteen)

Laughing through clouds, his milk-teeth still unshed,
Cities and men he smote from overhead.
His deaths delivered, he returned to play
Childlike, with childish things now put away.

The Refined Man

I was of delicate mind. I stepped aside for my needs,
  Disdaining the common office. I was seen from afar and killed. . . .
How is this matter for mirth? Let each man be judged by his deeds.
  I have paid my price to live with myself on the terms that I willed.

Native Water-Carrier (M.E.F.)

Prometheus brought down fire to men.
  This brought up water.
The Gods are jealous—now, as then,
  Giving no quarter.

Bombed in London

On land and sea I strove with anxious care
To escape conscription. It was in the air!

The Sleepy Sentinel

Faithless the watch that I kept: now I have none to keep.
I was slain because I slept: now I am slain I sleep.

Let no man reproach me again, whatever watch is unkept—
I sleep because I am slain. They slew me because I slept.

Batteries Out of Ammunition

If any mourn us in the workshop, say
We died because the shift kept holiday.

Common Form

If any question why we died,
Tell them, because our fathers lied.

A Dead Statesman

I could not dig: I dared not rob:
Therefore I lied to please the mob.
Now all my lies are proved untrue
And I must face the men I slew.
What tale shall serve me here among
Mine angry and defrauded young?

The Rebel

If I had clamored at Thy gate
For gift of life on earth,
And, thrusting through the souls that wait,
Flung headlong into birth—
Even then, even then, for gin and snare
About my pathway spread,
Lord, I had mocked Thy thoughtful care
Before I joined the dead!
But now?... I was beneath Thy hand
Ere yet the planets came.
And now—though planets pass, I stand
The witness to Thy shame!

The Obedient

Daily, though no ears attended,
Did my prayers arise.
Daily, though no fire descended,
Did I sacrifice.
Though my darkness did not lift,
Though I faced no lighter odds,
Though the Gods bestowed no gift,
Nonetheless,
Nonetheless, I served the Gods!

A Drifter Off Tarentum

He from the wind-bitten North with ship and companions descended,
  Searching for eggs of death spawned by invisible hulls.
Many he found and drew forth. Of a sudden the fishery ended
  In flame and a clamorous breath known to the eye-pecking gulls.

Destroyers in Collision

For fog and fate no charm is found
  To lighten or amend.
I, hurrying to my bride, was drowned—
  Cut down by my best friend.

Convoy Escort

I was a shepherd to fools
  Causelessly bold or afraid.
They would not abide by my rules.
  Yet they escaped. For I stayed.

Unknown Female Corpse

Headless, lacking foot and hand,
Horrible I come to land.
I beseech all women's sons
Know I was a mother once.

Raped and Revenged

One used and butchered me: another spied
Me broken—for which thing an hundred died.
So it was learned among the heathen hosts
How much a freeborn woman's favor costs.

Salonikan Grave

I have watched a thousand days
Push out and crawl into night
Slowly as tortoises.
Now I, too, follow these.
It is fever, and not the fight—
Time, not battle,—that slays.

The Bridegroom

Call me not false, beloved,
  If, from thy scarce-known breast
So little time removed,
  In other arms I rest.

For this more ancient bride,
  Whom coldly I embrace,
Was constant at my side
  Before I saw thy face.

Our marriage, often set—
  By miracle delayed—
At last is consummate,
  And cannot be unmade.

Live, then, whom life shall cure,
  Almost, of memory,
And leave us to endure
  Its immortality.

V.A.D. (Mediterranean)

Ah, would swift ships had never been, for then we ne'er had found,
These harsh Aegean rocks between, this little virgin drowned,
Whom neither spouse nor child shall mourn, but men she nursed
  through pain
And—certain keels for whose return the heathen look in vain.

Actors

ON A MEMORIAL TABLET IN HOLY TRINITY CHURCH,
STRATFORD-ON-AVON

We counterfeited once for your disport
  Men's joy and sorrow: but our day has passed.
We pray you pardon all where we fell short—
  Seeing we were your servants to this last.

Journalists

ON A PANEL IN THE HALL OF THE INSTITUTE OF JOURNALISTS

We have served our day.

RANDALL JARRELL

The Death of the Ball Turret Gunner

From my mother's sleep I fell into the State,
And I hunched in its belly till my wet fur froze.
Six miles from earth, loosed from its dream of life,

I woke to black flak and the nightmare fighters.
When I died they washed me out of the turret with a hose.

WILFRED OWEN

Anthem for Doomed Youth

What passing-bells for these who die as cattle?
Only the monstrous anger of the guns.
Only the stuttering rifles' rapid rattle
Can patter out their hasty orisons.

No mockeries for them; no prayers nor bells,
Nor any voice of mourning save the choirs,—
The shrill, demented choirs of wailing shells;
And bugles calling for them from sad shires.

What candles may be held to speed them all?
Not in the hands of boys, but in their eyes
Shall shine the holy glimmers of good-byes.
The pallor of girls' brows shall be their pall;
Their flowers the tenderness of patient minds,
And each slow dusk a drawing-down of blinds.

Dulce et Decorum Est

Bent double, like old beggars under sacks,
Knock-kneed, coughing like hags, we cursed through sludge,
Till on the haunting flares we turned our backs,
And towards our distant rest began to trudge.
Men marched asleep. Many had lost their boots,
But limped on, blood-shod. All went lame, all blind;
Drunk with fatigue; deaf even to the hoots
Of gas-shells dropping softly behind.

Gas! Gas! Quick, boys!—An ecstasy of fumbling,
Fitting the clumsy helmets just in time,
But someone still was yelling out and stumbling
And flound'ring like a man in fire or lime.
Dim through the misty panes and thick green light,
As under a green sea, I saw him drowning.

In all my dreams before my helpless sight
He plunges at me, guttering, choking, drowning.

If in some smothering dreams, you too could pace
Behind the wagon that we flung him in,
And watch the white eyes wilting in his face,
His hanging face, like a devil's sick of sin,
If you could hear, at every jolt, the blood
Come gargling from the froth-corrupted lungs
Bitten as the cud
Of vile, incurable sores on innocent tongues,—
My friend, you would not tell with such high zest
To children ardent for some desperate glory,
The old lie: *Dulce et decorum est
Pro patria mori.*

THOMAS MERTON

The Roots of War

The present war crisis is something we have made entirely for and by
ourselves. There is, in reality, not the slightest logical reason for war,
and yet the whole world is plunging headlong into frightful destruction, and doing so with the purpose of avoiding war and preserving
peace! This is a true war-madness, an illness of the mind and the spirit
that is spreading with a furious and subtle contagion all over the
world. Of all the countries that are sick, America is perhaps the most
grievously afflicted. On all sides we have people building bomb
shelters where, in case of nuclear war, they will simply bake slowly
instead of burning up quickly or being blown out of existence in a
flash. And they are prepared to sit in these shelters with machine guns
with which to prevent their neighbor from entering. This is a nation
that claims to be fighting for religious truth along with freedom and
other values of the spirit. Truly we have entered the "post-Christian
era" with a vengeance. Whether we are destroyed or whether we
survive, the future is awful to contemplate.

What is the place of the Christian in all this? Is he simply to fold his
hands and resign himself for the worst, accepting it as the inescapable
will of God and preparing himself to enter heaven with a sigh of relief?
Should he open up the Apocalypse and run out into the street to give
everyone his idea of what is happening? Or worse still, should he take a
hard-headed and "practical" attitude about it and join in the madness

of the warmakers, calculating how, by a "first strike," the glorious Christian West can eliminate atheistic communism for all time and usher in the millennium? . . . I am no prophet and no seer, but it seems to me that this last position may very well be the most diabolical of illusions, the great and not even subtle temptation of a Christianity that has grown rich and comfortable, and is satisfied with its riches.

STRIVE WITH HOPE

What are we to do? The duty of the Christian in this crisis is to strive with all his power and intelligence, with his faith, hope in Christ, and love for God and humanity, to do the one task which God has imposed upon us in the world today. That task is to work for the total abolition of war. There can be no question that unless war is abolished the world will remain constantly in a state of madness and desperation in which, because of the immense destructive power of modern weapons, the danger of catastrophe will be imminent and probably at every moment everywhere. Unless we set ourselves immediately to this task, both as individuals and in our political and religious groups, we tend by our very passivity and fatalism to cooperate with the destructive forces that are leading inexorably to war. It is a problem of terrifying complexity and magnitude, for which the Church herself is not fully able to see clear and decisive solutions. Yet she must lead the way on the road towards nonviolent settlement of difficulties and towards the gradual abolition of war as the way of settling international or civil disputes. Christians must become active in every possible way, mobilizing all their resources for the fight against war. First of all, there is much to be studied, much to be learned. Peace is to be preached, nonviolence is to be explained as a practical method, and not left to be mocked as an outlet for crackpots who want to make a show of themselves. Prayer and sacrifice must be used as the most effective spiritual weapons in the war against war, and, like all weapons, they must be used with deliberate aim: not just with a vague aspiration for peace and security, but against violence and against war. This implies that we are also willing to sacrifice and restrain our own instinct for violence and aggressiveness in our relations with other people. We may never succeed in this campaign, but, whether we succeed or not, the duty is evident. It is the great Christian task of our time. Everything else is secondary, for the survival of the human race itself depends upon it. We must at least face this responsibility and do something about it. And the first job of all is to understand the psychological forces at work in ourselves and in society.

At the root of all war is fear: not so much the fear people have of one another as the fear they have of *everything*. It is not merely that they do not trust one another: they do not even trust themselves. If they are not sure when someone else may turn around and kill them, they are still less sure when they may turn around and kill themselves. They cannot trust anything, because they have ceased to believe in God.

It is not only our hatred of others that is dangerous, but also, and above all, our hatred of ourselves: particularly that hatred of ourselves which is too deep and too powerful to be consciously faced. For it is this which makes us see our own evil in others and unable to see it in ourselves.

When we see crime in others, we try to correct it by destroying them or at least putting them out of sight. It is easy to identify the sin with the sinner when he is someone other than our own self. In ourselves, it is the other way around; we see the sin, but we have great difficulty in shouldering responsibility for it. We find it very hard to identify our sin with our own will and our own malice. On the contrary, we naturally tend to interpret our immoral act as an involuntary mistake, or as the malice of a spirit in us that is other than ourself. Yet, at the same time, we are fully aware that others do not make this convenient distinction for us. The acts that have been done are, in their eyes, "our" acts, and they hold us fully responsible.

What is more, we tend unconsciously to ease ourselves still more of the burden of guilt that is in us, by passing it on to somebody else. When I have done wrong, and have excused myself by attributing the wrong to "another" who is unaccountably "in me," my conscience is not yet satisfied. There is still too much left to be explained. The "other in myself" is too close to home. The temptation is, then, to account for my fault by seeing an equivalent amount of evil in someone else. Hence I minimize my own sins, and compensate for doing so by exaggerating the faults of others.

As if this were not enough, we make the situation much worse by artificially intensifying our sense of evil, and by increasing our propensity to feel guilt even for things which are not in themselves wrong. In all these ways we build up such an obsession with evil, both in ourselves and in others, that we waste all our mental energy trying to account for this evil, to punish it, to exorcise it, or to get rid of it in any way we can. We drive ourselves mad with our preoccupation and in the end there is no outlet left but violence. We have to destroy something or someone. By that time, we have created for ourselves a suitable enemy, a scapegoat in whom we have invested all the evil in the world. He is the cause of every wrong. He is the fomenter of all conflict. If he can only be destroyed, conflict will cease, evil will be done with, there will be no more war.

This kind of fictional thinking is especially dangerous when it is supported by a whole elaborate pseudo-scientific structure of myths, like those which Marxists have adopted as their ersatz for religion. But it is certainly no less dangerous when it operates in the vague, fluid, confused and unprincipled opportunism which substitutes in the west for religion, for philosophy and even for mature thought.

When the whole world is in moral confusion: when no one knows any longer what to think, and when, in fact, everybody is running away from the responsibility of thinking, when one makes rational thought about moral issues absurd by exiling oneself entirely from realities into the realm of fictions, and when we expend all our efforts in constructing more fictions with which to account for our ethical failures, then it becomes clear that the world cannot be saved from global war and global destruction by the mere efforts and good intentions of peace-makers. In actual fact, everyone is becoming more and more aware of the widening gulf between good purposes and bad results, between efforts to make peace and the growing likelihood of war. It seems that no matter how elaborate and careful the planning, all attempts at international dialogue end in more and more ludicrous failures. In the end, no one has any more faith in those who even attempt the dialogue. On the contrary, the negotiators, with all their pathetic good will, become the objects of contempt and of hatred. It is the "people of good will," those who have made their poor efforts to do something about peace, who will in the end be the most mercilessly reviled, crushed, and destroyed as victims of the universal self-hate of humans, which they have unfortunately only increased by the failure of their good intentions.

REALISTIC ACCEPTANCE

Perhaps we still have a basically superstitious tendency to associate failure with dishonesty and guilt—failure being interpreted as "punishment." Even if a person starts out with good intentions, if he fails we tend to think he was somehow "at fault." If he was not guilty, he was at least "wrong." And "being wrong" is something we have not yet learned to face with equanimity and understanding. We either condemn it with god-like disdain, or forgive it with god-like condescension. We do not manage to accept it with human compassion, humility and identification. Thus we never see the one truth that would help us begin to solve our ethical and political problems: that we are all more or less wrong, that we are all at fault, all limited and obstructed by our mixed motives, our self-deception, our greed, our self-righteousness and our tendency to aggressivity and hypocrisy.

In our refusal to accept the partially good intentions of others and work with them (of course prudently and with resignation to the inevitable imperfection of the result) we are unconsciously proclaiming our own malice, our own intolerance, our own lack of realism, our own ethical and political quackery.

Perhaps, in the end, the first real step toward peace would be a realistic acceptance of the fact that our political ideals are perhaps, to a great extent, illusions and fictions to which we cling out of motives that are not always perfectly honest: that because of this we prevent ourselves from seeing any good or any practicability in the political ideals of our enemies—which may, of course, be in many ways even more illusory and dishonest than our own. We will never get anywhere unless we can accept the fact that politics is an inextricable tangle of good and evil motives in which, perhaps, the evil predominate but where one must continue to hope doggedly in what little good can still be found.

But someone will say: "If we once recognize that we are all equally wrong, all political action will instantly be paralyzed. We can only act when we assume that we are in the right." On the contrary, I believe the basis for valid political action can only be the recognition that the true solution to our problems is not accessible to any one isolated party or nation but that all must arrive at it by working together.

TRUST

I do not mean to encourage the guilt-ridden thinking that is always too glad to be "wrong" in everything. This, too, is an evasion of responsibility, because every form of oversimplification tends to make decisions ultimately meaningless. We must try to accept ourselves, whether individually or collectively, not only as perfectly good or perfectly bad, but in our mysterious, unaccountable mixture of good and evil. We have to stand by the modicum of good that is in us without exaggerating it. We have to defend our real rights, because, unless we respect our own rights we will certainly not respect the rights of others. But, at the same time, we have to recognize that we have wilfully or otherwise trespassed on the rights of others. We must be able to admit this not only as the result of self-examination, but when it is pointed out unexpectedly, and perhaps not too gently, by somebody else.

These principles which govern personal moral conduct, which make harmony possible in small social units like the family, also apply in the wider area of the state and in the whole community of nations. It is, however, quite absurd, in our present situation or in any other, to expect these principles to be universally accepted as the result of moral exhortations. There is very little hope that the world will be run according to them all of a sudden, as a result of some hypothetical change of heart on the part of politicians. It is useless and even laughable to base political thought on the faint hope of a purely contingent and subjective moral illumination in the hearts of the world's leaders. But outside of political thought and action, in the religious sphere, it is not only permissible to hope for such a mysterious consummation, but it is necessary to pray for it. We can and must believe not so much that the mysterious light of God can "convert" the ones who are mostly responsible for the world's peace, but at least that they may, in spite of their obstinacy and their prejudices, be guarded against fatal error.

It would be sentimental folly to expect people to trust one another when they obviously cannot be trusted. But at least they can learn to trust God. They can bring themselves to see that the mysterious power of God can, quite independently of human malice and error, protect persons unaccountably against themselves, and that He can always turn evil into good, though perhaps not always in a sense that would be understood by the preachers of sunshine and uplift. If they can trust and love God, Who is infinitely wise and Who rules the lives of all, permitting them to use their freedom even to the point of almost incredible abuse, they can love people who are evil. They can learn to love them even in their sin, as God has loved them. If we can love those we cannot trust (without trusting them foolishly) and if we can, to some extent, share the burden of their sin by identifying ourselves with them, then perhaps there is some hope of a kind of peace on earth, based not on the wisdom and the manipulations of humans but on the inscrutable mercy of God.

For only love—which means humility—can exorcise the fear which is at the root of all war.

What is the use of postmarking our mail with the exhortations to "pray for peace" and then spending billions of dollars on atomic submarines, thermonuclear weapons, and ballistic missiles? This, I would think, would certainly be what the New Testament calls "mocking God"—and mocking Him far more effectively than the atheists do. The culminating horror of the joke is that we are piling up these weapons to protect ourselves against atheists who, quite frankly, believe there is no God and are convinced that one has to rely on bombs and missiles since nothing else offers any real security. Is it, then, because we have so much trust in the power of God that we are intent upon utterly destroying these people before they can destroy us? Even at the risk of destroying ourselves at the same time?

I do not mean to imply that prayer excludes the simultaneous use of ordinary human means to accomplish a naturally good and justifiable end. One can very well pray for a restoration of physical health and at the same time take medicine prescribed by a doctor. In fact, a believer should normally do both. And there would seem to be a reasonable and right proportion between the use of these two means to the same end.

But consider the utterly fabulous amount of money, planning, energy, anxiety and care which go into the production of weapons which almost immediately become obsolete and have to be scrapped. Contrast all this with the pitiful little gesture: "pray for peace" piously cancelling our four-cent stamps! Think, too, of the disproportion between our piety and the enormous act of murderous destruction, which we, at the same time, countenance without compunction and without shame! It does not even seem to enter our minds that there might be some incongruity in praying to the God of peace, the God Who told us to love one another as He had loved us, Who warned us that they who took the sword would perish by it, and, at the same time, planning to annihilate not thousands, but millions of civilians and soldiers, men, women and children, without discrimination, even with the almost infallible certainty of inviting the same annihilation for ourselves!

It may make sense for a sick person to pray for health and then take medicine, but I fail to see any sense at all in their praying for health and then drinking poison.

When I pray for peace, I pray God to pacify not only the Russians and the Chinese, but above all my own nation and myself. When I pray for peace, I pray to be protected not only from the Russians but also from the folly and blindness of my own country. When I pray for peace, I pray not only that the enemies of my country may cease to want war, but, above all, that my own country will cease to do the things that make war inevitable. In other words, when I pray for peace I am not just praying that the Russians will give up without a struggle and let us have our own way. I am praying that both we and the Russians may somehow be restored to sanity and learn how to work out our problems, as best we can, together, instead of preparing for global suicide.

I am fully aware that this sounds utterly sentimental, archaic and out of tune with an age of science. But I would like to submit that pseudo-scientific thinking in politics and sociology has so much less than this to offer. One thing I would like to add, in all fairness, is that the atomic scientists themselves are quite often the ones most concerned about the ethics of the situation, and that they are among the few who dare to open their mouths from time to time and say something about it. But who on earth listens?

PEACE

If people really wanted peace they would sincerely ask God for it, and

He would give it to them. But why should He give the world a peace which it does not really desire? The peace the world pretends to desire is really no peace at all.

To some, peace merely means the liberty to exploit other people without fear of retaliation or interference. To others, peace means the freedom to rob others without interruption. To still others, it means the leisure to devour the goods of the earth without being compelled to interrupt their pleasures to feed those whom their greed is starving. And, to practically everybody, peace simply means the absence of any physical violence that might cast a shadow over lives devoted to the satisfaction of their animal appetites for comfort and pleasure.

Many like these have asked God for what they thought was "peace," and wondered why their prayer was not answered. They could not understand that it actually *was* answered. God left them with what they desired, for their idea of peace was only another form of war. The "cold war" is simply the normal consequence of our corruption of a peace based on a policy of "everyone for himself" in ethics, economics and political life. It is absurd to hope for a solid peace based on fictions and illusions!

So instead of loving what you think is peace, love other people, and love God above all. And instead of hating the people you think are warmongers, hate the appetites and the disorder in your own soul, which are the causes of war. If you love peace, then hate injustice, hate tyranny, hate greed—but hate these things in yourself, not in another.

KARL RAHNER

Peace

In Scripture peace is simply the gift of God himself to men: as such it was promised to the chosen people in the Old Testament and brought to the world by Jesus Christ. For biblical theology peace has the more precise sense of that "well-being"—wholeness, health, safety—which Jesus' act of obedience, in "delivering" himself without reserve to God, has won, by totally defeating the power of evil and of the mere law, and of death, which held us in bondage, and graciously ending man's quarrel with and separation from God. Peace therefore is the peace which is Jesus Christ (Eph 2:14), the peace which Jesus Christ (as the revelation of God's unrepenting self-surrender) has made with man (Acts 10:36; Col 1:20): which he alone can bequeath (Jn 14:27); which remains in the world by the operation of the Spirit of Jesus Christ (Gal 5:22; Lk 2:14); which therefore, gift of God though it be, is the task of

Jesus Christ's Church and must be preserved by her (Rom 12:18; Eph 4:3). Scholastic philosophy specially emphasizes this last aspect: in St. Thomas peace is "the order of community life based on justice." This order of things is not preordained, but has always to be brought about anew. The requisite assurance of peace is a task for all those forces which can make a contribution. Those who claim to be Christians must hold in such deliberations to Jesus' requirements of nonviolence, unconditional forgiveness, and love of one's enemies.

6

WISDOM

DAME FREYA STARK

"Permissive" and the Negative Virtues

Pasan, serenas las horas, no hay guerra en el mundo y duerme
bien el labrador, viendo el cielo en el fondo alto de su sueño.
XIMENEZ. Platero y yo.

Obedience, chastity, strictness of duty—respectable virtues with a
medieval ancestry, encouraged by Dr. Arnold and flourishing under
Victoria—they have vanished underground like desert rivers and at
present show no sign of reappearing. In my own lifetime they have
become almost improper to mention—banished in any case from the
public scene and replaced after the First World War by the poor
alternative adjective *permissive.*

I am not out to defend them, for they are negative in themselves, and
meant to be used only as a boundary to retrench the vagabond
lawlessness of man. The enchantment, the beauty which a virtue must
have if it is to be a virtue indeed, is borrowed: it comes to them from a
presence outside themselves, a radiance which their fence is built to
protect and defend.

> There dwells sweet love, and constant chastity,
> Unspotted faith and comely womanhood,
> Regard of honour and mild modesty;
> There virtue raynes as queen in royal throne,

And giveth lawes alone,
The which the base affections doe obey,
And yield their services unto her will;
Ne thought of thing uncomely ever may
Thereto approach to tempt her mind to ill.
Had ye once seen these her celestial treasures,
And unrevealéd pleasures,
Then would ye wonder, and her prayses sing,
That al the woods should answer, and your echo ring.*

It is not possible to quarrel with words like these: but the loveliness that is so praised is not the subservient virtue but Love itself in its timeless light.

So with the other two. It is not so much Obedience as what is obeyed that has the "integra, consonantia, claritas"—the wholeness, harmony, radiance defined by St. Thomas Aquinas. And Duty as a virtue, *stern daughter of the voice of God,* must also get her halo from outside as it were, before the *Godhead's most benignant grace* can show.

She *preserves the stars from wrong,* says Wordsworth, who over-lapped into the Victorian age; and this negative touch, this quality of being a defence rather than an adventure, has robbed all the three virtues of their modern charm. To see them in their proper setting one must go back to the early Christianity when education, almost entirely monastic, was a jungle adventure surrounded by renunciations and dangers. These three were then helpful as the black and white stripes are helpful to motorists at dangerous corners: their warning kept one on the road. Like an athlete's training, their innate quality of boredom was lost in its objective, and their decline is due to the fact that the Faith which inspired and encouraged them has almost disappeared.

Far above their world, in flashes of a hidden sun, the bird of Faith was sailing in their sky. Its intimate, eternal fires lit their terrestrial efforts, their many abdications sacrificed to the inexpressible progress of light. The shadow of its wing, the safety of man's sunset in his West, were the prize of these renunciations; and when the great bird sped from our geography, the virtues that were meant to ease his visitations drooped and died.

Permissive was found instead, as a substitute in the shaken conditions that followed the First World War—a word in whose poor sky the only visible wings are those of Lucifer falling through Space towards Chaos and Night.

*Spenser—for his own wedding.

Into this wild abyss,
The womb of nature and perhaps her grave.*

A new fashion in adjectives is surely needed?

MARGUERITE OF NAVARRE

Autant en Emporte le Vent†

If someone insults you,
Endure him lightheartedly;
And if all slander you,
Give no heed to them:
    'Tis nothing new
To hear such frequent talk:
Autant en emporte le vent.

If someone speaks of Faith,
Minimizing its value
Compared with the works of the Law,
Judging these worthier,
    'Tis strange dogma.
Pass him by, go forth:
Autant en emporte le vent.

And if, to impair your Faith,
He lauds your noble deeds,
Declaring (to flatter you)
That he ranks you with the elect,
    Flee such talk
That leads to false pride:
Autant en emporte le vent.

If the world comes a-tempting
With riches, honours, pleasures,
And offers them all to you,
Deny it your heart and will,
    For temporal things
Return whence they came:
Autant en emporte le vent.

*Paradise Lost: Book II, 910-11.

†Something like: "all this is idle talk" or "it will all vanish into thin air."

If you are told of a place
(Not God's) where can be found
Solace and true salvation,
It is to murder your soul.
       Be a rebel.
Belie the most learned:
Autant en emporte le vent.

7

THE DESERT

HENRY NOUWEN

Silence
from *The Way of the Heart*

INTRODUCTION

When Arsenius, the Roman educator who exchanged his status and wealth for the solitude of the Egyptian desert, prayed, "Lord, lead me into the way of salvation," he heard a voice saying, "Be silent." Silence completes and intensifies solitude. This is the conviction shared by the Desert Fathers. A charming story about Abbot Macarius makes the point quite well. "Once the abbot Macarius, after he had given the benediction to the brethren in the church at Scete, said to them, 'Brethren, fly.' One of the elders answered him, 'How can we fly further than this, seeing we are here in the desert?' Then Macarius placed his finger on his mouth and said, 'Fly from this.' So saying, he entered his cell and shut the door."

Silence is the way to make solitude a reality. The Desert Fathers praise silence as the safest way to God. "I have often repented of having spoken," Arsenius said, "but never of having remained silent." One day Archbishop Theophilus came to the desert to visit Abba Pambo. But Abba Pambo did not speak to him. When the brethren finally said to Pambo, "Father, say something to the archbishop, so that he may be edified," he replied: "If he is not edified by my silence, he will not be edified by my speech."

Silence is an indispensable discipline in the spiritual life. Ever since

James described the tongue as a "whole wicked world in itself" and silence as putting a bit into the horse's mouth (James 3:3, 6) Christians have tried to practice silence as the way to self-control. Clearly silence is a discipline needed in many different situations: in teaching and learning, in preaching and worship, in visiting and counseling. Silence is a very concrete, practical, and useful discipline in all our ministerial tasks. It can be seen as a portable cell taken with us from the solitary place into the midst of our ministry. Silence is solitude practiced in action.

In this reflection I would like first to show how wordy our world has become. Then I want to describe the great value of silence in this wordy world. Finally I hope to indicate how silence can be a sign of God's presence in the different forms of ministry.

OUR WORDY WORLD

Over the last few decades we have been inundated by a torrent of words. Wherever we go we are surrounded by words: words softly whispered, loudly proclaimed, or angrily screamed; words spoken, recited, or sung; words on records, in books, on walls, or in the sky; words in many sounds, many colors, or many forms; words to be heard, read, seen, or glanced at; words which flicker off and on, move slowly, dance, jump, or wiggle. Words, words, words! They form the floor, the walls, and the ceiling of our existence.

It has not always been this way. There was a time not too long ago without radios and televisions, stop signs, yield signs, merge signs, bumper stickers, and the ever-present announcements indicating price increases or special sales. There was a time without the advertisements which now cover whole cities with words.

Recently I was driving through Los Angeles, and suddenly I had the strange sensation of driving through a huge dictionary. Wherever I looked there were words trying to take my eyes from the road. They said, "Use me, take me, buy me, drink me, smell me, touch me, kiss me, sleep with me." In such a world who can maintain respect for words?

All this is to suggest that words, my own included, have lost their creative power. Their limitless multiplication has made us lose confidence in words and caused us to think, more often than not, "They are just words."

Teachers speak to students for six, twelve, eighteen, and sometimes twenty-four years. But the students often emerge from the experience with the feeling, "They were just words." Preachers preach their sermons week after week and year after year. But their parishioners remain the same and often think, "They are just words." Politicians, businessmen, ayatollahs, and popes give speeches and make statements "in season and out of season," but those who listen say: "They are just words...just another distraction."

The result of this is that the main function of the word, which is communication, is no longer realized. The word no longer communicates, no longer fosters communion, no longer creates community, and therefore no longer gives life. The word no longer offers trustworthy ground on which people can meet each other and build society.

Do I exaggerate? Let us focus for a moment on theological education. What else is the goal of theological education than to bring us closer to the Lord our God so that we may be more faithful to the great commandment to love him with all our heart, with all our soul, and with all our mind, and our neighbor as ourselves (Matthew 22:37)? Seminaries and divinity schools must lead theology students into an ever-growing communion with God, with each other, and with their fellow human beings. Theological education is meant to form our whole person toward an increasing conformity with the mind of Christ so that our way of praying and our way of believing will be one.

But is this what takes place? Often it seems that we who study or teach theology find ourselves entangled in such a complex network of discussions, debates, and arguments about God and "God-issues" that a simple conversation with God or a simple presence to God has become practically impossible. Our heightened verbal ability, which enables us to make many distinctions, has sometimes become a poor substitute for a single-minded commitment to the Word who is life. If there is a crisis in theological education, it is first and foremost a crisis of the word. This is not to say that critical intellectual work and the subtle distinctions it requires have no place in theological training. But when our words are no longer a reflection of the divine Word in and through whom the world has been created and redeemed, they lose their grounding and become as seductive and misleading as the words used to sell Geritol.

There was a time when the obvious milieu for theological education was the monastery. There words were born out of silence and could lead one deeper into silence. Although monasteries are no longer the most common places of theological education, silence remains as indispensable today as it was in the past. The Word of God is born out of the eternal silence of God, and it is to this Word out of silence that we want to be witnesses.

SILENCE

Silence is the home of the word. Silence gives strength and fruitfulness to the word. We can even say that words are meant to disclose the mystery of the silence from which they come.

The Taoist philosopher Chuang Tzu expresses this well in the following way:

> The purpose of a fish trap is to catch fish and when the fish are caught, the trap is forgotten. The purpose of a rabbit snare is to catch rabbits. When the rabbits are caught, the snare is forgotten. The purpose of the word is to convey ideas. When the ideas are grasped, the words are forgotten. Where can I find a man who has forgotten words? He is the one I would like to talk to.

"I would like to talk to the man who has forgotten words." That could have been said by one of the Desert Fathers. For them, the word is the instrument of the present world and silence is the mystery of the future world. If a word is to bear fruit it must be spoken from the future world into the present world. The Desert Fathers therefore considered their going into the silence of the desert to be a first step into the future world. From that world their words could bear fruit, because there they could be filled with the power of God's silence.

In the sayings of the Desert Fathers, we can distinguish three aspects of silence. All of them deepen and strengthen the central idea that silence is the mystery of the future world. First, silence makes us pilgrims. Secondly, silence guards the fire within. Thirdly, silence teaches us to speak.

SILENCE MAKES US PILGRIMS

Abba Tithoes once said, "Pilgrimage means that a man should control his tongue." The expression "To be on pilgrimage is to be silent" *(peregrinatio est tacere)*, expresses the conviction of the Desert Fathers that silence is the best anticipation of the future world. The most frequent argument for silence is simply that words lead to sin. Not speaking, therefore, is the most obvious way to stay away from sin. This connection is clearly expressed by the apostle James: "... every one of us does something wrong, over and over again; the only man who could reach perfection would be someone who never said anything wrong—he would be able to control every part of himself" (James 3:2).

James leaves little doubt that speaking without sinning is very difficult and that, if we want to remain untouched by the sins of the world on our journey to our eternal home, silence is the safest way. Thus, silence became one of the central disciplines of the spiritual life. St. Benedict, the father of the monastic life in the West and the patron saint of Europe, puts great emphasis on silence in his Rule. He quotes the Psalmist who says, "I will keep a muzzle on my mouth... I will watch how I behave and not let my tongue lead me into sin" (Psalm

39:1). St. Benedict not only warns his brothers against evil talk, but also tells them to avoid good, holy, edifying words because, as it is written in the book of Proverbs, "A flood of words is never without its faults" (Proverbs 10:19). Speaking is dangerous and easily leads us away from the right path.

The central idea underlying these ascetic teachings is that speaking gets us involved in the affairs of the world, and it is very hard to be involved without becoming entangled in and polluted by the world. The Desert Fathers and all who followed in their footsteps, "knew that every conversation tended to interest them in this world, to make them in heart less of strangers here and more of citizens."

This might sound too unworldly to us, but let us at least recognize how often we come out of a conversation, a discussion, a social gathering, or a business meeting with a bad taste in our mouth. How seldom have long talks proved to be good and fruitful? Would not many if not most of the words we use be better left unspoken? We speak about the events of the world, but how often do we really change them for the better? We speak about people and their ways, but how often do our words do them or us any good? We speak about our ideas and feelings as if everyone were interested in them, but how often do we really feel understood? We speak a great deal about God and religion, but how often does it bring us or others real insight? Words often leave us with a sense of inner defeat. They can even create a sense of numbness and a feeling of being bogged down in swampy ground. Often they leave us in a slight depression, or in a fog that clouds the window of our mind. In short, words can give us the feeling of having stopped too long at one of the little villages that we pass on our journey, of having been motivated more by curiosity than by service. Words often make us forget that we are pilgrims called to invite others to join us on the journey. *Peregrinatio est tacere.* "To be silent keeps us pilgrims."

SILENCE GUARDS THE FIRE WITHIN

A second, more positive, meaning of silence is that it protects the inner fire. Silence guards the inner heat of religious emotions. This inner heat is the life of the Holy Spirit within us. Thus, silence is the discipline by which the inner fire of God is tended and kept alive.

Diadochus of Photiki offers us a very concrete image: "When the door of the steambath is continually left open, the heat inside rapidly escapes through it; likewise the soul, in its desire to say many things, dissipates its remembrance of God through the door of speech, even though everything it says may be good. Thereafter the intellect, though lacking appropriate ideas, pours out a welter of confused thoughts to anyone it meets, as it no longer has the Holy Spirit to keep its understanding free from fantasy. Ideas of value always shun verbosity, being foreign to confusion and fantasy. Timely silence, then, is precious, for it is nothing less than the mother of the wisest thoughts."

These words of Diadochus go against the grain of our contemporary life-style, in which "sharing" has become one of the greatest virtues. We have been made to believe that feelings, emotions, and even the inner stirrings of our soul have to be shared with others. Expressions such as "Thanks for sharing this with me," or "It was good to share this with you," show that the door of our steambath is open most of the time. In fact, people who prefer to keep to themselves and do not expose their interior life tend to create uneasiness and are often considered inhibited, asocial, or simply odd. But let us at least raise the question of whether our lavish ways of sharing are not more compulsive than virtuous; that instead of creating community they tend to flatten out our life together. Often we come home from a sharing session with a feeling that something precious has been taken away from us or that holy ground has been trodden upon. James Hannay, commenting on the sayings of the Desert Fathers, writes:

> The mouth is not a door through which any evil enters. The ears are such doors as are the eyes. The mouth is a door only for exit. What was it that they [the Desert Fathers] feared to let go out? What was it which someone might steal out of their hearts, as a thief takes the steed from the stable when the door is left open? It can have been nothing else than the force of religious emotion.

What needs to be guarded is the life of the Spirit within us. Especially we who want to witness to the presence of God's Spirit in the world need to tend the fire within with utmost care. It is not so strange that many ministers have become burnt-out cases, people who say many words and share many experiences, but in whom the fire of God's Spirit has died and from whom not much more comes forth than their own boring, petty ideas and feelings. Sometimes it seems that our many words are more an expression of our doubt than of our faith. It is as if we are not sure that God's Spirit can touch the hearts of people: we have to help him out and, with many words, convince others of his power. But it is precisely this wordy unbelief that quenches the fire.

Our first and foremost task is faithfully to care for the inward fire so that when it is really needed it can offer warmth and light to lost travelers. Nobody expressed this with more conviction than the Dutch painter Vincent van Gogh:

> There may be a great fire in our soul, yet no one ever comes to warm himself at it, and the passersby only see a wisp of smoke

coming through the chimney, and go along their way. Look here, now what must be done? Must one tend the inner fire, have salt in oneself, wait patiently yet with how much impatience for the hour when somebody will come and sit down—maybe to stay? Let him who believes in God wait for the hour that will come sooner or later.

Vincent van Gogh speaks here with the mind and heart of the Desert Fathers. He knew about the temptation to open all the doors so that the passersby could see the fire and not just the smoke coming through the chimney. But he also realized that if this happened, the fire would die and nobody would find warmth and new strength. His own life is a powerful example of faithfulness to the inner fire. During his life nobody came to sit down at his fire, but today thousands have found comfort and consolation in his drawings, paintings, and letters.

As ministers our greatest temptation is toward too many words. They weaken our faith and make us lukewarm. But silence is a sacred discipline, a guard of the Holy Spirit.

SILENCE TEACHES US TO SPEAK

The third way that silence reveals itself as the mystery of the future world is by teaching us to speak. A word with power is a word that comes out of silence. A word that bears fruit is a word that emerges from the silence and returns to it. It is a word that reminds us of the silence from which it comes and leads us back to that silence. A word that is not rooted in silence is a weak, powerless word that sounds like a "clashing cymbal or a booming gong" (1 Corinthians 13:1).

All this is true only when the silence from which the word comes forth is not emptiness and absence, but fullness and presence, not the human silence of embarrassment, shame, or guilt, but the divine silence in which love rests secure.

Here we can glimpse the great mystery in which we participate through silence and the Word, the mystery of God's own speaking. Out of his eternal silence God spoke the Word, and through this Word created and recreated the world. In the beginning God spoke the land, the sea, and the sky. He spoke the sun, the moon, and the stars. He spoke plants, birds, fish, animals wild and tame. Finally, he spoke man and woman. Then, in the fullness of time, God's Word, through whom all had been created, became flesh and gave power to all who believe to become the children of God. In all this, the Word of God does not break the silence of God, but rather unfolds the immeasurable richness of his silence.

By entering into the Egyptian desert, the monks wanted to partici-pate in the divine silence. By speaking out of this silence to the needs of their people, they sought to participate in the creative and recreative power of the divine Word.

Words can only create communion and thus new life when they embody the silence from which they emerge. As soon as we begin to take hold of each other by our words, and use words to defend ourselves or offend others, the word no longer speaks of silence. But when the word calls forth the healing and restoring stillness of its own silence, few words are needed: much can be said without much being spoken.

Thus silence is the mystery of the future world. It keeps us pilgrims and prevents us from becoming entangled in the cares of this age. It guards the fire of the Holy Spirit who dwells within us. It allows us to speak a word that participates in the creative and recreative power of God's own Word.

THE MINISTRY OF SILENCE

We are now left with the question of how to practice a ministry of silence in which our word has the power to represent the fullness of God's silence. This is an important question because we have become so contaminated by our wordy world that we hold to the deceptive opinion that our words are more important than our silence. Therefore it requires a strenuous discipline to make our ministry one that leads our people into the silence of God. That is the task Jesus has given us. The whole of Jesus' ministry pointed away from himself to the Father who had sent him. To his disciples Jesus said, "The words I say to you I do not speak as from myself; it is the Father, living in me, who is doing this work" (John 14:10). Jesus, the Word of God made flesh, spoke not to attract attention to himself but to show the way to his Father: "I came from the Father and have come into the world and now I leave the world to go to the Father (John 16:28). I am going to prepare a place for you . . . so that where I am you may be too" (John 14:2—3). In order to be a ministry in the Name of Jesus, our ministry must also point beyond our words to the unspeakable mystery of God.

One of our main problems is that in this chatty society, silence has become a very fearful thing. For most people, silence creates itchiness and nervousness. Many experience silence not as full and rich, but as empty and hollow. For them silence is like a gaping abyss which can swallow them up. As soon as a minister says during a worship service, "Let us be silent for a few moments," people tend to become restless and preoccupied with only one thought: "When will this be over?" Imposed silence often creates hostility and resentment. Many ministers who have experimented with silence in their services have soon found out that silence can be more demonic than divine and have quickly picked up the signals that were saying: "Please keep talking." It is quite understandable that most forms of ministry avoid silence precisely so as to ward off the anxiety it provokes.

But isn't the purpose of all ministry to reveal that God is not a God of fear but a God of love? And couldn't this be accomplished by gently and carefully converting the empty silence into a full silence, the anxious silence into a peaceful silence, and the restless silence into a restful silence, so that in this converted silence a real encounter with the loving Father could take place? What a power our word would have if it could enable people to befriend their silence! Let me describe a few concrete ways in which this might happen.

SILENCE AND PREACHING

Our preaching, when it is good, is interesting or moving, and sometimes both. It stimulates mind and heart and thus leads to a new insight or a new feeling. This is both valuable and necessary. But there is another option, one which is especially appropriate when we work with small groups. There is a way of preaching in which the word of Scripture is repeated quietly and regularly, with a short comment here and there, in order to let that word create an inner space where we can listen to our Lord. If it is true that the word of Scripture should lead us into the silence of God, then we must be careful to use that word not simply as an interesting or motivating word, but as a word that creates the boundaries within which we can listen to the loving, caring, gentle presence of God.

Most people who listen to a sermon keep their eyes directed toward the preacher, and rightly so, because he or she asks for attention to the word that is being spoken. But is it also possible for the word to be spoken in such a way that it slowly moves attention away from the pulpit to the heart of the listener and reveals there an inner silence in which it is safe to dwell.

The simple words "The Lord is my shepherd" can be spoken quietly and persistently in such a way that they become like a hedge around a garden in which God's shepherding can be sensed. These words, which at first might seem to be no more than an interesting metaphor, can slowly descend from the mind into the heart. There they may offer the context in which an inner transformation, by the God who transcends all human words and concepts, can take place. Thus, the words "The Lord is my shepherd" lead to the silent pastures where we can dwell in the loving presence of him in whose Name the preacher speaks. This meditative preaching is one way to practice the ministry of silence.

SILENCE AND COUNSELING

Counseling is understood by many to be a way in which one person listens to another and guides him or her to better self-understanding and greater emotional independence. But it is also possible to experience the relationship between pastor and counselee as a way of entering together into the loving silence of God and waiting there for the healing Word. The Holy Spirit is called the divine Counselor. He is actively present in the lives of those who come together to discern God's will. This is why human counselors should see as their primary task the work of helping their parishioners to become aware of the movements of the divine Counselor and encouraging them to follow these movements without fear. In this perspective, pastoral counseling is the attempt to lead fearful parishioners into the silence of God, and to help them feel at home there, trusting that they will slowly discover the healing presence of the Spirit.

This suggests that the human counselor needs to be very sensitive to the words of Scripture as words emerging from God's silence and directed to specific people in specific circumstances. When a word from Scripture is spoken by a counselor at that particular moment when the parishioner is able to hear it, it can indeed shatter huge walls of fear and open up unexpected perspectives. Such a word then brings with it the divine silence from which it came and to which it returns.

SILENCE AND ORGANIZING

Finally, I would like to stress the importance of silence in the ways a minister organizes his own life and that of others. In a society in which entertainment and distraction are such important preoccupations, ministers are also tempted to join the ranks of those who consider it their primary task to keep other people busy. It is easy to perceive the young and the elderly as people who need to be kept off the streets or on the streets. And ministers frequently find themselves in fierce competition with people and institutions who offer something more exciting to do than they do.

But our task is the opposite of distraction. Our task is to help people concentrate on the real but often hidden event of God's active presence in their lives. Hence, the question that must guide all organizing activity in a parish is not how to keep people busy, but how to keep them from being so busy that they can no longer hear the voice of God who speaks in silence.

Calling people together, therefore, means calling them away from the fragmenting and distracting wordiness of the dark world to that silence in which they can discover themselves, each other, and God. Thus organizing can be seen as the creation of a space where communion becomes possible and community can develop.

These examples of silence in preaching, counseling, and organizing are meant to illustrate how silence can help to determine the practical shape of our ministry. But let us not be too literal about silence. After all, silence of the heart is much more important than silence of the mouth. Abba Poemen said: "A man may seem to be silent, but if his heart is condemning others he is babbling ceaselessly. But there may be another who talks from morning till night and yet he is truly silent."

Silence is primarily a quality of the heart that leads to ever-growing charity. Once a visitor said to a hermit, "Sorry for making you break your rule." But the monk answered: "My rule is to practice the virtue of hospitality towards those who come to see me and send them home in peace."

Charity, not silence, is the purpose of the spiritual life and of ministry. About this all the Desert Fathers are unanimous.

CONCLUSION

This brings me to the end of my reflection on silence. In our chatty world, in which the word has lost is power to communicate, silence helps us to keep our mind and heart anchored in the future world and allows us to speak from there a creative and recreative word to the present world. Thus silence can also give us concrete guidance in the practice of our ministry.

There is little doubt that the Desert Fathers believed that simply not speaking is a very important practice. Too often our words are superfluous, inauthentic, and shallow. It is a good discipline to wonder in each new situation if people wouldn't be better served by our silence than by our words. But having acknowledged this, a more important message from the desert is that silence is above all a quality of the heart that can stay with us even in our conversation with others. It is a portable cell that we carry with us wherever we go. From it we speak to those in need and to it we return after our words have born fruit.

It is in this portable cell that we find ourselves immersed in the divine silence. The final question concerning our ministry of silence is not whether we say much or little, but whether our words call forth the caring silence of God himself. It is to this silence that we all are called: words are the instrument of the present world, but silence is the mystery of the future world.

CARLO CARRETTO

Under the Great Rock

The track, white in the sun, unwound ahead of me in a vague outline.

The furrows in the sand made by the wheels of the great oil trucks forced me to keep alert every second, if I was to keep the jeep on the move.

The sun was high in the sky, and I felt tired. Only the wind blowing on the hood of the car allowed the jeep to continue, although the temperature was like hell-fire and the water was boiling in the radiator. Every now and then I fixed my gaze on the horizon. I knew that in the area there were great blocks of granite embedded in the sand: they provided highly desirable sources of shade under which to pitch camp and wait the evening before proceeding with the journey.

In fact, towards mid-day, I found what I was looking for. Great rocks appeared on the left of the track. I approached, in the hope that I would find a little shade. I was not disappointed. On the north wall of the thirty foot high slab of stone, a knife of shade was thrown on to the red sand. I pulled the jeep against the wind to cool the engine and unloaded the *ghess*, the necessary equipment for pitching camp: a bag of food, two blankets, and a tripod for the fire.

But approaching the rock I realized that in the shade there were some guests already there: two snakes were curled up in the warm sand, watching me motionlessly. I leapt backwards and retreated to the jeep without taking my eyes off the two serpents. I took the gun, an old contraption lent me by a native who used it to get rid of jackals which, urged on by hunger and thirst, used to attack his flocks.

I loaded the gun, drew back a bit and took aim in order to try to hit the two snakes together, so as not to waste another bullet.

I fired, and saw the two beasts leap into the air in a cloud of sand. When I was cleaning up the blood and the remains of the snakes I saw, coming out of the mangled entrails of one of them, a bird he hadn't had time to digest. I spread out the mat. In the desert it is everything: chapel, dining-room, bedroom, drawing-room. It was the hour of Sext. I sat down, took out my breviary, and recited a few Psalms, but I had to force myself because I was so tired. Besides, every now and then the wind blew fragments of the two vipers I had killed onto the verses I was reading. Warm sultry air was coming from the south and my head ached. I got up. I calculated how much water I had to last me until I reached the well of Tit, and decided to sacrifice a little. From the goatskin gourd I drew a basinful of two pints and poured it on my head. The water soaked into my turban, ran down my neck and on to my clothes. The wind did the rest. From 115° the temperature descended in a few minutes to 80°. With that sense of refreshment I stretched out on the sand to sleep; in the desert you take your siesta before your meal.

In order to lie more comfortably I looked for a blanket to put under my head. I had two. One remained by my side unused, and as I looked at it I could not feel at ease.

But to understand you must hear my story.

The evening before I had passed through Irafog, a small village of Negroes, ex-slaves of the Tuareg. As usual when one reaches a village the people ran out to crowd round the jeep, either from curiosity, or to obtain the various things which desert-travellers bring with them: they may bring a little tea, distribute medicines or hand over letters.

That evening I had seen old Kada trembling with cold. It seems strange to speak of cold in the desert, but it is so; in fact the Sahara is often called 'a cold country where it is very hot in the sun.' The sun had gone down, and Kada was shivering. I had the idea of giving him one of the blankets I had with me, an essential part of my *ghess;* but I put the thought out of my mind. I thought of the night and I knew that I, too, would shiver. The little charity that was in me made me think again, though, reasoning that my skin wasn't worth more than his and that I had best give him one of the blankets. Even if I shivered a little that was the least a Little Brother could do.

When I left the village the blankets were still on the jeep; and now they were giving me a bad conscience.

I tried to get to sleep with my feet resting on the great rock,.but I couldn't manage it. I remembered that a month ago a Tuareg in the middle of his siesta had been crushed by a falling slab. I got up to make sure how stable the boulder was; I saw that it was a little off-balance, but not enough to be dangerous.

I lay down again on the sand. If I were to tell you what I dreamed of you would find it strange. The funny thing is that I dreamed that I was asleep under the great boulder and that at a given moment—it didn't seem to be a dream at all: I saw the rock moving, and I felt the boulder fall on top of me. What a nightmare! I felt my bones grating and I found myself dead. No, alive, but with my body crushed under the stone. I was amazed that not a bone hurt; but I could not move. I opened my eyes and saw Kada shivering in front of me at Irafog. I didn't hesitate for a minute to give him the blanket, especially as it was lying unused behind me, a yard away. I tried to stretch out my hand to offer it to him; but the stone made even the smallest movement impossible. I understood what purgatory was and that the suffering of the soul was "no longer to have the possibility of doing what before one could and should have done." Who knows for how many years afterwards I would be haunted by seeing that blanket near me as a witness to my selfishness and to the fact that I was too immature to enter the Kingdom of Love.

I tried to think of how long I was to remain under the rock: The reply was given me by the catechism: "Until you are capable of an act of perfect love." At that moment I felt quite incapable.

The perfect act of love is Jesus going up to Calvary to die for us all. As a member of his Mystical Body I was being asked to show if I was close enough to that perfect love to follow my master to Calvary for the salvation of my brethren. The presence of the blanket denied to Kada the evening before told me that I had still a long way to go. If I were capable of passing by a brother who was shivering with cold, how should I be capable of dying for him in imitation of Jesus who died for us all? In this way I understood that I was lost, and that if somebody had not come to my aid, I should have lain there, aeon after aeon, without being able to move.

I looked away and realized that all those great rocks in the desert were nothing more than the tombs of other men. They too, judged according to their ability to love and found cold, were there to await him who once said, "I shall raise you up on the last day."

JULIAN GREEN

From His Diary

MARCH 8. We are growing old and our decaying civilizations are going, one after the other, but God is always new, He is always there like a beautiful, fresh, clear morning, and that is how we will meet Him again after the night and storm of sin. His wealth of forgiveness is without limits. He is youth eternal.

NOVEMBER 21. Perhaps God wishes certain souls to live in a state of unbalance. There are times when I believe that a great many men will be saved in spite of their faults, and even through their faults, because they remained steadfast in faith and charity, amidst the most violent crises.

WILLIAM BUTLER YEATS

The Second Coming

Turning and turning in the widening gyre
The falcon cannot hear the falconer;
Things fall apart; the center cannot hold;
Mere anarchy is loosed upon the world,

The blood-dimmed tide is loosed, and everywhere
The ceremony of innocence is drowned;
The best lack all conviction, while the worst
Are full of passionate intensity.

Surely some revelation is at hand;
Surely the Second Coming is at hand;
The Second Coming! Hardly are those words out
When a vast image out of *Spiritus Mundi*
Troubles my sight: somewhere in sands of the desert
A shape with lion body and the head of a man,
A gaze blank and pitiless as the sun,
Is moving its slow thighs, while all about it
Reel shadows of the indignant desert birds.
The darkness drops again; but now I know
That twenty centuries of stony sleep
Were vexed to nightmare by a rocking cradle,
And what rough beast, its hour come round at last,
Slouches towards Bethlehem to be born?

8

THE COMIC SENSE
THE TRAGIC SENSE

ST. JOHN OF THE CROSS

The Song of the Soul

In darkness, on a night
Inflamed with love and sweet anxiety,
O daring! O delight!
I left—none noticed me—
My house was yielded to tranquillity.

In darkness, veiled from sight,
I took the secret stair unerringly,
O daring! O delight!
In dark and secrecy,
My house was yielded to tranquillity.

Upon that night of bliss,
When none beheld, I parted secretly,
Nor looked on that or this,
And nothing guided me
But light that brimmed my heart so ardently.

This was a surer guide
Than all the light of shining middle-day,
It took me to His side,

Who watched upon a way
On which I knew none else would ever stray.

O night that guided well!
O night of grace that day has never brought!
O night that in her spell
Beloved and Lover caught!
Into the Lover the beloved was wrought!

He lay upon the breast
I kept for Him immaculate and fair.
He closed His eyes in rest,
And I caressed Him there,
And fans of cedar branches moved the air.

And when the dawning flung
Her wind among His locks and spread them wide,
His gentle fingers clung
About my neck—O tide
Of ecstasy in which my senses died!

And then I bowed my head
On my Beloved, forgot my self, and all
Else ceased, my self I shed,
And shed was every pall:
Forgotten where the lilies hold in thrall.

SAMUEL BECKETT

That Time

Curtain. Stage in darkness. Fade up to Listener's face about ten feet above stage level midstage off centre.
Old white face, long flaring white hair as if seen from above outspread. Voices A B C are his own coming to him from both sides and above. They modulate back and forth without any break in general flow except where silence indicated. See note.
Silence 7 seconds. Listener's eyes are open. His breath audible, slow and regular.

A: that time you went back that last time to look was the ruin still
   there where you hid as a child when was that *(eyes close)* grey day
   took the eleven to the end of the line and on from there no no
   trams then all gone long ago that time you went back to look was

the ruin still there where you hid as a child that last time not a
tram left in the place only the old rails when was that

C: when you went in out of the rain always winter then always
raining that time in the Portrait Gallery in off the street out of the
cold and rain slipped in when no one was looking and through the
rooms shivering and dripping till you found a seat marble slab
and sat down to rest and dry off and on to hell out of there when
was that

B: on the stone together in the sun on the stone at the edge of the little
wood and as far as eye could see the wheat turning yellow vowing
every now and then you loved each other just a murmur not
touching or anything of that nature you one end of the stone she
the other long low stone like millstone no looks just there together
on the stone in the sun with the little wood behind gazing at the
wheat or eyes closed all still no sign of life not a soul abroad no
sound

A: straight off the ferry and up with the nightbag to the high street
neither right nor left not a curse for the old scenes the old names
straight up the rise from the wharf to the high street and there not
a wire to be seen only the old rails all rust when was that was your
mother ah for God's sake all gone long ago that time you went
back that last time to look was the ruin still there where you hid as
a child someone's folly

C: was your mother ah for God's sake all gone long ago all dust the
lot you the last huddled up on the slab in the old green greatcoat
with your arms round you whose else hugging you for a bit of
warmth to dry off and on to hell out of there and on to the next not
a living soul in the place only yourself and the odd attendant
drowsing around in his felt shufflers not a sound to be heard only
every now and then a shuffle of felt drawing near then dying away

B: all still just the leaves and ears and you too still on the stone in a
daze no sound not a word only every now and then to vow you
loved each other just a murmur one thing could ever bring tears
till they dried up altogether that thought when it came up among
the others floated up that scene

A: Foley was it Foley's Folly bit of a tower still standing all the rest
rubble and nettles where did you sleep no friend all the homes
gone was it that kip on the front where you no she was with you
then still with you then just the one night in any case off the ferry
one morning and back on her the next to look was the ruin still
there where none ever came where you hid as a child slip off when
no one was looking and hide there all day long on a stone among
the nettles with your picture-book

C: till you hoisted your head and there before your eyes when they opened a vast oil black with age and dirt someone famous in his time some famous man or woman or even child such as a young prince or princess some young prince or princess of the blood black with age behind the glass where gradually as you peered trying to make it out gradually of all things a face appeared had you swivel on the slab to see who it was was there at your elbow

B: on the stone in the sun gazing at the wheat or the sky or the eyes closed nothing to be seen but the wheat turning yellow and the blue sky vowing every now and then you loved each other just a murmur tears without fail till they dried up altogether suddenly there in whatever thoughts you might be having whatever scenes perhaps way back in childhood or the womb worst of all or that old Chinaman long before Christ born with long white hair

C: never the same after that never quite the same but that was nothing new if it wasn't this it was that common occurrence something you could never be the same after crawling about year after year sunk in your lifelong mess muttering to yourself who else you'll never be the same after this you were never the same after that

A: or talking to yourself who else out loud imaginary conversations there was childhood for you ten or eleven on a stone among the giant nettles making it up now one voice now another till you were hoarse and they all sounded the same well on into the night some moods in the black dark or moonlight and they all out on the roads looking for you

B: or by the window in the dark harking to the owl not a thought in your head till hard to believe harder and harder to believe you ever told anyone you loved them or anyone you till just one of those things you kept making up to keep the void out just another of those old tales to keep the void from pouring in on top of you the shroud

(Silence 10 seconds. Breath audible. After 3 seconds eyes open.)

C: never the same but the same as what for God's sake did you ever say I to yourself in your life come on now *(eyes close)* could you ever say I to yourself in your life turning-point that was a great word with you before they dried up altogether always having turning-points and never but the one the first and last that time curled up worm in slime when they lugged you out and wiped you off and straightened you up never another after that never looked back after that was that the time or was that another time

B: muttering that time together on the stone in the sun or that time together on the towpath or that time together in the sand that time that time making it up from there as best you could always together somewhere in the sun on the towpath facing downstream into the sun sinking and the bits of flotsam coming from behind and drifting on or caught in the reeds the dead rat it looked like came on you from behind and went drifting on till you could see it no more

A: that time you went back to look was the ruin still there where you hid as a child that last time straight off the ferry and up the rise to the high street to catch the eleven neither right nor left only one thought in your head not a curse for the old scenes the old names just head down press on up the rise to the top and there stood waiting with the nightbag till the truth began to dawn

C: when you started not knowing who you were from Adam trying how that would work for a change not knowing who you were from Adam no notion who it was saying what you were saying whose skull you were clapped up in whose moan had you the way you were was that the time or was that another time there alone with the portraits of the dead black with dirt and antiquity and the dates on the frames in case you might get the century wrong not believing it could be you till they put you out in the rain at closing-time

B: no sight of the face or any other part never turned to her nor she to you always parallel like on an axle-tree never turned to each other just blurs on the fringes of the field no touching or anything of that nature always space between if only an inch no pawing in the manner of flesh and blood no better than shades no worse if it wasn't for the vows

A: no getting out to it that way so what next no question of asking not another word to the living as long as you lived so foot it up in the end to the station bowed half double get out to it that way all closed down and boarded up Doric terminus of the Great Southern and Eastern all closed down and the colonnade crumbing away so what next

C: the rain and the old rounds trying making it up that way as you went along how it would work that way for a change never having been how never having been would work the old rounds trying to wangle you into it tottering and muttering all over the parish till the words dried up and the head dried up and the legs dried up whosoever they were or it gave up whoever it was

B: stock still always stock still like that time on the stone or that time in the sand stretched out parallel in the sand in the sun gazing up at the blue or eyes closed blue dark blue dark stock still side by side scene float up and there you were wherever it was

A: gave it up gave up and sat down on the steps in the pale morning sun no those steps got no sun somewhere else then gave up and off somewhere else and down on a step in the pale sun a doorstep say someone's doorstep for it to be time to get on the night ferry and out to hell out of there no need sleep anywhere not a curse for the old scenes the old names the passers pausing to gape at you quick gape then pass pass on pass by on the other side

B: stock still side by side in the sun then sink and vanish without your having stirred any more than the two knobs on a dumbbell except the lids and every now and then the lips to vow and all around too all still all sides wherever it might be no stir or sound only faintly the leaves in the little wood behind or the ears or the bent or the reeds as the case might be of man no sight of man or beast no sight or sound

C: always winter then always raining always slipping in somewhere when no one would be looking in off the street out of the cold and rain in the old green holeproof coat your father left you places you hadn't to pay to get in like the Public Library that was another great thing free culture far from home or the Post Office that was another another place another time

A: huddled on the doorstep in the old green greatcoat in the pale sun with the nightbag needless on your knees not knowing where you were little by little not knowing where you were or when you were or what for place might have been uninhabited for all you knew like that time on the stone the child on the stone where none ever came

(Silence 10 seconds. Breath audible. After 3 seconds eyes open.)

B: or alone in the same the same scenes making it up that way to keep it going keep it out on the stone *(eyes close)* alone on the end of the stone with the wheat and blue or the towpath alone on the towpath with the ghosts of the mules the drowned rat or bird or whatever it was floating off into the sunset till you could see it no more nothing stirring only the water and the sun going down till it went down and you vanished all vanished

A: none ever came but the child on the stone among the giant nettles with the light coming in where the wall had crumbled away poring on his book well on into the night some moods the moonlight and they all out on the roads looking for him or making up talk breaking up two or more talking to himself being together that way where none ever came

C: always winter then endless winter year after year as if it couldn't end the old year never end like time could go no further that time in the Post Office all bustle Christmas bustle in off the street when no one was looking out of the cold and rain pushed open the door

like anyone else and straight for the table neither right nor left
with all the forms and the pens on their chains sat down first
vacant seat and were taking a look round for a change before
drowsing away

B: or that time alone on your back in the sand and no vows to break
the peace when was that an earlier time a later time before she
came after she went or both before she came after she was gone and
you back in the old scene wherever it might be might have been the
same old scene before as then then as after with the rat or the wheat
the yellowing ears or that time in the sand the glider passing over
that time you went back soon after long after

A: eleven or twelve in the ruin on the flat stone among the nettles in
the dark or moonlight muttering away now one voice now another
there was childhood for you till there on the step in the pale sun
you heard yourself at it again not a curse for the passers pausing to
gape at the scandal huddled there in the sun where it had no
warrant clutching the nightbag drooling away out loud eyes
closed and the white hair pouring out down from under the hat
and so sat on in that pale sun forgetting it all

C: perhaps fear of ejection having clearly no warrant in the place to
say nothing of the loathsome appearance so this look round for
once at your fellow bastards thanking God for once bad and all as
you were you were not as they till it dawned that for all the
loathing you were getting you might as well not have been there at
all the eyes passing over you and through you like so much thin
air was that the time or was that another time another place
another time

B: the glider passing over never any change same blue skies nothing
ever changed but she with you there or not on your right hand
always the right hand on the fringe of the field and every now and
then in the great peace like a whisper so faint she loved you hard to
believe you even you made up that bit till the time came in the end

A: making it all up on the doorstep as you went along making
yourself all up again for the millionth time forgetting it all where
you were and what for Foley's Folly and the lot the child's ruin
you came to look was it still there to hide in again till it was night
and time to go till that time came

C: the Library that was another another place another time that time
you slipped in off the street out of the cold and rain when no one
was looking what was it then you were never the same after never
again after something to do with dust something the dust said
sitting at the big round table with a bevy of old ones poring on the
page and not a sound

B: that time in the end when you tried and couldn't by the window in
     the dark and the owl flown to hoot at someone else or back with a
     shrew to its hollow tree and not another sound hour after hour
     hour after hour not a sound when you tried and tried and couldn't
     any more no words left to keep it out so gave it up gave up there by
     the window in the dark or moonlight gave up for good and let it in
     and nothing the worse a great shroud billowing in all over you on
     top of you and little or nothing the worse little or nothing
A: back down to the wharf with the nightbag and the old green
     greatcoat your father left you trailing the ground and the white
     hair pouring out down from under the hat till that time came on
     down neither right nor left not a curse for the old scenes the old
     names not a thought in you head only get back on board and away
     to hell out of it and never come back or was that another time all
     that another time was there ever any other time but that time away
     to hell out of it all and never come back
C: not a sound only the old breath and the leaves turning and then
     suddenly this dust whole place suddenly full of dust when you
     opened your eyes from floor to ceiling nothing only dust and not a
     sound only what was it it said come and gone was that it
     something like that come and gone come and gone no one come
     and gone in no time gone in no time
     *(Silence 10 seconds. Breath audible. After 3 seconds eyes open.
     After 5 seconds smile, toothless for preference. Hold 5 seconds till
     fade out and curtain.)*

NOTE

Moments of one and the same voice A B C relay one another without
solution of continuity—apart from the two 10-second breaks. Yet the
switch from one to another must be clearly faintly perceptible. If
threefold source and context prove insufficient to produce this effect it
should be assisted mechanically (e.g. threefold pitch).

9

PRAYER

CHARLES DE FOUCAULD

Prayer of Abandonment

Father,
I abandon myself into your hands;
do with me what you will.
Whatever you may do, I thank you:
I am ready for all, I accept all.
Let only your will be done in me,
and in all your creatures.
I wish no more than this, O Lord.
Into your hands I commend my soul;
I offer it to you with all the love of my heart,
for I love you, Lord, and so need to give myself,
to surrender myself into your hands, without reserve,
and with boundless confidence,
for you are my Father.

ST. THERESA OF AVILA

Persistent Prayer

To persist in prayer without returns, this is not time lost, but a great
gain. It is endeavour without thought of self and only for the glory of

the Lord. Even though at first it seems that the effort is all in vain, it is not so, but it is as with children who work in their father's fields: they receive no daily wage, but when the year comes to an end, everything belongs to them...

He who sets out to pray must be as the husbandman. In the season of summer and fair weather he (as the ant) must not grow weary, so that he may be fed in the season of winter and stormy rains. He must have a full larder so that he may live and not (like the dumb beasts) die of hunger. For we must be prepared for the great storm of death and judgment.

In Albula I learned to know a certain saint who lived as it is fitting for a saint. After she had given away all for the sake of the Lord, she had left a cover to protect her from the cold, and this she gave also. Soon after this, God afflicted her with the greatest inner pain and a feeling of loneliness. Whereat she complained and said to Him: "Is this meet, dear Lord? You have taken all from me, and now You Yourself forsake me too!"

Here, then, God repaid the great services performed for Him, with sorrow. And there can, indeed, be no better payment, for the true meaning of it is that one is paid with the love of God.

Do not let your heart cling to inner solace. For that is in the manner of common soldiers: they demand their daily wage at once. Give you service as the noblest officers serve their king—for nothing!

CHARLES PEGUY

Abandonment

God Speaks:

I know man well. It is I who made him. A funny creature.
For in him that freedom is at work which is the mystery of mysteries.
You can still ask a lot of him. He is not too bad. You can't say that he is bad.
When you know how to handle him, you can still ask a lot of him.
You can get a lot out of him. And God knows that my grace
Knows how to handle him, that with my grace
I know how to handle him, that my grace is insidious, as clever as a thief
And like a man hunting a fox.
I know how to handle him. It's my business. And that freedom of his is my creation.

You can ask a lot of kindness of him, a lot of charity, a lot of sacrifice.
He has much faith and much charity.
But what you can't ask of him, by gum, is a little hope.
A little confidence, don't you know, a little relaxation.
A little yielding, a little abandonment into my hands,
A little giving in. He is always so stiff.
Now you, my daughter night, you sometime succeed, you sometimes obtain that very thing
Of rebellious man.
Let the gentleman consent, let him yield a little to me.
Let him stretch out his poor weary limbs on a bed of rest.
Let him ease his aching heart a little on a bed of rest.
Above all, let his head stop working. It works only too much, his head does. And he thinks it is work, when his head goes that way.
And his thoughts... Did you ever... What he calls his thoughts!
Let his thoughts stop moving about and struggling inside his head and rattling like calabash seeds,
Like a little bell in an empty gourd.
When you see what they are all about, those ideas of his, as he calls them!
Poor creature. I don't care for the man who doesn't sleep, says God.
The man who is all aglow in his bed, all aglow with unrest and fever.
I am all for making one's examination of conscience every night, says God.
It is a good exercise.
But after all, you mustn't torment yourself with it to the point of losing your sleep.
At that hour, the day is done, and well done. It doesn't have to be done over again.
It is all settled.
Those sins for which you are so sorry, my boy, well, it is plain enough,
My friend, you should not have committed them.
At the time when you were still free not to commit them.
Now it's over. So go to sleep, you won't do it again tomorrow.
But the man who, going to bed at night, makes plans for the next day,
That man I don't care for.
Jackass, how does he know what tomorrow will be like?
Does he even know what color the weather is going to take on?
He had much better say his prayers. I have never withheld tomorrow's bread.
The man who is in my hand like the staff in the traveller's hand,
That man is agreeable to me, says God.
The man who rests on my arm like the suckling child who laughs

And is not concerned with anything.
And sees the world in his mother's and his nurse's eyes,
And sees it nowhere else, and looks for it nowhere else,
That one is agreeable to me, says God.
But the one who concocts plans, the one who inside himself, in his own
    head,
Works for tomorrow like a hired laborer,
Works dreadfully like a slave making an everlasting wheel go round,
(And between you and me like a fool),
Well, that man is in no way agreeable to me, says God.
He who abandons himself, I love. He who does not abandon himself, I
    don't love. That's simple enough.
He who abandons himself does not abandon himself, and he is the only
    one who does not abandon himself.
He who does not abandon himself, abandons himself, and is the only
    one who does abandon himself.
Now you, my daughter night, my daughter of the great cloak, my
    daughter of the silver cloak,
You are the only one who sometimes overcomes that rebel and can
    bend that stiff neck of his.
It is then, O night, that you appear.
And what you have done once,
You do every time.
What you have done one day,
You do every day.
As you came down one evening,
So you come down every evening.
What you did for my son who was made man,
O great and charitable one, you do for all men his brothers,
You bury them in silence and shadow
And in the salutary oblivion
Of the mortal unrest
Of day.

RICHARD CRASHAW

On the Baptized Ethiopian

Let it no longer be a forlorn hope
    To wash an Ethiope;
He's washed, his gloomy skin a peaceful shade
    For his white soul is made,

> And now, I doubt not, the Eternal Dove
> A black-faced house will love.

To the Infant Martyrs

> Go, smiling souls, your new-built cages break,
> In heaven you'll learn to sing, ere here to speak,
> Nor let the milky fonts that bathe your thirst
>   Be your delay;
> The place that calls you hence is, at the worst,
>   Milk all the way.

Upon the Infant Martyrs

> To see both blended in one flood,
> The mothers' milk, the children's blood,
> Make me doubt if heaven will gather
> Roses hence, or lilies rather.

JULIAN GREEN

From His Diary

JUNE 23.   I don't think anyone suspects what forms the substance of my sadness. How can I express it? It is impossible to say and would seem ridiculous, but I'm going to say it just the same. I wanted to be a saint. That is all. I can add nothing to this. A great part of my life does not resemble me. I am very keenly aware of constantly passing by the man that I wanted to be, and in a certain way he exists, he is there, and he is sad, and his sadness is mine.

MAY 20.   A man can turn his room into a Paradise or a Hell without budging, simply by the thoughts he harbors.

GERARD MANLEY HOPKINS

Thou Art Indeed Just, Lord

Justus quidem tu es, Domine, si disputem tecum: verumtamen justa loquar ad te: Quare via impiorum prosperatur? & c.

Thou art indeed just, Lord, if I contend
With thee; but, sir, so what I plead is just.
Why do sinners' ways prosper? and why must
Disappointment all I endeavour end?
    Wert thou my enemy, O thou my friend,
How wouldst thou worse, I wonder, than thou dost
Defeat, thwart me? Oh, the sots and thralls of lust
Do in spare hours more thrive than I that spend,
Sir, life upon thy cause. See, banks and brakes
Now, leavèd how thick! lacèd they are again
With fretty chervil, look, and fresh wind shakes
Them; birds build—but not I build; no, but strain,
Time's eunuch, and not breed one work that wakes.
Mine, O thou lord of life, send my roots rain.

RALPH WALDO EMERSON

Grace

How much, preventing God! how much I owe
To the defenses thou hast round me set:
Example, custom, fear, occasion slow,
These scornéd bondmen were my parapet.
I dare not peep over this parapet
To gauge with glance the roaring gulf below,
The depths of sin to which I had descended,
Had not these me against myself defended.

ST. THERESA OF AVILA

Two Poems

Nothing move thee;
Nothing terrify thee;
Everthing passes;
God never changes.
Patience be all to thee.
Who trusts in God, he
Never shall be needy.
God alone suffices.

If, Lord, Thy love for me is strong
As this which binds me unto Thee,
What holds me from Thee, Lord, so long,
What holds Thee, Lord, so long from me?

O soul, what then desirest thou?
—Lord, I would see Thee, who thus choose Thee.
What fears can yet assail thee now?
—All that I fear is but to lose Thee.

Love's whole possession I entreat,
Lord, make my soul Thine own abode,
And I will build a nest so sweet
It may not be too poor for God.

O soul in God hidden from sin,
What more desires for thee remain,
Save but to love, and love again,
And, all on flame with love within,
Love on, and turn to love again?

ST. BERNARD

Prayer is hindered by too little light and by too much. He who neither
sees his sins nor confesses them is not illumined with light. But he for
whom his sins loom so large that he despairs of forgiveness is drowned
in light. Neither of these prays. What follows from this? The light must
be gentle.

THREE CELTIC PRAYERS

Compassionate God of life,
Forgiveness to me give,
    In my wanton talk,
    In my lying oath,
    In my foolish deed,
    In my empty speech.

Thou Father of the waifs,
    Thou Father of the naked,
Draw me to the shelter-house

Of the Saviour of the poor,
The Saviour of the poor.*

Be the pain of Christ betwixt me and each pain,
The love of Christ betwixt me and each love,
The dearness of Christ betwixt me and each dearness,
The kindness of Christ betwixt me and each kindness,
The wish of Christ betwixt me and each wish,
The will of Christ betwixt me and each will,
    And no venom can wound me.

*From Ann Livingstone, crofter, Bay, Taynuilt, Lorne

10

THINGS
OF
THIS WORLD

GERARD MANLEY HOPKINS

From His Journal

JULY 11.   Oats: hoary blue-green sheaths and stalks, prettily shadow-stroked spikes of pale green grain. Oaks: the organisation of this tree is difficult. Speaking generally no doubt the determining planes are concentric, a system of brief contiguous and continuous tangents, whereas those of the cedar wd. roughly be called horizontals and those of the beech radiating but modified by droop and by a screw-set towards jutting points. But beyond this since the normal growth of the boughs is radiating and the leaves grow some way in there is of course a system of spoke-wise clubs of green—sleeve-pieces. And since the end shoots curl and carry young and scanty leaf-stars these clubs are tapered, and I have seen also the pieces in profile with chiselled outlines, the blocks thus made detached and lessening towards the end. However the star knot is the chief thing: it is whorled, worked round, a little and this is what keeps up the illusion of the tree: the leaves are rounded inwards and figure out ball-knots. Oaks differ much, and much turns on the broadness of the leaf, the narrower giving the crisped and starry and catharine-wheel forms, the broader the flat-pieced mailed or shard-covered ones, in wh. it is possible to see composition in dips, etc., on wider bases than the single knot or cluster. But I shall study them further. See the 19th.

JULY 17 .... It was this night I believe but possibly the next that I saw clearly the impossibility of staying in the Church of England, but resolved to say nothing to anyone till three months are over, that is the end of the Long, and then of course to take no step till after my Degree.

JULY 18. Bright. Sunset over oaks a dapple of rosy clouds blotted with purple, sky round confused pale green and blue with faint horned rays, crimson sparkles through the leaves below....

JULY 19. Alone in the woods and in Mr. Nelthorpe's park, whence one gets such a beautiful view southwards over the country. I have now found the law of the oak leaves. It is of platter-shaped stars altogether; the leaves lie close like pages, packed, and as if drawn tightly to. But these old packs, wh. lie at the end of their twigs, throw out now long shoots alternately and slimly leaved, looking like bright keys. All the sprays but markedly these ones shape out and as it were embrace greater circles and the dip and toss of these make the wider and less organic articulations of the tree.

ABBIE HUSTON EVANS

Fact of Crystal

Who shall say that the rock feels not at all
In its obscure, slumbrous, geologic way
The pinprick of incipient demolition;
Or sensed not once the dream-faint, unremitting,
Electric stir of the crystal rising in its side—
The next-to-nothing gnat-sting, the dim prickle
Of flowering not-life making try at growth,
Prefiguring afar the flying fire
That runs in the veins of men, through coils of time
Bringing prodigious newness out of earth?

Motion, that far-off whisper—it was there
In quartz, in beryl, in the mica sheath.
In crystal-building and in fusion flash
The poles of speed declare themselves, and what
Is cataclysmic, loosed in a splintered second,
Innocuous creeps down its millionth year.

Locked in dragging ages black as Tophet,
Crammed into corners in split seams of the earth,

Down deep in torpor's dungeon lodged forgotten,
Accepting off-slant cramping of the facets
As incidental and of no importance,
These mounting shapes from formlessness arriving
Were not unmindful of their glorious axes
In at the center fixed, ordaining true
The ancient inmost pivots of pure selfhood.

Behold the beauteous sluggards and their work—
The slothful quartz, the lazing tourmaline,
And their great tardy dazzle. Envy rock's glory.
This that hung once thinner than breath in space,
Wraith of a wraith, earth's uncreated dust,
Now signals with the flung-down fact of crystal,
Its stern-decreed geometry achieved,
Its pattern worked out to a T, its tip atom in place.

Where current rode the illimitable streaming
Too slow for any swirl to break the surface,
At that old, creeping, archetypal snail pace,
With none to note it, chaos inched back, worsted.
How landfall-like august form stands delivered!
Here's most diffuse most pointed, peaked, compacted,
Here's most amorphous grappled into jewel.

PABLO NERUDA

Youth

Acid and sword blade: the fragrance
of plum in the pathways:
tooth's sweetmeat of kisses,
power and spilth on the fingers,
the yielding erotic of pulps,
hayricks and threshing floors, clandestine
recesses that tempt through the vastness of houses;
bolsters asleep in the past, the bitter green valley,
seen from above, from the glasses' concealment;
and drenching and flaring by turns, adolescence
like a lamp overturned in the rain.

Hunger in the South

Woe in the charcoals of Lota, I see:
the dishonored *chileno* like a black corrugation
rifling the bitter recesses,
dying or living, born to the pitiless cinder
in a posture of kneeling, felled
between fires and black powder,
as if worlds might create and undo themselves
for only a winter's survival of coughing,
or the step of a horse through the pitch-colored water, where lately
the perishing knives of the stripped eucalyptus have fallen.

Some Beasts

It was the twilight of the iguana:

From a rainbowing battlement,
a tongue like a javelin
lunging in verdure;
an ant heap treading the jungle,
monastic, on musical feet;
the guanaco, oxygen-fine
in the high places swarthy with distances,
cobbling his feet into gold;
the llama of scrupulous eye
that widens his gaze on the dews
of a delicate world.

A monkey is weaving
a thread of insatiable lusts
on the margins of morning:
he topples a pollen-fall,
startles the violet flight
of the butterfly, wings on the Muzo.

It was the night of the alligator:
snouts moving out of the slime,
in original darkness, pullulations,
a clatter of armor, opaque
in the sleep of the bog,
turning back to the chalk of the sources.

The jaguar touches the leaves
with his phosphorous absence,
the puma speeds through the branches
in the blaze of his hungers,
his eyeballs, a jungle of alcohol,
burn in his head.
Badgers are raking the river beds,
nuzzling the havens
for their warm delectation,
red-toothed, for assault.

And below, on the vastness of water,
like a continent circled,
drenched in the ritual mud,
rapacious, religious,
gigantic, the coiled anaconda.

Artichoke

The artichoke
of delicate heart
erect
in its battle-dress, builds
its minimal cupola;
keeps
stark
in its scallop of
scales.
Around it,
demoniac vegetables
bristle their thicknesses,
devise
tendrils and belfries,
the bulb's agitations;
while under the subsoil
the carrot
sleeps sound in its
rusty mustaches.
Runner and filaments
bleach in the vineyards,
whereon rise the vines.
The sedulous cabbage

arranges
its petticoats;
oregano
sweetens a world;
and the artichoke
dulcetly there in a gardenplot,
armed for a skirmish,
goes proud
in its pomegranate
burnishes.

Till, on a day,
each by the other,
the artichoke moves
to its dream
of a market place
in the big willow
hoppers:
a battle formation.
Most warlike
of defilades—
with men
in the market stalls,
white shirts
in the soup-greens,
artichoke
field marshals,
close-order conclaves,
commands, detonations,
and voices,
a crashing of crate staves.

And
Maria
come
down
with her hamper
to
make trial
of an artichoke:
she reflects, she examines,
she candles them up to the light like an egg,
never flinching;
she bargains,

she tumbles her prize
in a market bag
among shoes and a
cabbage head,
a bottle
of vinegar; is back
in her kitchen.
The artichoke drowns in an olla.

So you have it:
a vegetable, armed,
a profession
(call it an artichoke)
whose end
is millennial.
We taste of that
sweetness,
dismembering
scale after scale.
We eat of a halcyon paste:
it is green at the artichoke heart.

A Lemon

Out of lemon flowers
loosed
on the moonlight, love's
lashed and insatiable
essences,
sodden with fragrance,
the lemon tree's yellow
emerges,
the lemons
move down
from the tree's planetarium.

Delicate merchandise!
The harbors are big with it—
bazaars
for the light and the
barbarous gold.
We open
the halves
of a miracle,

and a clotting of acids
brims
into the starry
divisions:
creation's
original juices,
irreducible, changeless,
alive:
so the freshness lives on
in a lemon,
in the sweet-smelling house of the rind,
the proportions, arcane and acerb.

Cutting the lemon
the knife
leaves a little
cathedral:
alcoves unguessed by the eye
that open acidulous glass
to the light; topazes
riding the droplets,
altars,
aromatic façades.

So, while the hand
holds the cut of the lemon,
half a world
on a trencher,
the gold of the universe
wells
to your touch:
a cup yellow
with miracles,
a breast and a nipple
perfuming the earth;
a flashing made fruitage,
the diminutive fire of a planet.

WILLIAM BLAKE

Auguries of Innocence

To see a World in a Grain of Sand
And a Heaven in a Wild Flower

Hold Infinity in the palm of your hand
And Eternity in an hour
A Robin Red breast in a Cage
Puts all Heaven in a Rage
A dove house filld with doves & Pigeons
Shudders Hell thro all its regions
A dog starvd at his Masters Gate
Predicts the ruin of the State
A Horse misusd upon the Road
Calls to Heaven for Human blood
Each outcry of the hunted Hare
A fibre from the Brain does tear
A Skylark wounded in the wing
A Cherubim does cease to sing
The Game Cock clipd & armd for fight
Does the Rising Sun affright
Every Wolfs & Lions howl
Raises from Hell a Human Soul
The wild deer wandring here & there
Keeps the Human Soul from Care
The Lamb misusd breeds Public strife
And yet forgives the Butchers Knife
    The Bat that flits at close of Eve
Has left the Brain that wont Believe
The Owl that calls upon the Night
Speaks the Unbelievers fright
He who shall hurt the little Wren
Shall never be belovd by Men
He who the Ox to wrath has movd
Shall never be by Woman lovd
The wanton Boy that kills the Fly
Shall feel the Spiders enmity
He who torments the Chafers sprite
Weaves a Bower in endless Night
The Caterpiller on the Leaf
Repeats to thee thy Mothers grief
Kill not the Moth nor Butterfly
For the Last Judgment draweth nigh
He who shall train the Horse to War
Shall never pass the Polar Bar
The Beggers Dog & Widows Cat
Feed them & thou wilt grow fat
The Gnat that sings his Summers song

Poison gets from Slanders tongue
The poison of the Snake & Newt
Is the sweat of Envys Foot
The Poison of the Honey Bee
Is the Artists Jealousy
The Princes Robes & Beggars Rags
Are Toadstools on the Misers Bags
A truth thats told with bad intent
Beats all the Lies you can invent
It is right it should be so
Man was made for Joy & Woe
And when this we rightly know
Thro the World we safely go
Joy & Woe are woven fine
A Clothing for the Soul divine
Under every grief & pine
Runs a joy with silken twine
The Babe is more than swadling Bands
Throughout all these Human Lands
Tools were made & Born were hands
Every Farmer Understands
Every Tear from Every Eye
Becomes a Babe in Eternity
This is caught by Females bright
And returned to its own delight
The Bleat the Bark Bellow & Roar
Are Waves that Beat on Heavens Shore
The Babe that weeps the Rod beneath
Writes Revenge in realms of death
The Beggars Rags fluttering in Air
Does to Rags the Heavens tear
The Soldier armd with Sword & Gun
Palsied strikes the Summers Sun
The poor Mans Farthing is worth more
Than all the Gold on Africs Shore
One Mite wrung from the Labrers hands
Shall buy & sell the Misers Lands
Or if protected from on high
Does that whole Nation sell & buy
He who mocks the Infants Faith
Shall be mock'd in Age & Death
He who shall teach the Child to Doubt
The rotting Grave shall neer get out

He who respects the Infants faith
Triumphs over Hell & Death
The Childs Toys & the Old Mans Reasons
Are the Fruits of the Two seasons
The Questioner who sits so sly
Shall never know how to Reply
He who replies to words of Doubt
Doth put the Light of Knowledge out
The Strongest Poison ever known
Came from Caesars Laurel Crown
Nought can deform the Human Race
Like to the Armours iron brace
When Gold & Gems adorn the Plow
To peaceful Arts shall Envy Bow
A Riddle or the Crickets Cry
Is to Doubt a fit Reply
The Emmets Inch & Eagles Mile
Make Lame Philosophy to smile
He who Doubts from what he sees
Will neer Believe do what you Please
If the Sun & Moon should doubt
Theyd immediately Go out
To be in a Passion you Good many do
But no Good if a Passion is in you
The Whore & Gambler by the State
Licencd build that Nations Fate
The Harlots cry from Street to Street
Shall weave Old Englands winding Sheet
The Winners Shout the Losers Curse
Dance before dead Englands Hearse
Every Night & every Morn
Some to Misery are Born
Every Morn & every Night
Some are Born to sweet delight
Some are Born to sweet delight
Some are Born to Endless Night
We are led to Believe a Lie
When we see not Thro the Eye
Which was Born in a Night to perish in a Night
When the Soul Slept in Beams of Light
God Appears & God is Light
To those poor Souls who dwell in Night

But does a Human Form Display
To those Who Dwell in Realms of day

DAME FREYA STARK

Joy

The difference lies in the listener's heart.
If he would forget he lives at the world's end
The bird would sing as it sang in the palace of old.
    PO CHU-I: "Hearing the Oriole." A.D. 818,
    Arthur Waley trans.

Joy is a queen of virtues, apt to be neglected by theologians, or anyway relegated to a world other than ours. Christianity, apart from some mystics and the earliest Greek Fathers, often forgets her earthly divinity, though her opposite (despondency or accidia) is numbered among the seven deadly sins. Basic as love, Joy does, I believe, keep its virtue both inside and outside of Time; and when we have shed all else that helped our earthly life Love and Joy remain, and must have warmed a roughly sketched universe long before immortality diclosed itself on our planet. The sea-anemones in their dim gardens, where the rhythm of waves drops and lifts their acquiescent petals, perhaps already registered the unconscious arrival of joy.

When *possessions* came and, being girt with limitation, grew by their nature into prisons, they were able to give pleasure rather than joy, and the true art of living came to be largely centred on keeping them in their proper place—sustaining but subordinate. The people I have most loved and admired were never distracted by them: enjoyments could be bought but Joy was independent, and the thought of it brings back to me the picture of an old and happy man, Admiral Sir William Goodenough, who was President of the Royal Geographical Society and gave me the first award I ever got—the Back grant of £40 (which seemed a large sum then) for my first Persian journey.

The Royal Geographical Society's beautiful house looked upon its task in the light of helping those eager to help themselves, and Sir William, "The Old Admiral," believing in this excellent principle, took every promising new traveller to his heart. I think with affection of all the years that followed, when one would find him in the little office where he sat, and talk about any adventure in one's mind at the moment. Much loved, he and his wife, both blue-eyed and white-haired, would sit every Sunday at either end of their long luncheon table in the country, and entertain people who had done this or that in most corners of the world.

"He has just come from the Shan States"—would introduce some shy and promising young man: "Oh, you turn from Burma to the right"—if more detail was asked for.

I saw him last on a summer morning when the Second World War was still moaning above us with V.1's while he showed me the bits of his ship from the battle of Jutland, which he cherished. When very ill, some old shipmate said to him: "You must be unhappy, tied to your bed?"

"Oh no," said the Old Admiral. "I've got to be ill, but I won't be unhappy too."

I often think of him and of the steadfastness of his tough generation, and how his happiness, planted so deep below vicissitude, could be thought of as the very substance of delight. He welcomed it as if it were roses on his path—to be welcomed and not clung to—(for the plucked rose must die).

> "Oh, no man knows
> Through what wild centuries
> Roves back the rose"*

Blossom upon blossom through its ages, into a future with the hands of unknown gardeners upon it, even to the rose of men's imagination and the end of Time—when so looked at, Joy in its freedom embraces and enhances all happy ownerships and temporary pleasures inherent in whatever loveliness or riches the world can pour upon us: to lose sight of their evanescence pushes the possessive moment too far.

For Joy belongs to that Unity in which, without usually knowing it, we live. It meets itself suddenly in small things as in great, and recognizing itself sets off this delight. Its variety is endless—words hitherto dormant, or the recognition of human strangers one with another; or runs of music that wander through our hearts; or a wayside view, or the taste of seasons, or the mere sparkle of sunlight on a stream. Sometimes it is a gesture, and I can remember a long and weary waiting-room in the highlands of Turkey when a woman's hand set this off as she adjusted her baby in its shawl; the wind was howling outside and suddenly this hand, this magic, so beautiful and tender, shaped itself through the ages, embodying the thoughts and loves and wickedness of man; until, at a meeting of lives so different, this woman and I smiled at each other over the little Turk wrapped in his shawl between us.

*Walter de la Mare.

Most things animate or inanimate can thus be a stimulus to joy if there is warmth in the heart to receive and answer their implicit unity. Some awareness is required to show that we recognize and love, or at any rate are pleasantly surprised by any small note in the great welter that surrounds us. If we do not respond, the spark falls dead for lack of feeling, and with such wasted joys the paths of life are strewn. A cherry tree grew against our wall in a London garden. We would wait for its blossom in spring and pause to look up as we walked beneath it, and on one occasion, returning from some absence, tired and with a headache, I stopped to gaze as usual, and the magic had gone. It was there, but I could not see it: the cherry was wasting its beauty and we could not *unite.* Husbands and wives and lovers come upon these moments and waste the spark which runs through all things, which only unity engenders from the beginning and probably before the beginning of Time: its gentle divinity, so inextricably mixed with all that our world has ever contained and much beyond it, is, with love, the chief ally we have in this world's war.

For whatever our God may be, He takes no ostensible side in our battles, apart from the strength He gives intrinsic to Himself: but Joy is our ally, and the bond of all union through the ages, and not to be parted from whatever sorrowful frontier we may have to cross.

Love and Delight

Love and Delight alone may be called immortal and shed their brightness from an unlimited horizon. Through them we share a divine freedom, the temporal enjoyment of temporary things. Any genuine artist or even craftsman can know this in the unpossessive realms where his dreams lead him, any lover must learn to know it as he grows to where self is forgotten. In these two ways of dedication and creation the simplest creature by its own native impulse touches the unchanging shores.

KARL RAHNER

Doctrine of Creation

The theological doctrine of the creatureliness of man, which is based on creation. It treats not only in general of the createdness of all that is not God (Gen 1:1) but especially of that creatureliness which is proper to man and thus becomes the fundamental structure of man's relationship with God: humility, adoration, trust in him who sustains the life we can no longer control, readiness to believe, hiddenness in God, docility to God, the inner dialectic of the attitude which accepts both utter dependence on God and real, responsible autonomy and independence in dialogue with God. The doctrine of creation does not merely state what human nature is, but in elaborating the notion of the creaturely, embraces every sphere of human life—and therefore also man's supernatural elevation by grace. The doctrine of creation is closely connected with theological anthropology since creatureliness is only fully realized in man.

Life

In philosophy, an analogical mode of being which is progressively realized at each ascending stage of reality as a whole (in the perspective of the natural sciences, life is associated with protoplasm as the highest known form of organization of matter). On the basis of our experience of animate bodies life connotes the ordered unity of a multiple being which coheres and persists in space and time as a singe thing *vis-à-vis* the environment despite the real plurality of the elements composing it; so that, containing within itself the principle of its movement and direction, it is not a mere dependent function of the environment, but the whole is always something more than the sum of its parts and their interaction. If the task of the living being, accordingly, is spontaneously to preserve and develop its spatio-temporal form, then (whenever it rightly understands itself and its rightly understood) it must by that very fact be more open than that which is dead (death is a *limit*) to the environment by "expectation"; by accepting and modulating impressions from without in its own characteristic way; by placing its self-fulfilment, only now become possible, at the service of others; by increasingly drawing the milieu into the field of its own being and extending its scope within the milieu. From the theological point of view this fragile "miracle" of life is evidently the gift of God because contingency and creatureliness are more keenly experienced in living being than in the inanimate world. Life is evidently verified on an essentially higher plane in the operations peculiar to the personal spirit: conscious free agency—as history, personal responsibility and ultimate self-realization, and as transcendence towards God's absolute mystery, through which the environment becomes a world of personal communion (and can thus become the kingdom of God)—is life in an eminent degree. Henceforth, God is finally conceived analogously and metaphorically as the "living God": Life itself and the ever creative primordial source of all life. He is not unreal, like the dead, like the dead idols, he can act with absolute power in perfect freedom. His world is at once in his presence and in him, its Creator, in absolute otherness and absolute intimacy (Gen 2:7; Ps 36:10; Acts 17:24-28). He perfectly abides with himself in exhaustive knowledge and love of his being, which is inexhaustible because it is infinite, which proceeds only from himself and therefore knows and loves all else in selfless communication. God's radical self-communication in Jesus Christ, therefore, is life in the supreme degree, which "now" indeed must still be lived by dying together with Christ (Rom 6:3f.; Gal 2:20; 2 Cor 6:9; Col 2:12), and so is "hid with Christ in God" (Col 3:3). But "I live, now not I, but Christ liveth in me" (Gal 2:20). The Christian shares the life of the Risen Lord in the Pneuma (Rom 5-6; 2 Cor 5; Jn 3:15f.; 5:24; 6:40, and *passim*), a life which continually grows and unfolds until it becomes manifest as the glory of eternal life (Rom 5:17; 6:5, 22; 2 Cor 2:16; Jn 14:2f.; 17:24, 26). Since "eternal life" begins, is anticipated and may become open to experience in earthly life, from the theological point of view, *all* human beings also have a right to authentic life.

Time, Temporality

If we wish to acquire a genuine understanding of time we must not first think of the time told by the clock, for this is an external measure of physical processes which is extrinsic to temporal things in their temporality and their intrinsic time. Furthermore, it would conceal the fact that the measure can only be used by an intelligent being who knows by his own interior activity of growth what time is, and who can draw comparisons. Time is primarily the mode of becoming of finite freedom: coming from a beginning beyond one's control, personally and selectively realizing the potentiality of one's own being, attaining the unique, irrevocable completion of its institution. The unity and differentiation of these elements is the time being—which does not mean that they form a mere succession of one different thing after another (in which case they would not be phases of a single occur-rence), for in fact they form a single temporal complex. The experi-enced "succession" of these elements, cannot be "explained," that is synthetically constructed out of other more intelligible elements, since the being and experience of these other elements would still be temporal. Given this inescapable involvement in time, which is experienced but not overcome, a true notion of eternity can neither be had by imagining time "indefinitely" continued (which would still be mere time) nor yet by denying time (in which case it would not be clear whether the idea of "something existing, minus time" would mean anything at all), but by reflexion on that conclusiveness which is sought as the fruit of time in freedom and which this desire experiences even in time. Insofar as these elements are disjoined and the beginning is not simply in free possession of the end but "conceives" it while bringing itself to birth, temporality is a hallmark of creatureliness. Insofar as it is not the concluded but the conclusive which comes about with time, time is the positive means by which creatures participate in God's eternity. Thus in this perspective the temporality of the individual biological being and the temporality that is proper to the world as a whole are seen to be diminished modes of the interior time characteristic of the history of free personal beings.

11

THE SENSUOUS PERIL
THE SENSUOUS
DELIGHT

FÉNELON

Love is chaste when we are devoted to God Himself, and have ceased to
cherish those things He lets us taste through our senses. We follow
Him, but not that we may have more loaves.

HÉLOÏSE AND ABÉLARD

Two Letters

HÉLOÏSE TO ABÉLARD

To her Lord, her Father, her Husband, her Brother; his Servant, his
Child, his Wife, his Sister, and to express all that is humble, respectful
and loving to her Abélard, Héloïse writes this.

A Consolatory letter of yours to a friend happened some days since to
fall into my hands; my knowledge of the writing and my love of the
hand gave me the curiosity to open it. In justification of the liberty I
took, I flattered myself I might claim a sovereign privilege over
everything which came from you. Nor was I scrupulous to break

through the rules of good breeding when I was to hear news of Abélard. But how dear did my curiosity cost me! What disturbance did it occasion, and how surprised I was to find the whole letter filled with a particular and melancholy account of our misfortunes! I met with my name a hundred times; I never saw it without fear—some heavy calamity always followed it. I saw yours too, equally unhappy.... What reflections did I not make! I began to consider the whole afresh, and perceived myself pressed with the same weight of grief as when we first began to be miserable. Though length of time ought to have closed up my wounds, yet the seeing them described by your hand was sufficient to make them all open and bleed afresh....

I reproached myself for having been so long without venting my sorrows, when the rage of our unrelenting enemies still burns with the same fury. Since length of time, which disarms the strongest hatred, seems but to aggravate theirs; since it is decreed that your virtue shall be persecuted till it takes refuge in the grave—and even then, perhaps, your ashes will not be allowed to rest in peace!—let me always meditate on your calamities, let me publish them through all the world, if possible, to shame an age that has not known how to value you....

Let me have a faithful account of all that concerns you; I would know everything, be it ever so unfortunate. Perhaps by mingling my sighs with yours I may make your sufferings less, for it is said that all sorrows divided are made lighter.

Tell me not by way of excuse you will spare me tears; the tears of women shut up in a melancholy place and devoted to penitence are not to be spared.... Write to me then immediately and wait not for miracles; they are too scarce, and we too much accustomed to misfortunes to expect a happy turn. I shall always have this, if you please, and this will always be agreeable to me, that when I receive any letter from you I shall know you still remember me....

We may write to each other; so innocent a pleasure is not denied us. Let us not lose through negligence the only happiness which is left us, and the only one perhaps which the malice of our enemies can never ravish from us. I shall read that you are my husband and you shall see me sign myself your wife. In spite of all our misfortunes you may be what you please in your letter. Letters were first invented for consoling such solitary wretches as myself. Having lost the substantial pleasures of seeing and possessing you, I shall in some measure compensate this loss by the satisfaction I shall find in your writing. There I shall read your most sacred thoughts; I shall carry them always about with me, I shall kiss them every moment....

You cannot but remember (for lovers cannot forget) with what pleasure I have passed whole days in hearing your discourse. How when you were absent I shut myself from everyone to write to you; how uneasy I was till my letter had come to your hands; what artful management it required to engage messengers. This detail perhaps surprises you, and you are in pain for what may follow. But I am no longer ashamed that my passion had no bounds for you, for I have done more than all this. I have hated myself that I might love you. I came hither to ruin myself in a perpetual imprisonment that I might make you live quietly and at ease.

Nothing but virtue, joined to a love perfectly disengaged from the senses, could have produced such effects. Vice never inspires anything like this: it is too much enslaved to the body. When we love pleasures we love the living and not the dead. We leave off burning with desire for those who can no longer burn for us. This was my cruel uncle's notion; he measured my virtue by the frailty of my sex, and thought it was the man and not the person I loved. But he has been guilty to no purpose. I love you more than ever; and so revenge myself on him. I will still love you with all the tenderness of my soul till the last moment of my life. If, formerly, my affection for you was not so pure, if in those days both mind and body loved you, I often told you even then that I was more pleased with possessing your heart than with any other happiness, and the man was the thing I least valued in you.

You cannot but be entirely persuaded of this by the extreme unwillingness I showed to marry you, though I knew that the name of wife was honorable in the world and holy in religion; yet the name of your mistress had greater charms because it was more free. The bonds of matrimony, however honorable, still bear with them a necessary engagement, and I was very unwilling to be necessitated to love always a man who would perhaps not always love me. I despised the name of wife that I might live happy with that of mistress; and I find by your letter to your friend you have not forgot that delicacy of passion which loved you always with the utmost tenderness—and yet wished to love you more!

But oh! where is that happy time? I now lament my lover, and of all my joys have nothing but the painful memory that they are past. Now learn, all you my rivals who once viewed my happiness with jealous eyes, that he you once envied me can never more be mine. I loved him; my love was his crime and the cause of his punishment. My beauty once charmed him; pleased with each other, we passed our brightest days in tranquillity and happiness. If that were a crime, 'tis a crime I am yet fond of, and I have no other regret save that against my will I must now be innocent.

But what do I say? My misfortune was to have cruel relatives whose malice destroyed the calm we enjoyed; had they been reasonable I had now been happy in the enjoyment of my dear husband. Oh! how cruel were they when their blind fury urged a villain to surprise you in your sleep! Where was I—where was your Héloïse then? What joy should I have had in defending my lover; I would have guarded you from violence at the expense of my life. Oh! whither does this excess of passion hurry me? Here love is shocked and modesty deprives me of words.

But tell me whence proceeds your neglect of me since my being professed?* You know nothing moved me to it but your disgrace, nor did I give my consent, but yours. Let me hear what is the occasion of your coldness, or give me leave to tell you now my opinion. Was it not the sole thought of pleasure which engaged you to me? And has not my tenderness, by leaving you nothing to wish for, extinguished your desires?

Wretched Héloïse! you could please when you wished to avoid it; you merited incense when you could remove to a distance the hand that offered it: but since your heart has been softened and has yielded, since you have devoted and sacrificed yourself, you are deserted and forgotten!

I am convinced by a sad experience that it is natural to avoid those to whom we have been too much obliged, and that uncommon generosity causes neglect rather than gratitude. My heart surrendered too soon to gain the esteem of the conqueror; you took it without difficulty and threw it aside with ease. But ungrateful as you are I am no consenting party to this, and though I ought not to retain a wish of my own, yet I still preserve secretly the desire to be loved by you.

When I pronounced my sad vow I then had about me your last letters in which you protested your whole being wholly mine, and would never live but to love me. It is to you therefore I have offered myself; you had my heart and I had yours; do not demand anything back. You must bear with my passion as a thing which of right belongs to you, and from which you can be no ways disengaged....

Is it so hard for one who loves to write? I ask for none of your letters filled with learning and writ for your reputation; all I desire is such letters as the heart dictates, and which the hand cannot transcribe fast enough. How did I deceive myself with hopes that you would be wholly mine when I took the veil, and engaged myself to live forever under your laws? For in being professed I vowed no more than to be yours only, and I forced myself voluntarily to a confinement which you desired for me. Death only then can make me leave the cloister where you have placed me; and then my ashes shall rest here and wait for

*Having taken religious vows.

yours in order to show to the very last my obedience and devotion to you.

Why should I conceal from you the secret of my call? You know it was neither zeal nor devotion that brought me here. Your conscience is too faithful a witness to permit you to disown it. Yet here I am, and here I will remain; to this place an unfortunate love and a cruel relation have condemned me. But if you do not continue your concern for me, if I lose your affection, what have I gained by my imprisonment? What recompense can I hope for? The unhappy consequences of our love and your disgrace have made me put on the habit of chastity, but I am not penitent of the past. Thus I strive and labor in vain. Among those who are wedded to God I am wedded to a man; among the heroic supporters of the Cross I am the slave of a human desire; at the head of a religious community I am devoted to Abélard alone.

What a monster am I! Enlighten me, O Lord, for I know not if my despair of Thy grace draws these words from me! I am, I confess, a sinner, but one who, far from weeping for her sins, weeps only for her lover; far from abhorring her crimes, longs only to add to them; and who, with a weakness unbecoming my state, please myself continually with the remembrance of past delights when it is impossible to renew them.

Good God! What is all this? I reproach myself for my own faults, I accuse you for yours, and to what purpose? Veiled as I am, behold in what a disorder you have plunged me! How difficult it is to fight for duty against inclination. I know what obligations this veil lays upon me, but I feel more strongly what power an old passion has over my heart....

Oh, for pity's sake help a wretch to renounce her desires—her self— and if possible even to renounce you! If you are a lover—a father, help a mistress, comfort a child! These tender names must surely move you; yield either to pity or to love. If you gratify my request I shall continue a religious, and without longer profaning my calling....

I expect this from you as a thing you cannot refuse me. God has a peculiar right over the hearts of great men He has created. When He pleases to touch them He ravishes them, and lets them not speak nor breathe but for His glory. Till that moment of grace arrives, O think of me—do not forget me—remember my love and fidelity and constancy: love me as your mistress, cherish me as your child, your sister, your wife! Remember I still love you, and yet strive to avoid loving you. What a terrible saying is this! I shake with horror, and my heart revolts against what I say. I shall blot all my paper with tears. I end my long letter wishing you, if you desire it (would to Heaven I could!), forever adieu!

ABÉLARD TO HÉLOÏSE

Could I have imagined that a letter not written to yourself would fall into your hands, I had been more cautious not to have inserted anything in it which might awaken the memory of our past misfortunes. I described with boldness the series of my disgraces to a friend, in order to make him less sensible to a loss he had sustained.

If by this well-meaning device I have disturbed you, I purpose now to dry up those tears which the sad description occasioned you to shed; I intend to mix my grief with yours, and pour out my heart before you: in short, to lay open before your eyes all my trouble, and the secret of my soul, which my vanity has hitherto made me conceal from the rest of the world, and which you now force from me, in spite of my resolutions to the contrary.

It is true, that in a sense of the afflictions which have befallen us, and observing that no change of our condition could be expected; that those prosperous days which had seduced us were now past, and there remained nothing but to erase from our minds, by painful endeavors, all marks and remembrances of them. I had wished to find in philosophy and religion a remedy for my disgrace; I searched out an asylum to secure me from love. I was come to the sad experiment of making vows to harden my heart.

But what have I gained by this? If my passion has been put under a restraint my thoughts yet run free. I promise myself that I will forget you, and yet cannot think of it without loving you. My love is not at all lessened by those reflections I make in order to free myself. The silence I am surrounded by makes me more sensible to its impressions, and while I am unemployed with any other things, this makes itself the business of my whole vocation. Till after a multitude of useless endeavors I begin to persuade myself that it is a superfluous trouble to strive to free myself; and that it is sufficient wisdom to conceal from all but you how confused and weak I am.

I remove to a distance from your person with an intention of avoiding you as an enemy; and yet I incessantly seek for you in my mind; I recall your image in my memory, and in different disquietudes I betray and contradict myself. I hate you! I love you! Shame presses me on all sides.

Religion commands me to pursue virtue since I have nothing to hope for from love. But love still preseves its dominion over my fancies and entertains itself with past pleasures. Memory supplies the place of a mistress. Piety and duty are not always the fruits of retirement; even in deserts, when the dew of heaven falls not on us, we love what we ought no longer to love.

The passions, stirred up by solitude, fill these regions of death and silence; it is very seldom that what ought to be is truly followed here and that God only is loved and served. Had I known this before I had instructed you better. You call me your master; it is true you were entrusted to my care. I saw you, I was earnest to teach you vain sciences; it cost you your innocence and me my liberty.

Your uncle, who was fond of you, became my enemy and revenged himself on me. If now having lost the power of satisfying my passion I had also lost that of loving you, I should have some consolation.... How miserable am I! I find myself much more guilty in my thoughts of you, even amidst my tears, than in possessing you when I was in full liberty. I continually think of you; I continually call to mind your tenderness.

In this condition, O Lord! if I run to prostrate myself before your altar, if I beseech you to pity me, why does not the pure flame of the Spirit consume the sacrifice that is offered? Cannot this habit of penitence which I wear interest Heaven to treat me more favorably? But Heaven is still inexorable, because my passion still lives in me; the fire is only covered over with deceitful ashes, and cannot be extinguished but by extraordinary grace. We deceive men, but nothing is hid from God.

You tell me that it is for me you live under that veil which covers you; why do you profane your vocation with such words? Why provoke a jealous God with a blasphemy? I hoped after our separation you would have changed your sentiments; I hoped too that God would have delivered me from the tumult of my senses. We commonly die to the affections of those we see no more, and they to ours; absence is the tomb of love. But to me absence is an unquiet remembrance of what I once loved which continually torments me. I flattered myself that when I should see you no more you would rest in my memory without troubling my mind; that Brittany and the sea would suggest other thoughts; that my fasts and studies would by degrees delete you from my heart. But in spite of severe fasts and redoubled studies, in spite of the distance of three hundred miles which separates us, your image, as you describe yourself in your veil, appears to me and confounds all my resolutions.

What means have I not used! I have armed my hands against myself; I have exhausted my strength in constant exercises; I comment upon Saint Paul; I contend with Aristotle: in short, I do all I used to do before I loved you, but all in vain; nothing can be successful that opposes you. Oh! do not add to my miseries by your constancy.... Why use your eloquence to reproach me for my flight and for my silence? Spare the recital of our assignations and your constant exactness to them; without calling up such disturbing thoughts I have enough to suffer. What great advantages would philosophy give us over other men, if by studying it we could learn to govern our passions? What efforts, what relapses, what agitations do we undergo! And how long are we lost in this confusion, unable to exert our reason, to possess our souls, or to rule our affections?...

How can I separate from the person I love the passion I should detest? Will the tears I shed be sufficient to render it odious to me? I know not how it happens, there is always a pleasure in weeping for a beloved object. It is difficult in our sorrow to distinguish penitence from love. The memory of the crime and the memory of the object which has charmed us are too nearly related to be immediately separated. And the love of God in its beginning does not wholly annihilate the love of the creature.

But what excuses could I not find in you if the crime were excusable? Unprofitable honor, troublesome riches, could never tempt me: but those charms, that beauty, that air, which I yet behold at this instant, have occasioned my fall. Your looks were the beginning of my guilt; your eyes, your discourse, pierced my heart; and in spite of that ambition and glory which tried to make a defense, love was soon the master.

God, in order to punish me, forsook me. You are no longer of the world; you have renounced it: I am a religious devoted to solitude; shall we not take advantage of our condition? Would you destroy my piety in its infant state? Would you have me forsake the abbey into which I am but newly entered? Must I renounce my vows? I have made them in the presence of God; whither shall I fly from His wrath should I violate them? Suffer me to seek ease in my duty....

Regard me no more, I entreat you, as a founder or any great personage; your praises ill agree with my many weaknesses. I am a miserable sinner, prostrate before my Judge, and with my face pressed to the earth I mix my tears with the earth. Can you see me in this posture and solicit me to love you? Come, if you think fit, and in your holy habit thrust yourself between my God and me, and be a wall of separation. Come and force from me those sighs and thoughts and vows I owe to Him alone. Assist the evil spirits and be the instrument of their malice. What cannot you induce a heart to do whose weakness you so perfectly know?

Nay, withdraw yourself and contibute to my salvation. Suffer me to avoid destruction, I entreat you by our former tender affection and by our now common misfortune. It will always be the highest love to show none; I here release you from all your oaths and engagements. Be God's wholly, to whom you are appropriated; I will never oppose so

pious a design. How happy shall I be if I thus lose you! Then shall I
indeed be a religious and you a perfect example of an abbess....

I will confess to you I have thought myself hitherto an abler master
to instill vice than to teach virtue. My false eloquence has only set off
false good. My heart, drunk with voluptuousness, could only suggest
terms proper and moving to recommend that. The cup of sinners
overflows with so enchanting a sweetness, and we are naturally so
much inclined to taste it, that it needs only to be offered to us.

On the other hand the chalice of saints is filled with a bitter draught
and nature starts from it.* And yet you reproach me with cowardice for
giving it to you first. I willingly submit to these accusations. I cannot
enough admire the readiness you showed to accept the religious habit;
bear therefore with courage the Cross you so resolutely took up. Drink
of the chalice of saints, even to the bottom, without turning your eyes
with uncertainty upon me....

To make it more easy consider why I pressed you to your vow before I
took mine; and pardon my sincerity and the design I have of meriting
your neglect and hatred if I conceal nothing from you. When I saw
myself oppressed by my misfortune I was furiously jealous, and
regarded all men as my rivals. Love has more of distrust than
assurance. I was apprehensive of many things because of my many
defects, and being tormented with fear because of my own example I
imagined your heart so accustomed to love that it could not be long
without entering on a new engagement. Jealousy can easily believe the
most terrible things.

I was desirous to make it impossible for me to doubt you. I was very
urgent to persuade you that propriety demanded your withdrawal from
the eyes of the world; that modesty and our friendship required it; and
that your own safety obliged it. After such a revenge taken on me you
could expect to be secure nowhere but in a convent.

I will do you justice, you were very easily persuaded. My jealousy
secretly rejoiced in your innocent compliance; and yet, triumphant as I
was, I yielded you up to God with an unwilling heart. I still kept my
gift as much as was possible, and only parted with it in order to keep it
out of the power of other men. I did not persuade you to religion out of
any regard to your happiness, but condemned you to it like an enemy
who destroys what he cannot carry off. And yet you heard my
discourses with kindness, you sometimes interrupted me with tears,
and pressed me to acquaint you with those convents I held in the
highest esteem. What a comfort I felt in seeing you shut up. I was now
at ease and took a satisfaction in considering that you continued no

*Revolts against it.

longer in the world after my disgrace, and that you would return to it no more.... Till then I thought your youth and beauty would foil my design and force your return to the world. Might not a small temptation have changed you? Is it possible to renounce oneself entirely at the age of two-and-twenty? At an age which claims the utmost liberty could you think the world no longer worth your regard? How much did I wrong you, and what weakness did I impute to you?... I watched your eyes, your every movement, your air; I trembled at everything. You may call such self-interested conduct treachery, perfidy, murder. A love so like to hatred should provoke the utmost contempt and anger.

I went every day trembling to exhort you to this sacrifice; I admired without daring to mention it then, a brightness in your beauty which I had never observed before. Whether it was the bloom of a rising virtue, or an anticipation of the great loss I was to suffer, I was not curious in examining the cause, but only hastened your being professed. I engaged your prioress in my guilt by a criminal bribe with which I purchased the right of burying you. The professed of the house were alike bribed and concealed from you, at my directions, all their scruples and disgusts. I omitted nothing, either little or great; and if you had escaped my snares I myself would not have retired; I was resolved to follow you everywhere. The shadow of myself would always have pursued your steps and continually have occasioned either your confusion or your fear, which would have been a sensible gratification to me.

But, thanks to Heaven, you resolved to take the vows. I accompanied you to the foot of the altar, and while you stretched out your hand to touch the sacred cloth I heard you distinctly pronounce those fatal words that forever separated you from man....

Necessity and despair were at the root of my proceedings, and thus I offered an insult to Heaven rather than a sacrifice. God rejected my offering and my prayer, and continued my punishment by suffering me to continue my love. Thus I bear alike the guilt of your vows and of the passion that preceded them, and must be tormented all the days of my life.

If God spoke to your heart as to that of a religious whose innocence had first asked Him for favors, I should have matter of comfort; but to see both of us the victims of a guilty love, to see this love insult us in our very habits and spoil our devotions, fills me with horror and trembling. Is this a state of reprobation? Or are these the consequences of a long drunkenness in profane love?

We cannot say love is a poison and a drunkenness till we are illuminated by grace; in the meantime it is an evil we dote on. When we are under such a mistake, the knowledge of our misery is the first step towards amendment. Who does not know that 'tis for the glory of God to find no other reason in man for His mercy than man's very weakness? When He has shown us this weakness and we have bewailed it, he is ready to put forth His omnipotence and assist us. Let us say for our comfort that what we suffer is one of those terrible temptations which have sometimes disturbed the vocations of the most holy.

God can grant His presence to men in order to soften their calamities whenever He shall think fit. It was His pleasure when you took the veil to draw you to Him by His grace. I saw your eyes, when you spoke your last farewell, fixed upon the Cross. It was more than six months before you wrote me a letter, nor during all that time did I receive a message from you. I admired this silence, which I durst not blame, but could not imitate. I wrote to you, and you returned me no answer: your heart was then shut, but this garden of the spouse is now opened; He is withdrawn from it and has left you alone.

By removing from you He has made trial of you; call Him back and strive to regain Him. We must have the assistance of God, that we may break our chains; we are too deeply in love to free ourselves.

Our follies have penetrated into the sacred places; our amours have been a scandal to the whole kingdom. They are read and admired; love which produced them has caused them to be described. We shall be a consolation to the failings of youth forever; those who offend after us will think themselves less guilty. We are criminals whose repentance is late; oh, let it be sincere! Let us repair as far as is possible the evils we have done, and let France, which has been the witness of our crimes, be amazed at our repentance. Let us confound all who would imitate our guilt; let us take the side of God against ourselves, and by so doing prevent His judgment.

Our former lapses require tears, shame, and sorrow to expiate them. Let us offer up these sacrifices from our hearts, let us blush and let us weep. If in these feeble beginnings, O Lord, our hearts are not entirely Thine, let them at least feel that they ought to be so.

Deliver yourself, Héloïse, from the shameful remains of a passion which has taken too deep root. Remember that the least thought for any other than God is an adultery. If you could see me here with my meager face and melancholy air, surrounded with numbers of persecuting monks, who are alarmed at my reputation for learning and offended at my lean visage, as if I threatened them with a reformation, what would you say of my base sighs and of those unprofitable tears which deceive these credulous men? Alas! I am humbled under love, and not under the Cross. Pity me and free yourself. If your vocation be, as you say, my work, deprive me not of the merit of it by your continual inquietudes. . . .

I have been indeed your master, but it was only to teach sin. You call me your father; before I had any claim to the title, I deserved that of parricide. I am your brother, but it is the affinity of sin that brings me that distinction. I am called your husband, but it is after a public scandal.

If you have abused the sanctity of so many holy terms in the superscription of your letter to do me honor and flatter your own passion, blot them out and replace them with those of murderer, villain, and enemy, who has conspired against your honor, troubled your quiet, and betrayed your innocence. You would have perished through my means but for an extraordinary act of grace, which, that you might be saved, has thrown me down in the middle of my course.

This is the thought you ought to have of a fugitive who desires to deprive you of the hope of ever seeing him again. But when love has once been sincere how difficult it is to determine to love no more! 'Tis a thousand times more easy to renounce the world than love. I hate this deceitful, faithless world; I think no more of it; but my wandering heart still eternally seeks you, and is filled with anguish at having lost you, in spite of all the powers of my reason....

There are some whom God saves by suffering. Let my salvation be the fruit of your prayers; let me owe it to your tears and your exemplary holiness. Though my heart, Lord, be filled with the love of Thy creature, Thy hand can, when it pleases, empty me of all love save for Thee.

To love Héloïse truly is to leave her to that quiet which retirement and virtue afford. I have resolved it: this letter shall be my last fault. Adieu.

If I die here I will give orders that my body be carried to the house of the Paraclete. You shall see me in that condition, not to demand tears from you, for it will be too late; weep rather for me now and extinguish the fire which burns me.

You shall see me in order that your piety may be strengthened by horror of this carcass, and my death be eloquent to tell you what you brave when you love a man. I hope you will be willing, when you have finished this mortal life, to be buried near me. Your cold ashes need then fear nothing, and my tomb shall be the more rich and renowned.

C. P. CAVAFY

Che Fece ... Il Gran Rifiuto

For some people the day comes
when they have to declare the great Yes

or the great No. It's clear at once who has the Yes
ready within him; and saying it,
he goes from honor to honor, strong in his conviction.
He who refuses does not repent. Asked again,
he'd still say no. Yet that no—the right no—
drags him down all his life.

Longings

Like the beautiful bodies of those who died before growing old,
sadly shut away in a sumptuous mausoleum,
roses by the head, jasmine at the feet—
so appear the longings that have passed
without being satisfied, not one of them granted
a single night of pleasure, or one of its radiant mornings.

In the Same Space

The setting of houses, cafés, the neighborhood
that I've seen and walked through years on end:

I created you while I was happy, while I was sad,
with so many incidents, so many details.

And, for me, the whole of you has been transformed into feeling.

GERARD MANLEY HOPKINS

My Own Heart Let Me More Have Pity On

My own heart let me more have pity on; let
Me live to my sad self hereafter kind,
Charitable; not live this tormented mind
With this tormented mind tormenting yet.

I cast for comfort I can no more get
By groping round my comfortless, than blind
Eyes in their dark can day or thirst can find
Thirst's all-in-all in all a world of wet.

Soul, self; come, poor Jackself, I do advise ·
You, jaded, let be; call off thoughts awhile
Elsewhere; leave comfort root-room, let joy size

At God knows when to God knows what; whose smile
's not wrung, see you; unforeseen times rather—as skies
Betweenpie mountains—lights a lovely mile.

JOHN DONNE

I Am a Little World

I am a little world made cunningly
Of elements, and an angelic sprite;
But black sin hath betrayed to endless night
My world's both parts, and O, both parts must die.
You which beyond that heaven which was most high
Have found new spheres, and of new lands can write,
Pour new seas in mine eyes, that so I might
Drown my world with my weeping earnestly,
Or wash it if it must be drowned no more.
But O, it must be burnt! Alas, the fire
Of lust and envy'have burnt it heretofore,
And made it fouler; let their flames retire,
And burn me, O Lord, with a fiery zeal
Of Thee'and Thy house, which doth in eating heal.

Thou Hast Made Me

Thou hast made me, and shall Thy work decay?
Repair me now, for now mine end doth haste;
I run to death, and death meets me as fast,
And all my pleasures are like yesterday.
I dare not move my dim eyes any way,
Despair behind, and death before doth cast
Such terror, and my feeble flesh doth waste
By sin in it, which it towards hell doth weigh.
Only Thou art above, and when towards Thee
By Thy leave I can look, I rise again;
But our old subtle foe so tempteth me
That not one hour myself I can sustain.

Thy grace may wing me to prevent his art,
And Thou like adamant draw mine iron heart.

JULIAN GREEN

From His Diary

JANUARY 23. AT GSTAAD.   Everything in our lives being, it seems, of a
sexual nature, our gestures, our way of sitting down, the most innocent
of our litle manias, the good and bad books we read, the manner in
which we soap our bodies, everything, in fact, how can we not see that
when a man gives up physical pleasure, he replaces it instantly and
unconsciously by thousands of small things that are a sort of
compensation to him for what he misses? Am I wrong? I don't think so.
I believe that taking a nap, or eating a cake, or settling into a
comfortable armchair simply means cheating one's hunger. A hunger
that one doesn't even wish to name. Mortal sin is sent packing, escorted
to the city gate with a great beating of drums (the devil does the
drumming), but sensuality tiptoes back, creeps in at the back door,
duly disguised. Saints who sleep on the floor and fast so severely have
understood this. You don't win the game by confiscating the body's
sexual organs, to speak plainly. Sexuality looks elsewhere for shelter, it
can even conceal itself in mortifications.

DAME FREYA STARK

Love

The women of Cyprus are, on the whole, rather plain. They walk up
and down among their steep vineyards in the sun, labouring with
kilted skirts, and laced boots to keep their ankles firm on the rough
paths, and weights of hay or faggots on their backs. When a stranger
rose among them from the sea, she had no need to be superlatively
lovely: and one goes with some misgiving westward to Paphos,
wondering whether Aphrodite was not perhaps overpraised in her day?
New Paphos itself is a dull and orphaned shore, more reminiscent of
the landing of St. Paul, and of the toil and disappointments of life,
than of the Mother of Gods and men. Aphrodite, however, did not land
exactly there but at a place a little farther to the east, called White
Rocks, where the remains of a temple are on a headland, above a bay of
polished boulders and white sand.

Here the long waves still lift their backs as if they carried the queen of the world, and come in ranks with a space between them, regiments saluting, with the morning shining through the pennants and the plumes, the tossing spray. The water has the gem-like lucidity of the Levant and shows every pebble clean-cut through the advancing wave. There are no trees about, but the swelling shapes of grassy hills heavy with spicy odours in the sun; and a simplicity, an absence of clefts or crannies, an open-ness not cooled by shadows, but by the movement of the air and water, the bare world rolling. Here someone, a shepherd or a seaman, saw Loveliness, and gave to the surrounding rocks for ever, to the sapphire horizon and the whispering foam, the secret which the human being is happy to know, perhaps only once—when he sees the eyes of his beloved deeper than ocean and the Goddess herself in their radiance, miraculous and alas! unembraceable as the whiteness that bore her.

No creature can ever be derelict who has had this moment. He is an initiate. He has seen the well of life rising suddenly within its fleshly walls; out of the dark unknown foundations of the world, emerging from chaos, the glowing stream has risen stronger, more ancient, more divine, than the sweet human form that contains it; and the current has met above his being and carried him along its dark perennial way....

Love, and the beloved, are different. The lightness, the grace, the breath of divinity, are no intrinsic part of the shape which they inhabit. They radiate from it and lie like enchantment on all the world around. He is not completely happy who cannot remember this fugitive visit, this murmur of doves about him in his spring; when the skies are doors just opening and the grass lies like gold upon the hills; and the cries in the street are music, and the old men smile as they pass and remember their days.

The Goddess soon or late gathers the hem of sea and sky about her and departs; the colours fade; the White Rocks remain bare in the sun; the magic is over. The veil of divinity no longer hides the form of the beloved, and all is common day.

Then comes love as we chiefly know it in our lives, and as Botticelli painted his later Venus, with sad young eyes too innocent, that look out shrinkingly on toil and sorrow. The sea still ridges her shell with little flecks of foam; the winds still wrap their gentle mantles round her; yet she is conscious of nakedness, no longer triumphant, and weak in a fearful world. This is the love that walks in our lives and shares their toil and stumbles; and clothes itself, if it is wise, in the memory of that other time when all things were divine.

The whole human endeavour is to keep intact at least the outward adornments of that first visitation: like the riderless horse, or the empty armour, they are borne through the slow funeral procession of the life that follows Love when it departs.

Where men and women are wise and fortunate they have allowed no break between the vision and its memory, so that these merge imperceptibly, and no one, least of all themselves, can tell when the light that was unearthly turned into day. But even where this is not so, and death or division or the rashness of the heart or the grinding of need have stained the memory and spoiled it—the colours that remain, however few and however eaten into and effaced almost by time, still keep the divine quality that first made them alive. This divinity often leaves the form it once made beautiful; it shines on other loves, or illuminates even the unexpected details and trivial daily things that one would think incapable of answering to that glow. So, on a low flat coast, the presence of the sea is felt far inland and out of sight of the sea: salt is on the lips, and the salt-loving tamarisk blossoms in the ditches, and lavender or thrift cling to chalky ledges: the colour-wash on houses is bleached and bitten on one side by the prevailing wind; the rivers slow down as they meet sandbanks, and there is a gleam of sea-shells on the gravel of paths that tend to sand: in the softness and the freshness of the air, in the clouds wreathed in high spirals from their flat watery base, the lover who once has known it recognizes the nearness of the sea. And prhaps in a gap between dull houses and fences of allotments, and labelled pleasures, he may get a glimpse of that deeper blue horizon where he once saw the free Aphrodite born of foam.

Everything therefore depends on the visitation of the Gods and, as this is unpredictable, separate human arrangements have had to be made. It is no fault of theirs, and yet a thing to be remembered, that at every moment their pattern must cut across the divine.

For this reason every sort of social code is unsatisfactory, and the chances of happiness in love appear to be more or less equal under any dispensation that gives to the human creature a reasonable degree of freedom. Tacitly, under most systems, an allowance is made for the interruption of the Gods.

In Latin countries it is expected on the whole to come after, in the northern ones before marriage: in the Muslim East it is hampered altogether and only now beginning to uncoil itself from the too inelastic supremacy of man (though it was in the East that the words of forgiveness were spoken to the woman who "loved much"). The Latin way has a great deal to recommend it; it concentrates on the accessories, on teaching, as it were, the mechanism of love, so that the years may run smoothly in their grooves and, if the vision comes, may find ground tilled and weeded and ready to bear easily whatever the seed may be. If fortune favours and the parents' judgment was careful, and the young themselves were free and candid in their amount of choice, love follows marriage as faithfully and deeply as it does in more independent lands: otherwise it will come as a stranger, and fit itself with more or less disturbance—but on the whole rather less—into the normal rut of things. The easy habitual sex life makes for indulgence, but it prevents the miseries of repression, the solitary twists that happen too often with northern natures: and I think that men and women live more easily together in the south.

Yet we in the north have dreams. We may wait fruitless years on an arid shore, but when love comes we hope to see the Goddess herself. Like all devotees, we risk our temporal chances for hopes that have a measure of eternity. And though many fail altogether, and most fail in part—their enduring moment has been. It is a bond between them, too, for all that it is often a bond of failure, and is strong in human ways; for many lives, unconsciously, in their dull habitual reaches, still remember that forgotten glow of dawn. Perhaps the *only* reason for preferring our northern system to the more practical methods of the south is the isolation, as it were, of this moment: it is not crowded out and made unimportant by habits of more easy intercourse: it is put into an open space of our youth, cleared and empty, where—if it has come at all—it may be seen for ever down the vista of years. In respect of this moment alone it becomes a sin for human beings to unite, whether in marriage or without it, except in love. And what happens after matters very little, and will indeed be richer by the riches of that time.

I have figured this division of north and south, but it is independent of latitude, and is one of those unbridgeable clefts of the human race, such as the division between women who wear real lace or none upon their underwear, and those who, like the lady in Meredith, "prefer twenty shillings to one sovereign." As in the contrast of religions, it is not a difference of good and bad, but it is important to live in the category to which one naturally belongs.

Each has its own danger. The moment may be waited for, and because of the very ignorance produced by the waiting may pass unrecognized when it comes; or else it may come when a life too full of unimportant things has blunted the power to receive it and accidents, or the callousness of others, are there to interfere. No crime short of murder can be comparable to the crime of destroying in another the capacity to love: and this happens sometimes through the rashness of parents, or the sight of misery in adolescence, but more often through some bitterness of experience when youth is still defenceless, "nullo contusus aratro," and wounds leave a scar difficult to heal.

But when all is said and done the choice lies in ourselves. We are suitors to love, and life is more generous than Bassanio's father-in-law:

the caskets it presents are just as enigmatic, the choice as difficult and full of doom, but the result is not usually quite so final, and the Prince of Morocco was no doubt able to open another box in his time.

Safety lies in awareness of love: not in this person nor in that, by some private shore or secret enclosed harbour, but in the consciousness of all as a part of its embracing sea. All continents and islands, not our shore alone, are surrounded by the network of those streams; the tides that fill the creeks are swung by the whole globe in commerce with its stars, and by their planetary motion the smallest clinging shell-fish of the rocks is fed; nor is there any division between the shallower girdle of the coasts and those depths where hurricanes and blind monsters as well as the friendly dews and rains of earth are born. Embraced by this infinitude, we step for our summer pleasure into the wayward foam; and think of love in the same way, when it fills our pools and roams with its light and echo in our caves. Its tides come from distances far greater than the coastline they embrace can dream; and when they recede we can but keep our faith and feed our eyes with a horizon enriched with what lies beyond it, and rest in the certainty that at any moment, in youth or age or sorrow, in small ways or great, the divine Aphrodite may return with the splendour of the world iridescent and fragile as foam in her arms. The waves will laugh and cover the bare rocks and worn shabby places of our hearts; and we shall know how to welcome her, because we have known her long ago.

EMILY DICKINSON

I Cannot Live with You

I cannot live with You—
It would be Life—
And Life is over there—
Behind the Shelf

The Sexton keeps the Key to—
Putting up
Our Life—His Porcelain—
Like a Cup—

Discarded of the Housewife—
Quaint—or Broke—
A newer Sevres pleases—
Old Ones crack—

I could not die—with You—
For One must wait
To shut the Other's Gaze down—
You—could not—

And I—Could I stand by
And see You—freeze—
Without my Right of Frost—
Death's privilege?

Nor could I rise—with You—
Because Your Face
Would put out Jesus'—
That New Grace

Glow plain—and foreign
On my homesick Eye—
Except that You than He
Shone closer by—

They'd judge Us—How—
For You—served Heaven—You know,
Or sought to—
I could not—

Because You saturated Sight—
And I had no more Eyes
For sordid excellence
As Paradise

And were You lost, I would be—
Though My Name
Rang loudest
On the Heavenly fame—

And were You—saved—
And I—condemned to be
Where You were not—
That self—were Hell to Me—

So We must meet apart—
You there—I—here—
With just the Door ajar
That Oceans are—and Prayer—
And that White Sustenance—
Despair—

STENDHAL

The Crystallization of Love

CHAPTER I

ON LOVE

I am trying to account for that passion all of whose developments are inherently beautiful.

There are four different kinds of love:

1. Passion-love, that of the Portuguese Nun, of Héloïse for Abélard, of Captain de Vésel, of the Cento man-at-arms.*

2. Sympathy-love, such as was prevalent in Paris in 1760, and is found in the memoirs and romances of that period, in Crébillon, Lauzun, Duclos, Marmontel, Chamfort, Madame d'Épinay, etc., etc.

It is a picture in which everything, even to the shadows, must be rose coloured, and into which nothing unpleasant must intrude under any pretext whatever, at the risk of infringing custom, fashion, refinement, etc. A well-bred man knows in advance everything that he must do and expect in the various stages of this kind of love; as there is nothing passionate or unexpected about it, it is often more refined than real love, for it is always sprightly; it is like a cold and pretty miniature compared with a picture by the Caracci; and, whereas passion-love carries us away against all our interests, sympathy-love always knows how to adjust itself to them. It is true that if you strip this poor form of love of its vanity, very little remains; without its vanity, it is like a feeble convalescent who is scarcely able to drag himself along.

3. Sensual love.

Whilst out shooting, to meet a fresh, pretty country girl who darts away into a wood. Every one knows the love founded on pleasures of this kind; however unromantic and wretched one's character, it is there that one starts at the age of sixteen.

4. Vanity-love.

The great majority of men, especially in France, desire and possess a fashionable woman as they would possess a fine horse, as a necessary luxury for a young man. Their vanity, more or less flattered and more or less stimulated, gives rise to rapture. Sometimes sensual love is present also, but not always; often there is not even sensual pleasure.

---

*The *Letters of a Portuguese Nun,* unfolding the true story of a woman seduced, abandoned, and still passionately in love, went into many French and English editions in the seventeenth and eighteenth centuries. As for the captain and the man-at-arms mentioned here, Stendhal, when asked about them, said he had forgotten their story.

The Duchesse de Chaulnes used to say that a duchess is never more than thirty years old to a snob; and people who frequented the Court of that upright man, King Louis of Holland, still recall with amusement a pretty woman at the Hague who could never bring herself to think a man anything but charming if he was a Duke or a Prince. But, faithful to the monarchic principle, as soon as a Prince arrived at Court she dropped the Duke. She was a kind of insignia of the Corps Diplomatique.

The most agreeable form of this rather insipid relationship is the one in which sensual pleasure is increased by habit. In that case past memories make it seem something like real love; there is piqued vanity and sadness on being abandoned; and, becoming seized by romantic ideas, you begin to think you are in love and melancholy, for your vanity always aspires to have a great passion to its credit. The one thing certain is that to whatever kind of love one owes one's pleasures, so long as they are accompanied by mental exhilaration, they are very keen and their memory is entrancing; and in this passion, contrary to most others, the memory of what we have lost always seems sweeter than anything that we can hope for in the future.

Sometimes, in vanity-love, habit and the despair of finding anything better produces a kind of friendship, the least agreeable of all its kinds; it prides itself on its *security*, etc.

Sensual pleasure, being part of our nature, is within the grasp of every one, but it only holds a very low place in the eyes of tender and passionate beings. Although they may be ridiculous in drawing-rooms, although worldly people may often make them unhappy by their intrigues, on the other hand they taste pleasures utterly inaccessible to those hearts who only thrill to vanity or to gold.

Some virtuous and affectionate women have almost no idea at all of sensual pleasure; they have only very rarely laid themselves open to it, if I may put it so, and even then the raptures of passion-love have almost made them forget the pleasures of the body.

Some men are the victims and instruments of a satanic pride, a sort of Alfieri pride. These people, who are perhaps cruel because, like Nero, they live in constant fear, judging every one by their own heart, these people, I say, cannot obtain any sensual pleasure unless it is accompanied by circumstances which flatter their pride abnormally, that is to say, unless they can perpetrate some cruelty on the companion of their pleasures.... These men cannot feel the emotion of security with anything less.

However, instead of distinguishing four different kinds of love, one could easily adopt eight or ten shades. There are perhaps as many different ways of feeling as of seeing amongst men; but these differences in terms do not affect the reasoning that follows. Every kind of love that one meets here below is born, lives, dies or becomes immortal, according to the same laws.

CHAPTER II

THE BIRTH OF LOVE

This is what goes on in the mind:

1. Admiration.
2. One says to one's self: "How delightful to kiss her, to be kissed in return," etc.
3. Hope.

One studies her perfections. It is at this moment that a woman should surrender herself, to get the greatest possible sensual pleasure. The eyes of even the most modest women light up the moment hope is born; passion is so strong and pleasure is so acute that they betray themselves in the most obvious manner.

4. Love is born.

To love is to derive pleasure from seeing, touching and feeling through all one's senses and as closely as possible, a lovable person who loves us.

5. The first crystallization begins.

We take a joy in attributing a thousand perfections to a woman of whose love we are sure; we analyze all our happiness with intense satisfaction. This reduces itself to giving ourselves an exaggerated idea of a magnificent possession which has just fallen to us from Heaven in some way we do not understand, and the continued possession of which is assured to us.

This is what you will find if you let a lover turn things over in his mind for twenty-four hours.

In the salt mines of Salzburg a bough stripped of its leaves by winter is thrown into the depths of the disused workings; two or three months later it is pulled out again, covered with brilliant crystals: even the tiniest twigs, no bigger than a tomtit's claw, are spangled with a vast number of shimmering, glittering diamonds, so that the original bough is no longer recognizable.

I call crystallization that process of the mind which discovers fresh perfections in its beloved at every turn of events.*

For instance, should a traveller speak of the coolness of Genoese orange groves by the seashore on a scorching summer day, you

---

*What Stendhal calls "crystallization" we would probably call "projection." The lover projects upon the beloved qualities which exist only in his imagination and which have little or no relation to the actual person.

immediately think how delightful it would be to enjoy this coolness in her company!

One of your friends breaks his arm out hunting: how sweet, you think, to be nursed by a woman you love! To be with her always and to revel in her constant love would almost make your pain blessèd; and you leave your friend's broken arm still more firmly convinced of the angelic sweetness of your mistress. In short, it is sufficient to think of a perfection in order to see it in the person you love.

This phenomenon which I have allowed myself to call *crystallization*, arises from the promptings of Nature which urge us to enjoy ourselves and drive the blood to our brains, from the feeling that our delight increases with the perfections of the beloved, and from the thought: "She is mine." The savage has no time to get beyond the first step. He grasps his pleasures, but his brain is concentrated on following the buck fleeing from him through the forest, and with whose flesh he must repair his own strength as quickly as possible, at the risk of falling beneath the hatchet of his enemy.

At the other extreme of civilization, I have no doubt that a sensitive woman arrives at the point of experiencing no sensual pleasure except with the man she loves. This is in direct opposition to the savage. But, amongst civilized communities woman has plenty of leisure, whilst the savage lives so close to essentials that he is obliged to treat his female as a beast of burden. If the females of many animals have an easier lot, it is only because the subsistence of the males is more assured.

But let us leave the forests and return to Paris. A passionate man sees nothing but perfection in the woman he loves; and yet his affections may still wander, for the spirit wearies of monotony, even in the case of the most perfect happiness.

So what happens to rivet his attention is this:

6. Doubt is born.

When his hopes have first of all been raised and then confirmed by ten or a dozen glances, or a whole series of other actions which may be compressed into a moment or spread over several days, the lover, recovering from his first amazement and growing used to his happiness, or perhaps merely guided by theory which, based always on his most frequent experiences, is really only correct in the case of light women, the lover, I say, demands more positive proofs of love and wants to advance the moment of his happiness.

If he takes too much for granted he will be met with indifference, coldness or even anger: in France there will be a suggestion of irony which seems to say: "You think you have made more progress than you really have." A woman behaves in this way either because she is recovering from a moment of intoxication and obeys the behests of modesty, which she is alarmed at having transgressed, or merely from prudence or coquettishness.

The lover begins to be less sure of the happiness which he has promised himself; he begins to criticize the reasons he gave himself for hoping.

He tries to fall back on the other pleasures of life. *He finds they no longer exist.* He is seized with a dread of appalling misery, and his attention becomes concentrated.

7. Second crystallization.

Now he begins the second crystallization, producing as its diamonds various confirmations of the following idea:

"She loves me."

Every quarter of an hour, during the night following the birth of doubt, after a moment of terrible misery, the lover says to himself: "Yes, she loves me"; and crystallization sets to work to discover fresh charms; then gaunt-eyed doubt grips him again and pulls him up with a jerk. His heart misses a beat; he says to himself: "But does she love me?" Through all these harrowing and delicious alternations the poor lover feels acutely: "With her I would experience joys which she alone in the world could give me."

It is the clearness of this truth and the path he treads between an appalling abyss and the most perfect happiness, that make the second crystallization appear to be so very much more important than the first.

The lover hovers incessantly amongst these three ideas:

1. She is perfect in every way.

2. She loves me.

3. How can I get the strongest possible proof of her love for me?

The most heart-rending moment in love that is still young is when it finds that it has been wrong in its chain of reasoning and must destroy a whole agglomeration of crystals.

Even the fact of crystallization itself begins to appear doubtful.

CHAPTER III

... The thing that ensures the duration of love is the second crystallization, during which at every moment one realizes that one must either be loved or perish. How, with this conviction ever present in one's mind, and grown into a habit by several months of love, can one bear even the thought of ceasing to love? The more determined a man's character, the less liable is he to be inconstant.

This second crystallization is practically non-existent in love inspired by women who surrender themselves too quickly.

As soon as the crystallizations have taken place, especially the second one, which is much the stronger, indifferent eyes no longer recognize the bough:

For, 1. It is adorned by perfections or diamonds which they do not see;

2. It is adorned by perfections which are not perfections in their sight....

CHAPTER IV

In the mind of a completely unbiased person, that, for instance, of a young girl living in a country house in an isolated part of the country—the most insignificant unexpected event may lead to a little admiration, and if this is followed by the slightest ray of hope, it causes the birth of love and crystallization.

In a case of this kind, the first attraction of love is that it is a distraction.

Surprise and hope are powerfully assisted by the need of love and the melancholy which one has at the age of sixteen. It is fairly clear that the main anxiety of that age is a thirst for love, and it is characteristic of that thirst not to be unreasonably particular about the kind of draught that chance may offer to slake it....

CHAPTER V

Man is not free to refuse to do the thing which gives him more pleasure than any other conceivable action.

Love is like a fever; it comes and goes without the will having any part in the process. That is one of the principal differences between sympathy-love and passion-love, and one can only congratulate one's self on the fine qualities of the person one loves as on a lucky chance.

Love, indeed, belongs to every age: take, for instance, the passion of Madame du Deffand for the unattractive Horace Walpole....

CHAPTER VI

THE SALZBURG BOUGH

During love, crystallization hardly ever stops. This is its history: so long as you are on a distant footing with the person you love, crystallization takes place from an *imaginary solution;* it is only in your imagination that you are certain of the existence of any particular perfection in the woman you love. After you have arrived at terms of intimacy, constantly renewed fears are calmed by more real solutions. In this way, happiness is never uniform except in its source. Every day has a different flower.

If the loved woman surrenders to the passion she feels and falls into the grievous error of killing fear by the ardour of her transports, crystallization stops for a moment; but, when love loses its ardour, that is to say, its fears, it acquires the charm of complete unconstraint, of boundless confidence, and a sweet familiarity comes to deaden all the sorrows of life and bring fresh interest into one's pleasures.

If you are deserted, crystallization starts again; and the thought of every act of admiration and each delight which she can bestow on you and of which you had ceased to think, ends in this harrowing reflection: "That rapturous joy will *never* be mine again! And it is through my own fault that I have lost it!" If you try to find happiness in emotions of a different kind your heart refuses to react to them. . . .

CHAPTER VII

DIFFERENCES BETWEEN THE BIRTH OF LOVE IN THE TWO SEXES

Women attach themselves by their favours. As nineteen-twentieths of their ordinary day-dreams are connected with love, these day-dreams are all concentrated on one person after intimacy; they endeavour to justify such an extraordinary proceeding, so decisive and so contrary to all the habits of modesty. Men have no task of this kind to perform; later, a woman's imagination pictures minutely and at her leisure such moments of delight.

Since love makes one doubt even the most clearly proven things, the woman who before intimacy was so sure that her lover was a man above the common herd, is terrified lest he has only been trying to add another woman to his list of conquests, as soon as she thinks she has nothing more to refuse him.

That is the moment for the appearance of the second crystallization which, because of the fear that accompanies it, is much the stronger.

A woman thinks that from being a queen she has made herself a slave. This state of mind and soul is encouraged by the nervous intoxication which is the result of indulgence in pleasures which are all the more emotional in proportion to the rarity of their occurrence. Again, a woman seated before her embroidery frame, a dull form of work which only occupies her hands, dreams of her lover, whereas he, galloping across the plains with his squadron, is in a position where the slightest miscalculation may lead to his being placed under arrest.

I should imagine, therefore, that the second crystallization is much stronger in the case of women, because they have more to fear, their vanity and honour are at stake, and they have less to distract them from it. . . .

GREGORY CORSO

Marriage

Should I get married? Should I be good?
Astound the girl next door with my velvet suit and faustus hood?
Don't take her to movies but to cemeteries
tell all about werewolf bathtubs and forked clarinets
then desire her and kiss her and all the preliminaries
and she going just so far and I understanding why
not getting angry saying You must feel! It's beautiful to feel!
Instead take her in my arms lean against an old crooked tombstone
and woo her the entire night the constellations in the sky—

When she introduces me to her parents
back straightened, hair finally combed, strangled by a tie,
should I sit knees together on their 3rd degree sofa
and not ask Where's the bathroom?
How else to feel other than I am,
often thinking Flash Gordon soap—
O how terrible it must be for a young man
seated before a family and the family thinking
We never saw him before! He wants our Mary Lou!
After tea and homemade cookies they ask What do you do for a living?

Should I tell them? Would they like me then?
Say All right get married, we're losing a daughter
but we're gaining a son—
And should I then ask Where's the bathroom?

O God, and the wedding! All her family and her friends
and only a handful of mine all scroungy and bearded
just wait to get at the drinks and food—
And the priest! he looking at me as if I masturbated
asking me Do you take this woman for your lawful wedded wife?
And I trembling what to say say Pie Glue!
I kiss the bride all those corny men slapping me on the back
She's all yours, boy! Ha-ha-ha!
And in their eyes you could see some obscene honeymoon going on—
Then all that absurd rice and clanky cans and shoes
Niagara Falls! Hordes of us! Husbands! Wives! Flowers! Chocolates!
All streaming into cozy hotels
All going to do the same thing tonight
The indifferent clerk he knowing what was going to happen

The lobby zombies they knowing what
The whistling elevator man he knowing
The winking bellboy knowing
Everybody knowing! I'd be almost inclined not to do anything!
Stay up all night! Stare that hotel clerk in the eye!
Screaming: I deny honeymoon! I deny honeymoon!
running rampant into those almost climactic suites
yelling Radio belly! Cat shovel!

O I'd live in Niagara forever! in a dark cave beneath the Falls
I'd sit there the Mad Honeymooner
devising ways to break marriages, a scourge of bigamy
a saint of divorce—

But I should get married I should be good
How nice it'd be to come home to her
and sit by the fireplace and she in the kitchen
aproned young and lovely wanting my baby
and so happy about me she burns the roast beef
and comes crying to me and I get up from my big papa chair
saying Christmas teeth! Radiant brains! Apple deaf!
God what a husband I'd make! Yes, I should get married!
So much to do! like sneaking into Mr. Jones' house late at night
and cover his golf clubs with 1920 Norwegian books
Like hanging a picture of Rimbaud on the lawnmower
like pasting Tannu Tuva postage stamps all over the picket fence
like when Mrs. Kindhead comes to collect for the Community Chest
grab her and tell her There are unfavorable omens in the sky!
And when the mayor comes to get my vote tell him
When are you going to stop people killing whales!
And when the milkman comes leave him a note in the bottle
Penguin dust, bring me penguin dust, I want penguin dust—

Yet if I should get married and it's Connecticut and snow
and she gives birth to a child and I am sleepless, worn,
up for nights, head bowed against a quiet window, the past behind me,
finding myself in the most common of situations a trembling man
knowledged with responsibility not twig-smear nor Roman coin
    soup—
O what would that be like!
Surely I'd give it for a nipple a rubber Tacitus
For a rattle a bag of broken Bach records
Tack Della Francesca all over its crib
Sew the Greek alphabet on its bib
And build for its playpen a roofless Parthenon

No, I doubt I'd be that kind of father
Not rural not snow no quiet window
but hot smelly tight New York City
seven flights up, roaches and rats in the walls
a fat Reichian wife screeching over potatoes Get a job!
And five nose running brats in love with Batman
And the neighbors all toothless and dry haired
like those hag masses of the 18th century
all wanting to come in and watch TV
The landlord wants his rent
Grocery store Blue Cross Gas & Electric Knights of Columbus
Impossible to lie back and dream Telephone snow, ghost parking—
No! I should not get married I should never get married!
But—imagine If I were married to a beautiful sophisticated woman
tall and pale wearing an elegant black dress and long black gloves
holding a cigarette holder in one hand and a highball in the other
and we lived high up in a penthouse with a huge window
from which we could see all of New York and ever farther on clearer
    days
No, can't imagine myself married to that pleasant prison dream—

O but what about love? I forget love
not that I am incapable of love
it's just that I see love as odd as wearing shoes—
I never wanted to marry a girl who was like my mother
And Ingrid Bergman was always impossible
And there's maybe a girl now but she's already married
And I don't like men and—
but there's got to be somebody!
Because what if I'm 60 years old and not married,
all alone in a furnished room with pee stains on my underwear
and everybody else is married! All the universe married but me!

Ah, yet well I know that were a woman possible as I am possible
then marriage would be possible—
Like SHE in her lonely alien gaud waiting her Egyptian lover
so I wait—bereft of 2,000 years and the bath of life.

12

DEATH AND ITS MASKS

WILLIAM BLAKE

A Poison Tree

I was angry with my friend:
I told my wrath, my wrath did end.
I was angry with my foe:
I told it not, my wrath did grow.

And I watered it in fears,
Night & morning with my tears;
And I sunnéd it with smiles,
And with soft deceitful wiles.

And it grew both day and night,
Till it bore an apple bright.
And my foe beheld it shine,
And he knew that it was mine,

And into my garden stole,
When the night had veild the pole;
In the morning glad I see
My foe outstretchd beneath the tree.

CHARLES BAUDELAIRE

Spleen LXXX

I'm like the King of some damp, rainy clime,
Grown impotent and old before his time,
Who scorns the bows and scrapings of his teachers
And bores himself with hounds and all such creatures.
Naught can amuse him, falcon, steed, or chase:
No, not the mortal plight of his whole race
Dying before his balcony. The tune,
Sung to this tyrant by his pet buffoon,
Irks him. His couch seems far more like a grave.
Even the girls, for whom all kings seem brave,
Can think no toilet up, nor shamelesss rig,
To draw a smirk from this funereal prig.
The sage who makes him gold could never find
The baser element that rots his mind.
Even those blood-baths the old Romans knew,
And later tyrants imitated too,
Can't warm this skeleton to deeds of slaughter,
Whose only blood is Lethe's cold, green water.

Spleen LXXVIII

Old Pluvius, month of rains, in peevish mood
Pours from his urn chill winter's sodden gloom
On corpses fading in the near graveyard,
On foggy suburbs pours life's tedium.

My cat seeks out a litter on the stones,
Her mangy body turning without rest.
An ancient poet's soul in monotones
Whines in the rain-spouts like a chilblained ghost.

A great bell mourns, a wet log wrapped in smoke
Sings in falsetto to the wheezing clock,
While from a rankly perfumed deck of cards

(A dropsical old crone's fatal bequest)
The Queen of Spades, the dapper Jack of Hearts
Speak darkly of dead loves, how they were lost.

JOHN DONNE

At the Round Earth's Imagined Corners

At the round earth's imagined corners, blow
Your trumpets, angels, and arise, arise
From death, you numberless infinities
Of souls, and to your scattered bodies go;
All whom the flood did, and fire shall, o'erthrow,
All whom war, dearth, age, agues, tyrannies,
Despair, law, chance hath slain, and you whose eyes
Shall behold God, and never taste death's woe.
But let them sleep, Lord, and me mourn a space;
For, if above all these, my sins abound,
'Tis late to ask abundance of Thy grace
When we are there. Here on this lowly ground,
Teach me how to repent; for that's as good
As if Thou'hadst sealed my pardon with Thy blood.

JULIAN GREEN

From His Diary

DECEMBER 14.   That the body can suffer and the soul be happy, and very happy, is an aspect of life that unbelievers cannot even imagine.

VERA LACHMANN

The Eternal Playing

No longer whole is the world when the dearest has gone to rest, although you have acknowledged it with reverence. The pain, the sore longing for what was, and the grief for what never was fulfilled, reject consolation.
Now the enternal playing must begin.

DAME FREYA STARK

Death

Pictures of one's childhood are as fragmentary as the relics of the sailor's way which wanders through the south of England; a stretch emerges here and there, though most of it has vanished or been transformed. Amid these half-obliterated memories I can see, quite sharply, my first meeting with the image of death.

I must have been about four years old and a nurse in our grandmother's house was putting me to bed. It was a Victorian house where fireplaces had tall brass fenders highly polished, and the black metal bed-rails ended in knobs of brass; many pillows, beginning with bolsters, were piled up towards a chintz canopy from which curtains descended, securely lined against draughts, tied with tasselled ropes of red and green. Standing there on the eiderdown, being buttoned into a long nightgown that lay about my feet, I asked if my mother would live for ever.

"No," said nurse, "not for ever; but for a long time."

"How long?" said I. "A thousand years?"

"No," said nurse. "Not a thousand years."

The finality of Time was borne in upon me. Hours afterwards my parents, coming up to bed, found me half asleep but still sobbing at the top of the stairs, where I had crept a little nearer to those dear ones who in a thousand years would be dead.

This feeling has never really changed. If the world is not to last for ever, it seems to make no difference whether its time is to be counted in millions or billions of years; what matters is that there is an end. There can be no safe happiness until the fact has been faced and assimilated; and an absolute condition of all successful living, whether for an individual or a nation, is the acceptance of death.

What remnant of old darkness makes us fear? In all things else we recognize the values of black and white, the strength of contrast.

> Night, the shadow of light,
> And life, the shadow of death.*

Death, too, is an enhancer. Through him, life gains its colour, clinging precarious like some Alpine flower that digs its tenuous and tenacious roots in the rock face against the darkness of the drop below. The secret joy of peril comes from the veiled presence, without which most savour goes; and this is no morbid feeling, for the ecstasy belongs not to death

---

*SWINBURNE. *Atalanta in Calydon.*

in itself, but to *life*, suddenly enriched to know itself alive. So, after a summer dawn and climb till noon, among clefts and icy triangles or wind-scooped crannies, the mountaineer returning sets foot again on the short turf and flowers; and the breeze that cools him is the same breeze that sways the harebells; the blood that tramples in his ears and runs like chariots through his veins is the kind, swift, temporary stuff by which the smaller things of earth are fed; he is back in the community of his kind and descends, light-footed, among the pastures: but he remembers how in the high silences he has known himself on the edge of Silence and how its wing has brushed him. Once, looking down into a valley of the Lebanon, I have heard below me as it were a swish of silk and seen, within a pebble's drop, an eagle's wings outspread; and so we watch death's flight, in our sunlight.

The presence enters far more than one would imagine into commonplace things. Last year, in the cold that comes with the lengthening days, Turin kept her first carnival after the war among her bombed streets and dingy snows; and a wide square was filled in the pale winter daylight with merry-go-rounds and bumping motor-bugs, toy-stands, and sweetmeat booths, and swings. The most popular show was in a wooden cylinder built like a tower, about thirty feet both in breadth and height. We paid to climb by a wooden stair and to look down to where a young blonde, dressed like a Johann Strauss hussar, stood waiting beside a motor bicycle in a pit below. One push with her neat black boot on the sanded floor, and she was off, climbing vertical at first and then gradually horizontal, in quickening spirals, round the smooth plank sides towards her audience. The wooden tower resounded, swaying to the thumps of the engine, and with every hissing upward curve the crowd against the parapet drew back. Another female hussar soon appeared on another motor bicycle. They raced each other; they vied in audacity; they sat with arms akimbo, or placed a booted foot upon the handlebars:

> With life before and after
> And death beneath and above,*

It was a picture of our own existence—the progress of every creature on this earth between two gulfs of time. And did we not pay our sixpences in order, obscurely, to feel this foundation of ourselves?

Why, then, should there be a desire to keep from children the knowledge of death? When once it is obtained, all else falls into perspective; it is the chord to which the music of our life is played. No depth, no harmony, no realizing even of happiness, is possible without it. It makes the grace and dignity of small and trivial things.

*Swinburne. *Atalanta in Calydon.*

My darling's sparrow is dead:
The sparrow she delighted in
And loved more than her eyes.
For it was honey-sweet and knew her
As a child knows its mother;
Nor strayed from her lap,
But hopping here and there,
Piped only to its lady.
And now walks the dark way
Whence all are forbidden return.
Ah, evil be upon you, dark evil
Monsters, who devour all lovely things.
You have taken from me the pretty sparrow.
O evil deed! O luckless sparrow!
Now by your doing my darling
Has reddened and swollen her sweet eyes with tears.*

Great literature is saturated with a consciousness of death, which may come with personal directness as it did to Keats, when he woke with a spot of blood upon his pillow and recognized the sign:

When I behold, upon the night's starr'd face,
Huge cloudy symbols of a high romance,
And think that I may never live to trace
Their shadows, with the magic hand of chance;

Or the power of imagination alone may be sufficient. How it comes matters little; but the existence of the vision of death gives life and beauty to this world. This is the happy reason that carries humanity singing across the dark ages; and those are fortunate who see it early so that they may enjoy a sense of proportion for the remainder of their days. An awareness of death is as essential in education as the study of happiness, or beauty, or intellectual enjoyment.

Whether or no it is accompanied by a belief in future life, appears to be less important. Unbelievers face their end as peacefully as Christians, and the fear of death is independent of rational guidance. It is a fear that in sickness comes closer, like a long wave shining in the sun; its immense ridge gathers unavoidable, a vanguard of the sea; and terrifies as it approaches, and towers with facets of light over its darkening curve. But many that have been under its shadow and watched it breaking and felt its fear have suddenly known it to be no more than a physical barrier, a mere reluctance in their departure from

*CATULLUS. *Lesbia's Sparrow.*

familiar things; and tranquillity has come in sight beyond the aimless foam. If one can hold to the remembrance of such a revelation, one may hope to be free for ever.

No nation can be great, or even respectable, until it achieves such freedom; and it seems to me that the fault of our literature, and of much of our thought between the two wars, was the fear and distortion of death; so that when our moment came there was a good deal of uncertainty in what should have been the intellectual leadership of England. There is an emphasis on carnage in the poets who came after 1914 which is surely out of all proportion; for the horror of death and destruction is not in the thing itself but in the causes that bring it about. A book like *Cry Havoc* gives despicable reasons for disliking war; and the wise pacifist should be careful not to let even the hem of his argument flutter in the wind of fear. If peace cannot teach us that death is harmless, then war will ever be a benefit in some degree: and for this reason if for no other, such sports as riding, climbing, sailing, are better for children than games: for they help to show them, in a light of danger, their universe suspended, as it were a shield or an armorial bearing on some old gate of time—to whose quarterings and crest the ancient sculptors have given a place of honour, supported by two allegoric figures, that hold the weight of the shield between them, on brotherly arms outstretched. Such old and decorated gateways can be seen all over the Italian countryside, and I think of the two figures, baroque and ruinous but gay—as Life and Death, with our world and all its pomp held up between them.

EMILY DICKINSON

I Heard a Fly Buzz

I heard a Fly buzz—when I died—
The Stillness in the Room
Was like the Stillness in the Air—
Between the Heaves of Storm—

The Eyes around—had wrung them dry—
And Breaths were gathering firm
For that last Onset—when the King
Be witnessed—in the Room—

I willed my Keepsakes—Signed away
What portion of me be

Assignable—and then it was
There interposed a Fly—

With Blue—uncertain stumbling Buzz—
Between the light—and me—
And then the Windows failed—and then
I could not see to see—

The Bustle in a House

The Bustle in a House
The Morning after Death
Is solemnest of industries
Enacted upon Earth—

The Sweeping up the Heart
And putting Love away
We shall not want to use again
Until Eternity.

WALTER SAVAGE LANDOR

Death Stands Above Me, Whispering Low

Death stands above me, whispering low
I know not what into my ear:
Of his strange language all I know
Is, there is not a word of fear.

JOAN OF ARC

The Final Entry in the Trail

SHE IS THREATENED WITH TORTURE IN THE PRESENCE OF THE INSTRUMENTS

DONJON OF THE CASTLE, WEDNESDAY, MAY 9

Truly, if you were to have me torn limb from limb and send my soul out of my body, I would say nothing else. And if I did say anything, afterwards I should always say that you had made me say it by force.

I have asked my voices to counsel me whether I should submit to the

Church, because the churchmen were pressing me to submit to the Church. And my voices have told me that, if I want our Lord to help me, I must lay all my deeds before him.

LAST SESSION: SHE IS AGAIN ADMONISHED

WEDNESDAY, MAY 23

If I were at the place of execution, and I saw the fire lighted, and the faggots catching and the executioner ready to build up the fire, and if I were in the fire, even so I would say nothing else, and I would maintain what I have said at this trial until death.

I have nothing more to say.

KARL RAHNER

Death

Death is an event involving the whole man. But man is a unity of nature and person, that is, a being who exists antecedent to his free personal decision, who is subject to certain laws and a certain development, and on the other hand freely disposes of himself, is ultimately what he intends in his freedom to be. Thus death is at once a natural and a personal event. Since biology does not "really" know why all multicellular life, and especially man, dies, the only reason advanced to explain the indisputable universality of death is that advanced by faith—the moral catastrophe of mankind (Rom 5). And this theological basis itself provides the certainty that in all time to come the necessity of dying will continue to govern our lives, that we shall never be able to abolish death.

Resurrection of the Flesh

Man is the creature that awaits the future, which is fulfilment. Since he experiences himself as an entity, he cannot conceive this completion simply as fulfilment of the soul, even though he cannot imagine what true fulfilment would be "like." The Old Testament Scriptures and Later Judaism bear witness to a gradual emergence of belief in the resurrection of the flesh. The first certain evidence of it in the Old Testament is Dan 12:1bf. (Further evidence in 2 Macc 7; in the Old Testament apocrypha it figures especially as a privilege of the just, but is later extended to all, both good and bad.) In Jesus' time the resurrection of the flesh was denied in particular by the Sadducees because it is not found in the Pentateuch, and Jesus refuted them on scriptural grounds (Mk 12:18-27). The resurrection of the flesh is clearly taught in the preaching of Jesus, in Acts 24:15, in St. John's Gospel and in the Apocalypse, and St. Paul develops its theology while definitely rejecting the Hellenistic notion of the body (as the grave or prison of the soul). No trace is found in the New Testament of a beatitude with the Lord apart from the body. According to St. Paul the Christian's risen body is "spiritual" (as the whole resurrection is governed by the Spirit; Pneuma), conformed to Christ's glorious body (Phil 3:21; 1 Cor 15:35f.; Glory), but, analogous to Jesus' glorified body, preserving continuity with the earthly body, though changed (1 Cor 15:36f.; 51). St. Paul does not mention the resurrection of non-Christians and the unjust but presupposes it in his theology of Judgment.

Christian belief in the resurrection of the flesh was obscured for centuries by Greek depreciation of the body and individualistic concern for the salvation of the soul, and also by the cosmological theory of the ancients that represented heaven as a place prior and external to saving history which one could reach by emigrating upwards. Against his predecessor John XXII, Benedict XII defined the dogma that the human animating principle may attain the beatific vision even before its fulfilment in glorified corporeality and need not await the resurrection of the flesh.

In order to form an adequate conception of the resurrection of the flesh it is necessary to observe that flesh in Scripture means the whole man in his bodily reality. But this whole man in his unity is yet something plural, a being existing in various dimensions (matter—spirit, nature—person, action—passion, etc.) whose perfection need not necessarily be achieved in every dimension at once. Thus the permanent reality of the personal spirit can attain immediate union with God in death and the dead man yet remain bound up with the world's reality, its destiny, and therefore its time, the more so because the personal spirit must be seen as the sense of all terrestrial reality, and the end of the world—which is the end of its history but not of its existence—as a sharing in the completion of that spirit. This completion is only perfect when it embraces that dimension which inseparably belongs to the concreteness of the spirit as its matter, and which once perfect must no longer be conceived as occupying a place in our physical spatiality.

13

MARY

ADAM DE ST. VICTOR

In Hac Valle Lacrimarum

In hac valle lacrimarum
Nihil dulce, nihil carum,

   Suspecta sunt omnia;
Quid hic nobis erit tutum,

Cum nec ipsa vel virtutum

   Tuta sit victoria!

Caro nobis adversatur,
Mundus carni suffragatur

   In nostram perniciem;
Hostis instat, nos infestans,

Nunc se palam manifestans,

   Nunc occultans rabiem.

Et peccamus et punimur,

In this valley full of tears,
Nothing softens, nothing
   cheers,
   All is suspected lure;
What safety can we hope for,
   here,
When even virtue faints for
   fear
   Her victory be not sure!

Within, the flesh a traitor is,
Without, the world
   encompasses,
   A deadly wound to bring.
The foe is greedy for our
   spoils,
Now clasping us within his
   coils,
   Or hiding now his sting.

We sin, and penalty must
   pay,

Et diversis irretimur	And we are caught, like beasts of prey,
Laqueis venantium.	Within the hunter's snares.
O Maria, mater Dei,	Nearest to God! oh, Mary Mother!
Tu, post Deum, summa spei,	Hope can reach us from none other,
Tu dulce refugium;	Sweet refuge from our cares;
Tot et tantis irretiti,	We have no strength to struggle longer
Non valemus his reniti	For our bonds are more and stronger
Ne vi nec industria;	Than our hearts can bear!
Consolatrix miserorum,	You who rest the heavy-laden,
Suscitatrix mortuorum,	You who lead lost souls to Heaven,
Mortis rompe retia!	Burst the hunter's snare!

GERARD MANLEY HOPKINS

The Blessed Virgin Compared to the Air We Breathe

Wild air, world-mothering air,
Nestling me everywhere,
That each eyelash or hair
Girdles; goes home betwixt
The fleeciest, frailest-flixed
Snowflake; that's fairly mixed
With, riddles, and is rife
In every least thing's life;
This needful, never spent,
And nursing element;
My more than meat and drink,
My meal at every wink;
This air, which, by life's law,
My lung must draw and draw
Now but to breathe its praise,
Minds me in many ways
Of her who not only

Gave God's infinity
Dwindled to infancy
Welcome in womb and breast,
Birth, milk, and all the rest
But mothers each new grace
That does now reach our race—
Mary Immaculate,
Merely a woman, yet
Whose presence, power is
Great as no goddess's
Was deemèd, dreamèd; who
This one work has to do—
Let all God's glory through,
God's glory which would go
Through her and from her flow
Off, and no way but so.

   I say that we are wound
With mercy round and round
As if with air: the same
Is Mary, more by name.
She, wild web, wondrous robe,
Mantles the guilty globe,
Since God has let dispense
Her prayers his providence:
Nay, more than almoner,
The sweet alms' self is her
And men are meant to share
Her life as life does air.

   If I have understood,
She holds high motherhood
Towards all our ghostly good
And plays in grace her part
About man's beating heart,
Laying, like air's fine flood,
The deathdance in his blood;
Yet no part but what will
Be Christ our Saviour still.
Of her flesh he took flesh:
He does take fresh and fresh,
Though much the mystery how,
Not flesh but spirit now
And makes, O marvellous!

New Nazareths in us,
Where she shall yet conceive
Him, morning, noon, and eve;
New Bethlems, and he born
There, evening, noon, and morn—
Bethlem or Nazareth,
Men here may draw like breath
More Christ and baffle death;
Who, born so, comes to be
New self and nobler me
In each one and each one
More makes, when all is done,
Both God's and Mary's Son.
   Again, look overhead
How air is azurèd;
O how! nay do but stand
Where you can lift your hand
Skywards: rich, rich it laps
Round the four fingergaps.
Yet such a sapphire-shot,
Charged, steepèd sky will not
Stain light. Yea, mark you this:
It does no prejudice.
The glass-blue days are those
When every colour glows,
Each shape and shadow shows.
Blue be it: this blue heaven
The seven or seven times seven
Hued sunbeam will transmit
Perfect, not alter it.
Or if there does some soft,
On things aloof, aloft,
Bloom breathe, that one breath more
Earth is the fairer for.
Whereas did air not make
This bath of blue and slake
His fire, the sun would shake,
A blear and blinding ball
With blackness bound, and all
The thick stars round him roll
Flashing like flecks of coal,
Quartz-fret, or sparks of salt,
In grimy vasty vault.

So God was god of old:
A mother came to mould
Those limbs like ours which are
What must make our daystar
Much dearer to mankind:
Whose glory bare would blind
Or less would win man's mind.
Through her we may see him
Made sweeter, not made dim,
And her hand leaves his light
Sifted to suit our sight.
　　Be thou then, O thou dear
Mother, my atmosphere;
My happier world, wherein
To wend and meet no sin;
Above me, round me lie
Fronting my froward eye
With sweet and scarless sky;
Stir in my ears, speak there
Of God's love, O live air.
Of patience, penance, prayer:
World-mothering air, air wild,
Wound with thee, in thee isled,
Fold home, fast fold thy child.

KARL RAHNER

from *Mary Mother of the Lord*

The absolutely unique Yes of consent of the blessed Virgin, which co-operated in determining the whole history of the world, is not a mere happening that has disappeared into the void of the past. It occurred as an event in a personal spiritual history, by grace, and therefore it is—it is eternally. She still utters her eternal Amen, her eternal *Fiat*, Let it be so, Let it be done, to all that God willed, to the whole great ordered plan of redemption, in which we all find place, built up on the foundation which is Christ. She says Amen to it all, because she consented once and for all to Jesus Christ, and because that consent of hers has entered eternity. When God looks upon the one community of the redeemed, and wills each with all the others and because he wills the others, he also looks upon this eternal Yes of the blessed Virgin, the

Yes on which he willed, in this order of creation, the salvation of us all, quite directly and absolutely once and for all, to depend. God, therefore, wills our salvation too, in this view of his of Mary as she is in eternal life. When he looks upon her, he sees in her too only the grace of the Word made flesh, and he wills us on her account only because he loves her as the mother of his Son. But because God gives what is his sheer grace to its recipient in such a way that it is truly possessed as the recipient's own, though it still continues inalienably to belong to God and to Christ, this special and individual grace of God is only really recognized and praised when those to whom it is given are aware of it. Such praise does not diminish, but increases the glory of the utter grace of the one mediator. For that reason, therefore, we can truly say of Mary, on account of what she did in the history of redemption, which has become eternal, that in the communion of saints she is the intercessor for all of us, the mediatrix of all graces.

We can quietly trust the average Catholic to grasp in his own way and bear in mind in his religious life, the difference there is between the mediation of Christ, and that of the blessed Virgin. He may not be able to express the difference in well-chosen theological concepts, but he knows it. For he knows, and in his prayer applies the fact, that Mary is a created person who has been favoured by grace, and for all the glory of her grace, only a creature. And he knows that Jesus Christ is the Son of God, the eternal Word of the Father, to whom alone in the Father and the Holy Spirit, worship is due. The Catholic is so thoroughly convinced of the divine majesty of his one mediator Jesus Christ, that he is more often in danger of overlooking in Jesus Christ the true man, who has the same nature as we have.

So there is no need for us to be nervous, sparing or niggardly when we honour Mary. It is a sign of a truly Catholic life, when there grows to maturity in our hearts, slowly but genuinely, cultivated humbly and faithfully, a personal and tender love of the blessed Virgin. That is yet another grace that must be prayed for. But since she is the mediatrix who has given us the Lord, since she thereby as intermediary bestows in him and through him all grace, the grace he himself is and the grace he has merited, we must sincerely love and honour her. We must keep on lighting candles on the Maytime altar of our own souls, and the greeting of the angel and Elizabeth in the gospel must rise up in our minds perpetually. "Hail, full of grace, the Lord is with thee; blessed art thou among women; and blessed is the fruit of thy womb!" And must also repeatedly say: Our Lady, our intercessor, advocate, reconcile us to your Son, and show us now after this life, the blessed fruit of your womb; pray for sinners, now and in the hour of our death. Amen.

JOSEPH BRODSKY

Nunc Dimittis

When Mary first came to present the Christ Child
to God in His temple, she found—of those few
who fasted and prayed there, departing not from it—
     devout Simeon and the prophetess Anna.

The holy man took the Babe up in his arms.
The three of them, lost in the grayness of dawn,
now stood like a small shifting frame that surrounded
     the Child in the palpable dark of the temple.

The temple enclosed them in forests of stone.
Its lofty vaults stooped as though trying to cloak
the prophetess Anna, and Simeon, and Mary—
     to hide them from men and to hide them from heaven.

And only a chance ray of light struck the hair
of that sleeping Infant, who stirred but as yet
was conscious of nothing and blew drowsy bubbles;
     old Simeon's arms held him like a stout cradle.

It had been revealed to this upright old man
that he would not die until his eyes had seen
the Son of the Lord. And it thus came to pass. And
     he said: "Now O Lord, lettest thou thy poor servant,

according to thy holy word, leave in peace,
for mine eyes have witnessed thine offspring: he is
thy continuation and also the source of
     thy Light for idolatrous tribes, and the glory

of Israel as well." Then old Simeon paused.
The silence, regaining the temple's clear space,
oozed from all its corners and almost engulfed them,
     and only his echoing words grazed the rafters,

to spin for a moment, with faint rustling sounds,
high over their heads in the tall temple's vaults,
akin to a bird that can soar, yet that cannot
     return to the earth, even if it should want to.

A strangeness engulfed them. The silence now seemed
as strange as the words of old Simeon's speech.

And Mary, confused and bewildered, said nothing—
    so strange had his words been. He added, while turning

directly to Mary: "Behold, in this Child,
now close to thy breast, is concealed the great fall
of many, the great elevation of others,
    a subject of strife and a source of dissension,

and that very steel which will torture his flesh
shall pierce through thine own soul as well. And that wound
will show to thee, Mary, as in a new vision
    what lies hidden, deep in the hearts of all people."

He ended and moved toward the temple's great door.
Old Anna, bent down with the weight of her years,
and Mary, now stooping, gazed after him, silent.
    He moved and grew smaller, in size and in meaning,

to these two frail women who stood in the gloom.
As though driven on by the force of their looks,
he strode through the cold empty space of the temple
    and moved toward the whitening blur of the doorway.

The stride of his old legs was steady and firm.
When Anna's voice sounded behind him, he slowed
his step for a moment. But she was not calling
    to him; she had started to bless God and praise Him.

The door came still closer. The wind stirred his robe
and fanned at his forehead; the roar of the street,
exploding in life by the door of the temple,
    beat stubbornly into old Simeon's hearing.

He went forth to die. It was not the loud din
of streets that he faced when he flung the door wide,
but rather the deaf-and-dumb fields of death's kingdom.
    He strode through a space that was no longer solid.

The rustle of time ebbed away in his ears.
And Simeon's soul held the form of the Child—
its feathery crown now enveloped in glory—
    aloft, like a torch, pressing back the black shadows,

to light up the path that leads into death's realm,
where never before until this present hour
had any man managed to lighten his pathway.
    The old man's torch glowed and the pathway grew wider.

DIALOGUE BETWEEN EVE AND THE DEVIL

Diabolus. Jo vi Adam mais trop est
  fols.
Eva. Un poi est durs.
Diabolus. Il serra mols.
Il est plus durs qui n'est enfers.
Eva. Il est mult francs.
Diabolus. Ainz est mult sers.
Cure ne volt prendre de sei
Car la prenge sevals de tei.

Tu es fieblette et tendre chose
E es plus fresche que n'est rose.
Tu es plus blanche que cristal
Que neif que chiet sor glace en val.

Mal cuple en fist li Criatur.
Tu es trop tendre e il trop dur.
Mais neporquant tu es plus sage

En grant sens as mis tun corrage
Por co fait bon traire a tei.
Parler te voil.
Eva. Ore ja fai.

Devil. Adam I've seen, but he's too
  rough.
Eve. A little hard!
Devil. He'll soon be soft enough!
Harder than hell he is till now.
Eve. He's very frank!
Devil. Say very low!
To help himself he does not care;
The helping you shall be my
  share;
For you are tender, gentle, true,
The rose is not so fresh as you;
Whiter than crystal, or than snow
That falls from heaven on ice
  below.
A sorry mixture God has brewed,
You too tender, he too rude.
But you have much the greater
  sense.
Your will is all intelligence.
Therefore it is I turn to you.
I want to tell you—
Eve. Do it now!

—Anonymous

14

RITUAL AND SIGN

PAUL RICOEUR

From *The Symbolism of Evil*

For us, moderns, a myth is *only* a myth because we can no longer connect that time with the time of history as we write it, employing the critical method, nor can we connect mythical places with our geographical space. This is why the myth can no longer be an explanation; to exclude its etiological intention is the theme of all necessary demythologization. But in losing its explanatory pretensions the myth reveals its exploratory significance and its contribution to understanding, which we shall later call its symbolic function—that is to say, its power of discovering and revealing the bond between man and what he considers sacred. Paradoxical as it may seem, the myth, when it is thus demythologized through contact with scientific history and elevated to the dignity of a symbol, is a dimension of modern thought.

What we are now seeking is not yet the philosophy of fault; it can only be a propaedeutic. Myth is already logos, but it has still to be taken up into *philosophic* discourse. This propaedeutic remains at the level of a purely descriptive phenomenology that permits the believing soul to speak. The philosopher adopts provisionally the motivations and intentions of the believing soul. He does not "feel" them in their first naïveté; he "re-feels" them in a neutralized mode, in the mode of "as if." It is in this sense that phenomenology is a re-enactment in sympathetic imagination. But this phenomenology falls short of reflection in the full sense, such as we pursued in the first part up to the concept of fallibility. The problem remains: how to integrate this re-enactment in sympathetic imagination into reflection? How give reflection a new start by means of a symbolics of liberty in bondage?

DAVID JONES

*Changes in the Coronation Service**

Harrow-on the-Hill.

Dear Sir,

When Fr. Crehan says that, in his opinion, few theologians would allow the substantive, "sacramental," to be used of the present English Coronation rite, is it implied that the word would be allowed of the rite used previous to the Reformation? Secondly, is there any objection to the use of the adjective, sacramental? For that would seem to be the most exact adjective by which to describe an action in which visible signs are employed with intent to signify that a person has herself been made the visible sign of something: in this case the sign of the Monarchy of Britain.

Turning from this particular instance to the question of kingship as such, would it not be true to say that with the condemnation of the theory of *persona mixta,* and the exclusion from the monarch of any suspicion of clerical character, the precise nature of his or her laic character became the primary question? Judging from the signs employed a sacredness of some sort was predicated of this extra-clerical and wholly laic person. For ritual strippings, anointings, the putting on of significant garments, the conveyance of rods and rings and such like cannot be done without giving a very positive impression. We are right to suppose that sign and what is signified should correspond. For it troubles the intelligence and is an artistic anomaly to employ signs that signify less than those signs warrant. And here the signs would seem to warrant some actual otherness, some setting apart, some making over to divine use, some placing in the state of a victim. All of this was unexpectedly made much more apparent by the actual sight of these rites. What emerged with surprising vividness was the dedicated and sacred figure of immemorial tradition. The impression of regal splendour, let alone of mere pomp, was altogether eclipsed by something far deeper, more primal and quite ageless. The impression was of something sacrificial. A person appeared to have been "made

*A letter to *The Tablet* published 18th July 1953.

sacra.'' This is indeed a subjective impression only, an affair of mere appearances. But the Church, by sanctioning such visible and tangible signs, has, to that degree, fostered such subjective impressions for many centuries. It is then of great importance that we should know how far these subjective impressions are warranted in the mind of the Church. What relationship does she envisage between these signs and what they appear to us to signify and which they did signify to our ancestors from remote times?

Yours faithfully,

David Jones

from Religion and the Muses

It is often remarked with a certain amount of perplexity that the modern artist, though he be a Catholic and of sensitivity and ability at his work, seems none the less to be not at his happiest when required to do a job closely connected with the liturgical life of the Church. His preoccupations and enthusiasms seem commonly to be of another sort. The artist himself may find this none too easy to explain. I was once asked: "Why does Mr. X. paint only chimneypots and pots of flowers when he has the whole Christian mythology, which he talks enough about, to inspire him?" This question, so put, is indeed many questions in one, but still it has bearing on our problem, and it asks for elucidation.

It is necessary to have in mind the position of our epoch on what may be called, for convenience, the graph of history. For the relationship between what the Church wants for her use, and the characteristic art of any given epoch, will determine what sort of art is available for the Church's requirements.

It is said that "the best" of what Mr. Wilfred Childe calls "Man's own creative power" should be, in any epoch, at the direct service of the sanctuary—yes—but in the arts "the best" can only easily and naturally be available to the hierarchic, corporate, symbolic demands of the Church if the epoch itself is characterized by those qualities. This cannot, by any means, be said of our epoch. The characteristic bents and virtues of modern painting, for instance, are not in fact easily amenable to these demands. This has little or nothing to do with the will or wishes of this or that artist. He cannot by taking thought change himself into an artist of some other culture-sequence. That path is, *in reality,* closed. That way lies, the "trying to recapture" this or that historic-past plastic reality, without *living* the reality which created that particular plastic. But here it is very important to distinguish. The traffic-control says dead-slow here. There have been and are, efforts which look like some such escape efforts, but which, in fact, are productive of real works of real beauty. They must be seen however for what they are. They are very far from being mere revivalisms. They can be the product of a special kind of sensitivity, and they depend on association-perceptions to a large extent. They can be very various in mode. While some of the very best work, and only the very best, of the Pre-Raphaelite School, was of this sort, and we give it the appellation "romantic," so also, is a certain amount of contemporary work, work of a kind not usually nor so easily included under that term. "Associative" is perhaps the safer word, and under that amended term (romantic-associative) we should have to include a fair percentage of our valid contemporary effort. And were we speaking of the making of writings rather than paintings, we could, in this way, put Joyce as the most supreme "romantic" artist that the West has so far known.

The real poser is to be found when we seek to employ the particular characteristic perfections of contemporary artistic effort at its intensest power, in such a way as not to dilute those qualities which make it valid. Modern painting tends, among other things, to be idiosyncratic and personal in expression and experimental in technique, intimate and private rather than public and corporate; even the fact that on the whole the best modern paintings are smallish as to size, is not without significance, for the artist is all out on some particular problem, and the tentative and the searching tends to modesty in dimension and requires a special kind of concentration. He is not without tradition, but the tradition is not that of a true corporate culture-style, nor yet again is it "school-of," still less of a grand-manner technique. It is rather a tradition of a feeling-toward, it is one of exploration and specialization. Here I suppose the artist shares something with the contemporary physicist; but beware of the analogy, for as Pablo Picasso says in this connection, the artist "does not seek, he finds." It is not a bad affirmation of the differing ways of love and knowledge, of the receptive and the measuring processes. It is an improvement upon Da Vinci's humanistic "We must know before we love." Not good for so great an artist.

There is *liaison* between the practitioners, but they rather tunnel in a network of inter-related saps, than move in imposing formation. The work is essentially one of infiltration—it is intensive, and usually seeks to resolve a limited problem; on the other hand it is eclectic, and draws upon (because it is aware of) many past deposits, from the most barbarous to the most sophisticated. While it affords certain obvious opportunities for the charlatans and the clever and the quick-in-the-uptake, its standards are, in hard fact, exacting in the extreme, and demand the most disinterested sensitivity. Its genuine expression has initiated some new juxtapositions of beauty—not seen before, however ephemeral. The Wise Man said: "there is no new thing under the sun; but the arts do at certain moments uncover relationships hidden since the foundation of the world; but this is only achieved by the single-eyed, vocation-integrity of chance individuals, directed wholly toward plastic, or by the equally chance corporate awakening to an unassuageable will to form in a whole culture." The Norman panzer-gangs are forgiven for the sake of the astonishing freedom by which the Norman vision made the stone leap-frog in the under-crofts and with slow-motion embrace the round apses. We are forcibly reminded of how Phryne's judges forgot her crime-sheet, awed by the splendour of form accidentally present in the body of the accused.

The men of ethic are insufficient here, only the men of contemplation have any potency, by uncovering a beauty more excellent still, only by showing the hierarchies can they convince us. Otherwise there is danger of us shouting the rowdy and irresponsible cry: "Verily we do deny that canonist and legist be wiser than the artist."

One can detect behind the exhausted patiences and the fratricide of the West today, moods and pressures and antipathies not unrelated to this Rabelaisian student-jibe, but alas for us all, they've put hard stones in their snow-balls. This is no academic rag.

It is the tradition of the individual artist which concerns us here, and although that tradition could only *be* in our sort of civilization, it is, paradoxically, a contradiction, a fifth-column, within that civilization, and here it shares the honours of sabotage with the tradition of religion, for both are disruptive forces, both own allegiance to values in any event irritant, and easily becoming toxic to those values which of necessity dominate the present world-orders. "Religion" is already cautioned, and under suspicion, and "art" will, in due time, be found out for the recalcitrant and wayward mistress that she is. Eric Gill used sometimes to quote the words of the parish priest, "You can be a good Catholic in a factory"—but the Muses in a factory would disturb the calculations of any Ministry of Production. In Caesar's or the People's State (to both misquote Milton's text and give it another context):

> The flocking shadows pale
> Troop from th'infernal jail.

The world of utility and technics can only tolerate the "yellow-skirted Fayes" out of hours, or dancing to the propaganda-pipes—in the end they will slip the registration, unseen in the cultural darkness, and wait with Proserpine for the renewal.

It is no new problem. It troubled Plato, and Tolstoy also, I understand. All Utopians, most moralists and the men of prudence, all the putters-to-rights, are in danger of having "two-bugbears": Religion and the Muses. In these latter days what has been a poser for "the thinkers" shows signs of emerging as a fact seen by all. The subject is an enormous one, and can only be hinted at here, but it is the most important subject of all. Any order, new or old, "ours or theirs," local or a world-state, which binds the Muses, breaks the totems, and withdraws the people from contemplation, is already dead in the judgement of history, no matter what fanatic vitality shines in its morale, or however reputable its ethic.

The disparity between artist and epoch has a history. If we consider J.M.W. Turner and Paul Cézanne (two pivotal and apostolic figures in the tradition of modern painting) we see, I think, that although both were "of their times," in many respects, neither was so, in the sense that Giotto was of his, or the Byzantine mosaic masters of theirs. Cézanne indeed might be said to be the prototype of the modern artist—the men of the diaspora from the cultures, misfits, difficult chaps, often respected and even pampered, and sometimes paid, but parasitic on, and captive to, civilization, when you came down to brass tacks. Yet it would be interesting to know what relationship there is between Cézanne's painful and glorious mastery of mass and recession and the troop-dispositions of the Franco-Prussian War—not much one tends to think, and yet, I wonder, it may be the affinity is more than appears.

But to return to the position of the Church: the manual acts and sacred buildings of Christian worship are heirs to a true culture-tradition. They are cast in a form which is itself an Art-form and a derivative of immemorial forms belonging to a fusion of cultures. The Christian rites and *impedimenta* have not been, however, directly influenced either by Impressionism or Post-impressionism, *but,* that picture there, above the altar, painted last year, could scarcely have been but for a synthesis of sorts arising out of those two movements— that is very largely why it is a good representative contemporary picture. That is also why Major John Bull, in his pew, has a new set of distractions at Mass. He would be equally distracted if the vocal worship itself reflected, to a similar degree "the best" contemporary poetic and metric forms and perceptions.

It is clear that we have *three* rather than two elements—the problem is triangular, but not permanent—it belongs to our kind of time, even if such times are recurrent. I attempt to name those elements roughly as follows:

1. The symbolic culture-life of the Church,
2. The preoccupations and tradition of contemporary art,

3. The world of technics and utility alien alike to that into which we are born (one and two above), and which informs and conditions us all, whether we like it or not.

Any endeavour toward a re-vitalizing of Christian Art must keep this situation in mind, or, better still, make a note of it and then forget it, but the note will be necessary when the impossible is expected, or the reason why it is impossible unappreciated, or the cause of futile effort and unnecessary disappointment.

Dom Wilfred Upson, in speaking for those whose right concern is with the liturgical inheritance of the Church, quotes from a passage in Canon Law. That canon, whenever it was compiled, implies the existence of a common tradition within which it can operate. With all due respect I would ask what are the "laws of sacred art" for the West in 1941? I can see that it would have meaning and application within, say, the Byzantine age, when a common art-form, a "Christian art-form" dominated all spheres, from the *signum* of a military formation to the iconography about the altar. If those canons are in no way dependent on some particular art-form, but are of such fluidity as to have universal application, e.g. this figure must have a distinguishing mark, that object must not exceed such and such dimensions—then, of course, there is little difficulty.

Actually the term "a Christian Art" is somewhat liable to be misleading. The Church, strictly speaking, does not create an art-form; she has used and given significance, or a new twist to, this or that cultural expression in differing connections. She can be either inimical to a particular creativity, or be an inspiration and patroness of its efflorescence. It depends on circumstances and conjunctions. As, in marriage she is witness to a sacrament, but cannot bestow it, still less determine in whom or when true love shall operate—so, in the arts, she can encourage and bless, or not bless and neglect, but she cannot dispose in whom or where a new creativeness shall surprise the world and invigorate the generations.

The springing to life of an art-form is subject to no constraint and no good-will can call it into being. It would seem to arise from breakdowns and fusions to produce a new and unexpected life. (Something of this sort seems sometimes to take place also when individual artsists turn a corner, or suddenly achieve something worth looking at.) But what is most important to remember is that the Church cannot by making rules or by any other direct means hope for an art congenial to her liturgical forms from a civilization that does not, and cannot, by its very nature, produce such an art. Today we live in a world where the symbolic life (the life of the true cultures, of "institutional" religion, and of *all artists*, in the last resort—however

much we may disavow the association) is progressively eliminated—
the technician is master. In a manner of speaking the priest and the
artist are already in the catacombs, but *separate* catacombs—for the
technician divides to rule. No integrated, widespread, religious art,
properly so-called, can be looked for outside enormous changes in the
character and orientation and nature of our civilization, and this is
beyond our horizon—however much such vistas may occupy our
speculative thoughts. All will at least admit that civilization has many
somersaults to turn before a corporate will can again project itself
materially in such forms as, to choose very casually, the *Dies Irae*, the
Prefaces, the Christ of the central tympanum at Vezelay, the Avignon
Pieta—or whatever you like from a thousand and one years of
integrated marvel.

With these considerations at all events registered, we are the freer to
consider what is possible, and to understand why other things are
impossible, and we shall be better able to assess both aesthetic and
liturgical attempts at recovery. Not unduly critical of what they may
achieve, but seeing them in their true relationship to each other within
the realities of our epoch and noting whether such recoveries preserve a
genuine continuity with "the bests" of their several traditions, or
whether we are forced to admit the thing is a pastiche after all. It is
necessary to face this with impartial eyes—just as we have to try,
painfully enough, to do, when sifting the real from the unreal in our
own work, whatever it should chance to be.

The reformer who not unnaturally feels that something must be
done when he surveys the interiors of our churches, must remember
that were his concern the reform of public-houses, his problem would,
in many respects, be similar. We are all enough acquainted with the
Edwardian paraphernalia of the saloon tradition to see immediately
the analogy—but when we consider the tasteful and functional
appointments of the "Road House" reform, with its swept and
garnished and artistic lounge-bar and its decorative *Blue Dog* sign, we
see the difficulties inherent in improving upon a dead or decaying
tradition by means of aesthetic injections; and the new pub often
enough, has its contemporary counterpart (has the same "look"* as
painters used to say) in the new church next door. There also the junk
and gewgaws are no more, and all that goodwill can do may have been
done, but it is small blame to those concerned that the decline and
shoddy finale of a whole common, everyday, corporate "plastic,"

*It is a useful expression. A painting by someone of the English Pre-
Raphaelites has not the same "look" as a painting by those Italians before
Raphael which the Pre-Raphaelites sought to emulate, for obvious reasons. To
employ the Petrine tag: where common "look" is, there is common culture.

affecting all things to be made, happens to characterize our age. In technics and the strictly utile, of course, a will to form* is yet producing new and significant and vital shapes—there is little shoddiness there, but a terrible certainty and sinister perfection—that's where the "treasure" of modern man is, and so his "heart also"—hence the formal integrity of the air-plane and the aesthetic of the weapons—their "look" is genuine enough. But when we glance from the airman's weapons to the airmen's mess—O what fall is here, my countrymen! No one is to blame. We are born into civilization at this date. Certainly no one can afford to be superior, for we all, in one way or another, are involved, and all seek differing compensatory means as each is best able. But in the absence of a coporate tradition there can be no corporate renewal. Individuals of this or that perception or vision, or even the collaboration or individuals, may locally and in a tentative and fluid manner make the desert blossom and in some way or other, I say it may be so. Those arts which demand the minimum of collaboration, which depend least for their existence on material—which remain more in the region of "the idea" would *seem* to stand most chance. It will seem more possible to write a good poem than build a good cathedral—although, of course, all these things are, in the end, inextricably related. There is no escape from incarnation. It's like a shunting train.

*I ought rather to have said a *pseudo* will to form, for in the age of technics the tendency is for creativeness to become dehumanized, for contrivance to usurp imagination, for the will toward shape to become almost indistinguishable from a mere will toward power. There is a deflection, a mass-deflection, from the proper "habit of art" toward forms which owe their existence and meaning to what they *effect* rather than to what they *are*. Power-extension and multiplication become the objectives, and the utile is the sole factor determining the forms, and the symbolic loses altogether its central and presiding position. Beauty, however, of a certain order, undeniably adheres to these forms, the beauty of a mathematical formula "made flesh," given material projection. Awe-inspiring in its power-perfection, and, in the case of weapons, becoming symbolic, however unconsciously. For the gods of the power-age are best symbolized by those objects which are themselves power-devices. In the weapons, pure function stands naked. A severe, disinterested, unalloyed "functional-art," directed altogether toward action at its most characteristic and most intense. Even "commercialism," which modifies and cheapens most contemporary forms, keeps its demeaning hands off the weapons. Such is the logic of necessity that they can't "place the inferior article," and they have no motive in "decorating" the superb instruments of death, the market is O.K. without any titivation. But although we gaze like John the Divine and wonder with a great admiration, yet our natures are far from satisfied. The *numina* which preside over these forms are masters of illusion—this is a magician's world—the living God, the life-giver is not, after all, projected from the machine.

Dr. Rothenstein's suggestion that there is opportunity for the employment of native and individual vision, should be noted by those who have jobs that need doing—and, as he says, the wartime curtailment of the Church-furnishing trade, itself perhaps provides an opportunity. It is rather in such chance ways that most is to be expected. Instinct rather than rule will have to serve. There can be no operation orders, and our flanks have been in the air long since. The collaboration between "priest" and "artist" (to use shorthand words for a whole complex of things) in the No-Man's-land of the historic-present, is sufficiently full of difficulties, and those difficulties are so hard to locate and put into words with any accuracy, that this alone may account for the "shelving" complained of by Dom Wilfred Upson.

I have tried here only to give some tentative expression to those ruminations which have been going on in my own mind and, I know, in the minds of some of my friends, for years past. Inaccuracy of statement and a certain catlike obliqueness of direction, and the leaving of this scent for that, may be excused. It is, after all, a bit of a hornets' nest—certainly a place of booby-traps, that we are investigating; and every statement becomes easily an over-statement, and every example or analogy suspect and leaking. Finally, I would repeat that as far as I can see we are all very like men forced into guerrilla tactics—we operate in a terrain over-run by the enemy—and pretty efficiently administered by him. And whether we are the kind of chaps who feel inclined to plan this or that local *coup,* or whether we feel we must go to earth with the yellow-skirted Fayes, that the nipping of our cultural December is a little too much, that a very private and secret labyrinthine life is indicated—in either case, the words in Professor Ker's *Dark Ages* may be remembered: "But the gods who are defeated, think that defeat no refutation."

We were then *homo faber, homo sapiens* before Lascaux and we shall be *homo faber, homo sapiens* after the last atomic bomb has fallen.

I offer this concrete suggestion: Let us suppose that a milliner made her reconnaissance among the bright entanglements of her utile, yet most extra-utile and highly significant, art, then suppose her findings were compared with those made by her reverend cousin whose art was equally, or rather to an infinite degree more, concerned with the actual handling of material substances whereby certain things are said to be shown forth under certain signs. Then let us suppose the findings of these two reconnaissances were compared with those made by a mutual friend whose art was that of the precision-tool maker and that these findings were in turn compared with those of an acquaintance of his, an ex-miner now at a conveyor-belt who paints pictures in his spare time. I don't know, but it is just possible that the collated findings of these four contemporary persons concerning their respective makings would illuminate to some degree the nature of Ars. It is conceivable at all events that someone or other of these thoroughly representative and familiar figures would, during their reconnaissance, secure identifications helping to establish more certainly where this line of dichotomy runs.

In the view of the present writer any data whatsoever which help toward our understanding of this dichotomy are data most necessary to us in our present fix.

A L I C E M O R R I S

The Angel Beings

There are among us angel beings.
Beyond doubt, without question.
Shrouded in angel light they move—
It cannot be hidden: it's manifest.

Even when they are downcast, ill,
Threatened, out of sorts,
The radiance persists
And a scent of honey.

They cannot be mistaken,
They cannot be denied:
They ride on tides of air
At which we only guess,
Casting about them grace.

And we must love them, yes:
Abashed and blessed, we have no choice.

A. D. H O P E

Imperial Adam

Imperial Adam, naked in the dew,
Felt his brown flanks and found the rib was gone.
Puzzled he turned and saw where, two and two,
The mighty spoor of Jahweh marked the lawn.

Then he remembered through mysterious sleep
The surgeon fingers probing at the bone,

The voice so far away, so rich and deep:
"It is not good for him to live alone."

Turning once more he found Man's counterpart
In tender parody breathing at his side.
He knew her at first sight, he knew by heart
Her allegory of sense unsatisfied.

The pawpaw drooped its golden breasts above
Less generous than the honey of her flesh;
The innocent sunlight showed the place of love;
The dew on its dark hairs winked crisp and fresh.

This plump gourd severed from his virile root,
She promised on the turf of Paradise
Delicious pulp of the forbidden fruit;
Sly as the snake she loosed her sinuous thighs,

And waking, smiled up at him from the grass;
Her breasts rose softly and he heard her sigh—
From all the beasts whose pleasant task it was
In Eden to increase and multiply

Adam had learned the jolly deed of kind:
He took her in his arms and there and then,
Like the clean beasts, embracing from behind,
Began in joy to found the breed of men.

Then from the spurt of seed within her broke
Her terrible and triumphant female cry,
Split upward by the sexual lightning stroke.
It was the beasts now who stood watching by:

The gravid elephant, the calving hind,
The breeding bitch, the she-ape big with young
Were the first gentle midwives of mankind;
The teeming lioness rasped her with her tongue;

The proud vicuña nuzzled her as she slept
Lax on the grass; and Adam watching too
Saw how her dumb breasts at their ripening wept,
The great pod of her belly swelled and grew,

And saw its water break, and saw, in fear,
Its quaking muscles in the act of birth,
Between her legs a pigmy face appear,
And the first murderer lay upon the earth.

KARL RAHNER

Mass

The memorial in thanksgiving and celebration in Christ's Church, according to his commandment (Lk 22:19f.; 1 Cor 11:24f.), of his sacrifice of life and death as the foundation of the Church and the hidden advent, in forgiveness and grace, of the *basileia*. This celebration is anamnesis; that is, it signifies that a genuine historical event which has happened once for all is truly made present. The ontological and logical questions raised by anamnesis need not be gone into here. Suffice it to say that this anamnesis is neither a mere "idealist" reminiscence on our own part, nor a successive repetition of Christ's death, nor a denial that this historical event really happened, and happened once only, in time, since (contrary to gnostic views) just this historical event bears our salvation. The anamnetic "celebration" takes place when the Church does in cultic gesture what Jesus himself did when celebrating the Last Supper: accepting in free obedience the real death whereby he offers himself to the Father, proclaiming in terms the saving power of his sacrifice and its application to the disciples by delivering to them the symbols of his body and blood. Without being a *new* sacrifice, except in the ritual dimension, this anamnesis of Christ's death is a sacrifice (an offering to God of gifts in which a change is effected) in that it makes his historically unique offering to the Father present (in an unbloody manner), and that through a rite which cultically speaking is itself a sacrifice. In the Mass the Lord is truly and substantially present under the empirical appearances of bread and wine, because Jesus expressly declares that what he distributes to the Apostles under the appearances of bread and wine is his flesh and blood, that is, according to Semitic usage, himself in person in the concrete reality of his sacrificial existence (which through the permanent validity of his death has attained its definitive, "glorified" state) (Mt 26:26, 28; Mk 14:22, 24; Lk 22:19f.; 1 Cor 11:24f.); and because the reality of the total presence of his salvific deed implies the true presence of the person on whose substantial reality and eternity the continued presence of the historical deed is based. The Church knows from Jesus' own words that what it proffers, re-enacting his gestures at the Last Supper, is the body and blood of Christ (for the defined teaching of the Church) and therefore not bread and wine; so it is all the more ready to affirm that nothing has changed in the sphere of sensory human experience (the "appearances," that is to say the "species"), including whatever is accessible to the natural sciences; it holds that the reality (called "substance") underlying the appearances is no longer that of earthly nourishment but that of Jesus Christ himself. The process by which this is brought about can be called transsubstantiation, and can be regarded as the sacrificial action itself: in virtue of Jesus Christ's commission a liturgical rite so transforms the intrinsic reality, the "substance," of a bit of mundane reality that the reality which displaces it (the body and blood of Jesus Christ under the appearances of bread and wine) is wholly dedicated to God and liturgically represents Jesus Christ's surrender of himself in sacrifice to God. But since this is the essence of cultic sacrifice in general, the Mass is rightly called a sacrifice in the sense just defined, Christ himself being both sacrifice in the sense just defined, Christ himself being both sacrificing priest and victim. The true presence of the efficaciousness of Jesus's life and death in the Mass affords an immanent critique of cultic worship: that is an end to mere liturgico-symbolic memorials and an entry into Christian practice as anticipation of the kingdom of God.

15

SOLUTIONS

C. P. CAVAFY

Waiting for the Barbarians

What are we waiting for, assembled in the forum?

    The barbarians are due here today.

Why isn't anything going on in the senate?
Why are the senators sitting there without legislating?

    Because the barbarians are coming today.
    What's the point of senators making laws now?
    Once the barbarians are here, they'll do the legislating.

Why did our emperor get up so early,
and why is he sitting enthroned at the city's main gate,
in state, wearing the crown?

    Because the barbarians are coming today
    and the emperor's waiting to receive their leader.
    He's even got a scroll to give him,
    loaded with titles, with imposing names.

Why have our two consuls and praetors come out today
wearing their embroidered, their scarlet togas?
Why have they put on bracelets with so many amethysts,
rings sparkling with magnificent emeralds?
Why are they carrying elegant canes
beautifully worked in silver and gold?

> Because the barbarians are coming today
> and things like that dazzle the barbarians.

Why don't our distinguished orators turn up as usual
to make their speeches, say what they have to say?

> Because the barbarians are coming today
> and they're bored by rhetoric and public speaking.

Why this sudden bewilderment, this confusion?
(How serious people's faces have become.)
Why are the streets and squares emptying so rapidly,
everyone going home lost in thought?

> Because night has fallen and the barbarians haven't come.
> And some of our men just in from the border say
> there are no barbarians any longer.

Now what's going to happen to us without barbarians?
Those people were a kind of solution.

Unfaithfulness

*So although we approve of many things in Homer, this we will not
approve of . . . nor will we approve of Aischylos when he makes
Thetis say that Apollo sang at her wedding in celebration of her
child:*

> *that he would not know sickness, would live long,*
> *and that every blessing would be his:*
> *and he sang such praises that he rejoiced my heart.*

And I had hopes that the divine lips of Apollo,
fluent with the art of prophecy, would not prove false
But he who proclaimed these things . . .
                                   he it is
who killed my son . . .

Plato. Republic, II. 383

When Thetis and Peleus got married
Apollo stood up at the sumptuous wedding feast
and blessed the bridal pair
for the son who would come from their union.
"Sickness will never visit him," he said,
"and his life will be a long one."
This pleased Thetis immensely:
the words of Apollo, expert in prophecies,
seemed a guarantee of security for her child.
And when Achilles grew up
and all Thessaly said how beautiful he was,
Thetis remembered the god's words.
But one day some elders came in with the news
that Achilles had been killed at Troy.
Thetis tore her purple robes,
pulled off rings, bracelets,
flung them to the ground.
And in her grief, remembering that wedding scene,
she asked what the wise Apollo was up to,
where was this poet who spouts
so eloquently at banquets, where was this prophet
when they killed her son in his prime.
And the elders answered that Apollo himself
had gone down to Troy
and with the Trojans had killed her son.

Things Ended

Engulfed by fear and suspicion,
mind agitated, eyes alarmed,
we try desperately to invent ways out,
plan how to avoid
the obvious danger that threatens us so terribly.
Yet we're mistaken, that's not the danger ahead:
the news was wrong

(or we didn't hear it, or didn't get it right).
Another disaster, one we never imagined,
suddenly, violently, descends upon us,
and finding us unprepared—there's no time now—
sweeps us away.

As Much as You Can

Even if you can't shape your life the way you want,
at least try as much as you can
not to degrade it
by too much contact with the world,
by too much activity and talk.

Do not degrade it by dragging it along,
taking it around and exposing it so often
to the daily silliness
of social·relations and parties,
until it comes to seem a boring hanger-on.

JULIAN GREEN

From His Diary

GOOD FRIDAY.   Thought of a sentence that I once read in an English
book. It seems to have no meaning and yet has a very great one: "How
close I was to God when I was far from Him!" An illusion, no doubt,
but nothing gives me a keener longing for God than sin.

FERNAND BRAUDEL

from *The Mediterranean*

I confess that, not being a philosopher, I am reluctant to dwell for long
on questions concerning the importance of events and of individual
freedom, which have been put to me so many times in the past and no
doubt will be in the future. How are we to interpret the very word
freedom, which has meant so many different things, never signifying
the same from one century to another? We should at least distinguish
between the freedom of groups, that is of economic and social units,

and that of individuals. What exactly is the freedom today of the unit we call France? What was Spain's "freedom" in 1571, in the sense of the courses open to her? What degree of freedom was possessed by Philip II, or by Don John of Austria as he rode at anchor among his ships, allies and troops? Each of these so-called freedoms seems to me to resemble a tiny island, almost a prison.

By stating the narrowness of the limits of action, is one denying the role of the individual in history? I think not. One may only have the choice between striking two or three blows: the question still arises: will one be able to strike them at all? To strike them effectively? To do so in the knowledge that only this range of choices is open to one? I would conclude with the paradox that the true man of action is he who can measure most nearly the constraints upon him, who chooses to remain within them and even to take advantage of the weight of the inevitable, exerting his own pressure in the same direction. All efforts against the prevailing tide of history—which is not always obvious— are doomed to failure.

So when I think of the individual, I am always inclined to see him imprisoned within a destiny in which he himself has little hand, fixed in a landscape in which the infinite perspectives of the long term stretch into the distance both behind him and before. In historical analysis as I see it, rightly or wrongly, the long run always wins in the end. Annihilating innumerable events—all those which cannot be accommodated in the main ongoing current and which are therefore ruthlessly swept to one side—it indubitably limits both the freedom of the individual and even the role of chance. I am by temperament a "structuralist," little tempted by the event, or even by the short-term conjuncture which is after all merely a grouping of events in the same area. But the historian's "structuralism" has nothing to do with the approach which under the same name is at present causing some confusion in the other human sciences. It does not tend towards the mathematical abstraction of relations expressed as functions, but instead towards the very sources of life in its most concrete, everyday, indestructible and anonymously human expression.

RICHARD WILBUR

Advice to a Prophet

When you come, as you soon must, to the streets of our city,
Mad-eyed from stating the obvious,

Not proclaiming our fall but begging us
In God's name to have self-pity,

Spare us all word of the weapons, their force and range,
The long numbers that rocket the mind;
Our slow, unreckoning hearts will be left behind,
Unable to fear what is too strange.

Nor shall you scare us with talk of the death of the race.
How should we dream of this place without us?—
The sun mere fire, the leaves untroubled about us,
A stone look on the stone's face?

Speak of the world's own change. Though we cannot conceive
Of an undreamt thing, we know to our cost
How the dreamt cloud crumbles, the vines are blackened by frost,
How the view alters. We could believe,

If you told us so, that the white-tailed deer will slip
Into perfect shade, grown perfectly shy,
The lark avoid the reaches of our eye,
The jack-pine lose its knuckled grip

On the cold ledge, and every torrent burn
As Xanthus once, its gliding trout
Stunned in a twinkling. What should we be without
The dolphin's arc, the dove's return,

These things in which we have seen ourselves and spoken?
Ask us, prophet, how we shall call
Our natures forth when that live tongue is all
Dispelled, that glass obscured or broken

In which we have said the rose of our love and the clean
Horse of our courage, in which beheld
The singing locust of the soul unshelled,
And all we mean or wish to mean.

Ask us, ask us whether with the wordless rose
Our hearts shall fail us: come demanding
Whether there shall be lofty or long standing
When the bronze annals of the oak-tree close.

JEAN PIAGET

Judgment and Reasoning

What then gives rise to the need for verification? Surely it must be the shock of our thought coming into contact with that of others, which produces doubt and the desire to prove. If there were not other people, the disappointments of experience would lead to overcompensation and dementia. We are constantly hatching an enormous number of false ideas, conceits, Utopias, mystical explanations, suspicions, and megalomaniacal fantasies, which disappear when brought into contact with other people. The social need to share the thought of others and to communicate our own with success is at the root of our need for verification. Proof is the outcome of argument.

E. F. SCHUMACHER

Epilogue from *Small Is Beautiful*

In the excitement over the unfolding of his scientific and technical powers, modern man has built a system of production that ravishes nature and a type of society that mutilates man. If only there were more and more wealth, everything else, it is thought, would fall into place. Money is considered to be all-powerful; if it could not actually buy non-material values, such as justice, harmony, beauty or even health, it could circumvent the need for them or compensate for their loss. The development of production and the acquisition of wealth have thus become the highest goals of the modern world in relation to which all other goals, no matter how much lip-service may still be paid to them, have come to take second place. The highest goals require no justification; all secondary goals have finally to justify themselves in terms of the service their attainment renders to the attainment of the highest.

This is the philosophy of materialism, and it is this philosophy—or metaphysic—which is now being challenged by events. There has never been a time, in any society in any part of the world, without its sages and teachers to challenge materialism and plead for a different order of priorities. The languages have differed, the symbols have varied, yet the message has always been the same: "Seek ye *first* the kingdom of God, and all these things [the material things which you also need] shall be *added* unto you." They shall be added, we are told, here on earth where we need them, not simply in an after-life beyond our imagination. Today, however, this message reaches us not solely from the sages and saints but from the actual course of physical events. It speaks to us in the language of terrorism, genocide, breakdown, pollution, exhaustion. We live, it seems, in a unique period of convergence. It is becoming apparent that there is not only a promise but also a threat in those astonishing words about the kingdom of God—the threat that "unless you seek first the kingdom, these other things, which you also need, will cease to be available to you." As a recent writer put it, without reference to economics and politics but nonetheless with direct reference to the condition of the modern world:

> If it can be said that man collectively shrinks back more and more from the Truth, it can also be said that on all sides the Truth is closing in more and more upon man. It might almost be said that, in order to receive a touch of It, which in the past required a lifetime of effort, all that is asked of him now is not to shrink back. And yet how difficult that is!

We shrink back from the truth if we believe that the destructive forces of the modern world can be "brought under control" simply by mobilising more resources—of wealth, education, and research—to fight pollution, to preserve wildlife, to discover new sources of energy, and to arrive at more effective agreements on peaceful coexistence. Needless to say, wealth, education, research, and many other things are needed for any civilisation, but what is most needed today is a revision of the ends which these means are meant to serve. And this implies, above all else, the development of a life-style which accords to material things their proper, legitimate place, which is secondary and not primary.

The "logic of production" is neither the logic of life nor that of society. It is a small and subservient part of both. The destructive forces unleashed by it cannot be brought under control, unless the "logic of production" itself is brought under control—so that destructive forces cease to be unleashed. It is of little use trying to suppress terrorism if the production of deadly devices continues to be deemed a legitimate employment of man's creative powers. Nor can the fight against pollution be successful if the patterns of production and consumption continue to be of a scale, a complexity, and a degree of violence which, as is becoming more and more apparent, do not fit into the laws of the universe, to which man is just as much subject as the rest of creation. Equally, the chance of mitigating the rate of resource depletion or of bringing harmony into the relationships between those in possession of wealth and power and those without is non-existent as long as there is no idea anywhere of enough being good and more-than-enough being evil.

It is a hopeful sign that some awareness of these deeper issues is gradually—if exceedingly cautiously—finding expression even in some official and semi-official utterances. A report, written by a committee at the request of the Secretary of State for the Environment, talks about buying time during which technologically developed societies have an opportunity "to revise their values and to change their political objectives." It is a matter of "moral choices," says the report; "no amount of calculation can alone provide the answers.... The fundamental questioning of conventional values by young people all over the world is a symptom of the widespread unease with which our industrial civilisation is increasingly regarded." Pollution must be brought under control and mankind's population and consumption of resources must be steered towards a permanent and sustainable equilibrium. "Unless this is done, sooner or later—and some believe that there is little time left—the downfall of civilisation will not be a matter of science fiction. It will be the experience of our children and grandchildren."

But how is it to be done? What are the "moral choices"? Is it just a matter, as the report also suggests, of deciding "how much we are willing to pay for clean surroundings"? Mankind has indeed a certain freedom of choice: it is not bound by trends, by the "logic of production," or by any other fragmentary logic. But it is bound by truth. Only in the service of truth is perfect freedom, and even those who today ask us "to free our imagination from bondage to the existing system" fail to point the way to the recognition of truth.

It is hardly likely that twentieth-century man is called upon to discover truth that has never been discovered before. In the Christian tradition, as in all genuine traditions of mankind, the truth has been stated in religious terms, a language which has become well-nigh incomprehensible to the majority of modern men. The language can be revised, and there are contemporary writers who have done so, while leaving the truth inviolate. Out of the whole Christian tradition, there is perhaps no body of teaching which is more relevant and appropriate to the modern predicament than the marvellously subtle and realistic doctrines of the Four Cardinal Virtues—*prudentia, justitia, fortitudo,* and *temperantia.*

The meaning of *prudentia,* significantly called the "mother" of all other virtues—*prudentia dicitur genitrix virtutum*—is not conveyed by the word "prudence," as currently used. It signifies the opposite of a small, mean, calculating attitude to life, which refuses to see and value anything that fails to promise an immediate utilitarian advantage.

The pre-eminence of prudence means that realisation of the good presupposes knowledge of reality. He alone can do good who knows what things are like and what their situation is. The pre-eminence of prudence means that so-called "good intentions" and so-called "meaning well" by no means suffice. Realisation of the good presupposes that our actions are appropriate to the real situation, that is to the concrete realities which form the "environment" of a concrete human action; and that we therefore take this concrete reality seriously, with clear-eyed objectivity.

This clear-eyed objectivity, however, cannot be achieved and prudence cannot be perfected except by an attitude of "silent contemplation" of reality, during which the egocentric interests of man are at least temporarily silenced.

Only on the basis of this magnanimous kind of prudence can we achieve justice, fortitude, and *temperantia*, which means knowing when enough is enough. "Prudence implies a transformation of the knowledge of truth into decisions corresponding to reality." What, therefore, could be of greater importance today than the study and cultivation of prudence, which would almost inevitably lead to a real understanding of the three other cardinal virtues, all of which are indispensable for the survival of civilisation?

Justice relates to truth, fortitude to goodness, and *temperantia* to beauty; while prudence, in a sense, comprises all three. The type of realism which behaves as if the good, the true, and the beautiful were too vague and subjective to be adopted as the highest aims of social or individual life, or were the automatic spin-off of the successful pursuit of wealth and power, has been aptly called "crackpot-realism." Everywhere people ask: "What can I actually *do?*" The answer is as simple as it is disconcerting: we can, each of us, work to put our own inner house in order. The guidance we need for this work cannot be found in science or technology, the value of which utterly depends on the ends they serve; but it can still be found in the traditional wisdom of mankind.

KARL RAHNER

from Neighbourly Love

This is a sanctifying Christian love, brought into being and sustained by God's grace, a true personal generosity which seeks out the other for his own sake and not as a means of securing private advantage or pleasure, and thus affirms his unique individuality without subjecting him to one's own "ideal": a love which refers one to the other, not the other to oneself. The "selflessness" of this love, which is the real and total achievement of the spiritual personality, does not imply coolness and distance; it means the bestowal of one's whole being, so far as this is possible and the other is capable of being the recipient of such a love. Love of one's neighbour "for God's sake" precisely does not mean making the neighbour into a mere external occasion for training oneself in the love of God; the expression indicates the context and the basis which make real neighbourly love possible, because in the supernatural order God himself is man's inmost mystery. Hence it is the common theological view that neighbourly love is an act of the virtue of divine love, and thus an active participation in the inner life of the Trinity, brought about by the grace of the Holy Ghost, the Pneuma which is God's personal Love.

16

THE MYSTERY
OF FAULT AND
THE REDEEMED
HEART

DIETRICH BONHOEFFER

Confession and Communion

"Confess your faults one to another" (Jas. 5:16). He who is alone with his sin is utterly alone. It may be that Christians, notwithstanding corporate worship, common prayer, and all their fellowship in service, may still be left to their loneliness. The final break-through to fellowship does not occur, because, though they have fellowship with one another as believers and as devout people, they do not have fellowhip as the undevout, as sinners. The pious fellowship permits no one to be a sinner. So everybody must conceal his sin from himself and from the fellowship. We dare not be sinners. Many Christians are unthinkably horrified when a real sinner is suddenly discovered among the righteous. So we remain alone with our sin, living in lies and hypocrisy. The fact is that we *are* sinners!

But it is the grace of the Gospel, which is so hard for the pious to understand, that it confronts us with the truth and says: You are a sinner, a great, desperate sinner; now come, as the sinner that you are, to God who loves you. He wants you as you are; He does not want anything from you, a sacrifice, a work; He wants you alone. "My son, give me thine heart" (Prov. 23:26). God has come to you to save the sinner. Be glad! This message is liberation through truth. You can hide nothing from God. The mask you wear before men will do you no good before Him. He wants to see you as you are, He wants to be gracious to you. You do not have to go on lying to yourself and your brothers, as if you were without sin; you can dare to be a sinner. Thank God for that; He loves the sinner but He hates sin.

Christ became our Brother in the flesh in order that we might believe in him. In him the love of God came to the sinner. Through him men could be sinners and only so could they be helped. All sham was ended in the presence of Christ. The misery of the sinner and the mercy of God—this was the truth of the Gospel in Jesus Christ. It was in this truth that his Church was to live. Therefore, he gave his followers the authority to hear the confession of sin and to forgive sin in his name. "Whose soever sins ye remit, they are remitted unto them; and whose soever sins ye retain, they are retained" (John 20:23).

When he did that Christ made the Church, and in it our brother, a blessing to us. Now our brother stands in Christ's stead. Before him I need no longer to dissemble. Before him alone in the whole world I dare to be the sinner that I am; here the truth of Jesus Christ and his mercy rules. Christ became our Brother in order to help us. Through him our brother has become Christ for us in the power and authority of the commission Christ has given to him. Our brother stands before us as the sign of the truth and the grace of God. He has been given to us to help us. He hears the confession of our sins in Christ's stead and he forgives our sins in Christ's name. He keeps the secret of our confession as God keeps it. When I go to my brother to confess, I am going to God.

So in the Christian community when the call to brotherly confession and forgiveness goes forth it is a call to the great grace of God in the Church.

BREAKING THROUGH TO COMMUNITY

In confession the break-through to community takes place. Sin demands to have a man by himself. It withdraws him from the community. The more isolated a person is, the more destructive will be the power of sin over him, and the more deeply he becomes involved in it, the more disastrous is his isolation. Sin wants to remain unknown. It shuns the light. In the darkness of the unexpressed it poisons the whole being of a person. This can happen even in the midst of a pious community. In confession the light of the Gospel breaks into the darkness and seclusion of the heart. The sin must be brought into the light. The unexpressed must be openly spoken and acknowledged. All that is secret and hidden is made manifest. It is a hard struggle until the sin is openly admitted. But God breaks gates of brass and bars of iron (Ps. 107:16).

Since the confession of sin is made in the presence of a Christian brother, the last stronghold of self-justification is abandoned. The sinner surrenders; he gives up all his evil. He gives his heart to God, and he finds the forgiveness of all his sin in the fellowship of Jesus Christ and his brother. The expressed, acknowledged sin has lost all its power. It has been revealed and judged as sin. It can no longer tear the fellowship asunder. Now the fellowship bears the sin of the brother. He is no longer alone with his evil for he has cast off his sin in confession and handed it over to God. It has been taken away from him. Now he stands in the fellowship of sinners who live by the grace of God in the Cross of Jesus Christ. Now he can be a sinner and still enjoy the grace of God. He can confess his sins and in this very act find fellowhip for the first time. The sin concealed separated him from the fellowship, made all his apparent fellowship a sham; the sin confessed has helped him to find true fellowship with the brethren in Jesus Christ.

Moreover, what we have said applies solely to confession between two Christians. A confession of sin in the presence of all the members of the congregation is not required to restore one to fellowship with the whole congregation. I meet the whole congregation in the one brother to whom I confess my sins and who forgives my sins. In the fellowship I find with this one brother I have already found fellowship with the whole congregation. In this matter no one acts in his own name nor by his own authority, but by the commission of Jesus Christ. This commission is given to the whole congregation and the individual is called merely to exercise it for the congregation. If a Christian is in the fellowship of confession with a brother he will never be alone again, anywhere.

BREAKING THROUGH TO CERTAINTY

In confession a man breaks through to certainty. Why is it that it is often easier for us to confess our sins to God than to a brother? God is holy and sinless, He is a just judge of evil and the enemy of all disobedience. But a brother is sinful as we are. He knows from his own experience the dark night of secret sin. Why should we not find it easier to go to a brother than to the holy God? But if we do, we must ask ourselves whether we have not often been deceiving ourselves with our confession of sin to God, whether we have not rather been confessing our sins to ourselves and also granting ourselves absolution. And is not the reason perhaps for our countless relapses and the feebleness of our

Christian obedience to be found precisely in the fact that we are living on self-forgiveness and not a real forgiveness? Self-forgiveness can never lead to a breach with sin; this can be accomplished only by the judging and pardoning Word of God itself.

Who can give us the certainty that, in the confession and the forgiveness of our sins, we are not dealing with ourselves but with the living God? God gives us this certainty through our brother. Our brother breaks the circle of self-deception. A man who confesses his sins in the presence of a brother knows that he is no longer alone with himself; he experiences the presence of God in the reality of the other person. As long as I am by myself in the confession of my sins everything remains in the dark, but in the presence of a brother the sin has to be brought into the light. But since the sin must come to light some time, it is better that it happens today between me and my brother, rather than on the last day in the piercing light of the final judgment. It is a mercy that we can confess our sins to a brother. Such grace spares us the terrors of the last judgment.

Our brother has been given me that even here and now I may be made certain through him of the reality of God in His judgment and His grace. As the open confession of my sins to a brother insures me against self-deception, so, too, the assurance of forgiveness becomes fully certain to me only when it is spoken by a brother in the name of God. Mutual, brotherly confession is given to us by God in order that we may be sure of divine forgiveness.

But it is precisely for the sake of this certainty that confession should deal with *concrete* sins. People usually are satisfied when they make a general confession. But one experiences the utter perdition and corruption of human nature, in so far as this ever enters into experience at all, when one sees his own specific sins. Self-examination on the basis of all Ten Commandments will therefore be the right preparation for confession. Otherwise it might happen that one could still be a hypocrite even in confessing to a brother and thus miss the good of the confession. Jesus dealt with people whose sins were obvious, with publicans and harlots. They knew why they needed forgiveness, and they received it as forgiveness of their specific sins. Blind Bartimaeus was asked by Jesus: What do you want me to do for you? Before confession we must have a clear answer to this question. In confession we, too, receive the forgiveness of the particular sins which are here brought to light, and by this very token the forgiveness of all our sins, known and unknown.

Does all this mean that confession to a brother is a divine law? No, confession is not a law, it is an offer of divine help for the sinner. It is possible that a person may by God's grace break through to certainty, new life, the Cross, and fellowship without benefit of confession to a brother. It is possible that a person may never know what it is to doubt his own forgiveness and despair of his own confession of sin, that he may be given everything in his own private confession to God. We have spoken here for those who cannot make this assertion. Luther himself was one of those for whom the Christian life was unthinkable without mutual, brotherly confession. In the *Large Catechism* he said: "Therefore when I admonish you to confession I am admonishing you to be a Christian." Those who, despite all their seeking and trying, cannot find the great joy of fellowship, the Cross, the new life, and certainty should be shown the blessing that God offers us in mutual confession. Confession is within the liberty of the Christian. Who can refuse, without suffering loss, a help that God has deemed it necessary to offer?

TO WHOM CONFESS?

To whom shall we make confession? According to Jesus' promise, every Christian brother can hear the confession of another. But will he understand? May he not be so far above us in his Christian life that he would only turn away from us with no understanding of our personal sins?

Anybody who lives beneath the Cross and who has discerned in the Cross of Jesus the utter wickedness of all men and of his own heart will find there is no sin that can ever be alien to him. Anybody who has once been horrified by the dreadfulness of his own sin that nailed Jesus to the Cross will no longer be horrified by even the rankest sins of a brother. Looking at the Cross of Jesus, he knows the human heart. He knows how utterly lost it is in sin and weakness, how it goes astray in the ways of sin, and he also knows that it is accepted in grace and mercy. Only the brother under the Cross can hear a confession.

It is not experience of life but experience of the Cross that makes one a worthy hearer of confessions. The most experienced psychologist or observer of human nature knows infinitely less of the human heart than the simplest Christian who lives beneath the Cross of Jesus. The greatest psychological insight, ability, and experience cannot grasp this one thing: what sin is. Worldy wisdom knows what distress and weakness and failure are, but it does not know the godlessness of men. And so it also does not know that man is destroyed only by his sin and can be healed only by forgiveness. Only the Christian knows this. In the presence of a psychiatrist I can only be a sick man; in the presence of a Christian brother I can dare to be a sinner. The psychiatrist must first search my heart and yet he never plumbs its ultimate depth. The Christian brother knows when I come to him: here is a sinner like myself, a godless man who wants to confess and yearns for God's forgiveness. The psychiatrist views me as if there were no God. The brother views me as I am before the judging and merciful God in the Cross of Jesus Christ. It is not lack of psychological knowledge but lack of love for the crucified Jesus Christ that makes us so poor and inefficient in brotherly confession.

In daily, earnest living with the Cross of Christ the Christian loses the spirit of human censoriousness on the one hand and weak indulgence on the other, and he receives the spirit of divine severity and divine love. The death of the sinner before God and life that comes out of that death through grace become for him a daily reality. So he loves the brothers with the merciful love of God that leads through the death of the sinner to the life of the child of God. Who can hear our confession? He who himself lives beneath the Cross. Wherever the message concerning the Crucified is a vital, living thing, there brotherly confession will also avail.

TWO DANGERS

There are two dangers that a Christian community which practices confession must guard against. The first concerns the one who hears confessions. It is not a good thing for one person to be the confessor for all the others. All too easily this one person will be overburdened; thus confession will become for him an empty routine, and this will give rise to the disastrous misuse of the confessional for the exercise of spiritual domination of souls. In order that he may not succumb to this sinister danger of the confessional every person should refrain from listening to confession who does not himself practice it. Only the person who has so humbled himself can hear a brother's confession without harm.

The second danger concerns the confessant. For the salvation of his soul let him guard against ever making a pious work of his confession. If he does so, it will become the final, most abominable, vicious, and impure prostitution of the heart; the act becomes an idle, lustful babbling. Confession as a pious work is an invention of the devil. It is only God's offer of grace, help, and forgiveness that could make us dare to enter the abyss of confession. We can confess solely for the sake of the promise of absolution. Confession as a routine duty is spiritual death; confession in reliance upon the promise is life. The forgiveness of sins is the sole ground and goal of confession.

THE JOYFUL SACRAMENT

Though it is true that confession is an act in the name of Christ that is complete in itself and is exercised in the fellowship as frequently as there is desire for it, it serves the Christian community especially as a preparation for the common reception of the holy Communion. Reconciled to God and men, Christians desire to receive the body and blood of Jesus Christ. It is the command of Jesus that none should come to the altar with a heart that is unreconciled to his brother. If this command of Jesus applies to every service of worship, indeed, to every prayer we utter, then it most certainly applies to reception of the Lord's Supper.

The day before the Lord's Supper is administered will find the brethren of a Christian fellowship together and each will beg the forgiveness of the others for the wrongs committed. Nobody who avoids this approach to his brother can go rightly prepared to the table of the Lord. All anger, strife, envy, evil gossip, and unbrotherly conduct must have been settled and finished if the brethren wish to receive the grace of God together in the sacrament. But to beg a brother's pardon is still not confession, and only the latter is subject to the express command of Jesus.

But preparation for the Lord's Supper will also awaken in the individual the desire to be completely certain that the particular sins which disturb and torment him and are known only to God are forgiven. It is this desire that the offer of brotherly confession and absolution fulfills. Where there is deep anxiety and trouble over one's own sins, where the certainty of forgiveness is sought, there comes the invitation in the name of Jesus to come to brotherly confession. What brought upon Jesus the accusation of blasphemy, namely, that he forgave sinners, is what now takes place in the Christian brotherhood in the power of the presence of Jesus Christ. One forgives the other all his sins in the name of the triune God. And there is joy in the presence of the angels of God over the sinner who repents. Hence the time of preparation for the Lord's Supper will be filled with brotherly admonition and encouragement, with prayers, with fear, and with joy.

The day of the Lord's Supper is an occasion of joy for the Christian community. Reconciled in their hearts with God and the brethren, the congregation receives the gift of the body and blood of Jesus Christ, and, receiving that, it receives forgiveness, new life, and salvation. It is given new fellowship with God and men. The fellowship of the Lord's Supper is the superlative fulfillment of Christian fellowship. As the members of the congregation are united in body and blood at the table of the Lord so will they be together in eternity. Here the community has reached its goal. Here joy in Christ and his community is complete. The life of Christians together under the Word has reached its perfection in the sacrament.

JULIAN OF NORWICH

from *Revelations of Divine Love*

*God is all that is good, and gently enfolds us; in comparison
with almighty God creation is nothing; man can have no
rest until he totally denies himself and everything else for
love of God*

It was at this time that our Lord showed me spiritually how intimately
he loves us. I saw that he is everything that we know to be good and
helpful. In his love he clothes us, enfolds and embraces us; that tender
love completely surrounds us, never to leave us. As I saw it he is
everything that is good.

And he showed me more, a little thing, the size of a hazelnut, on the
palm of my hand, round like a ball. I looked at it thoughtfully and
wondered, "What is this?" And the answer came, "It is all that is
made." I marvelled that it continued to exist and did not suddenly
disintegrate; it was so small. And again my mind supplied the answer,
"It exists, both now and for ever, because God loves it." In short,
everything owes its existence to the love of God.

In this "little thing" I saw three truths. The first is that God made it;
the second is that God loves it; and the third is that God sustains it. But
what he is who is in truth Maker, Keeper, and Lover I cannot tell, for
until I am essentially united with him I can never have full rest or real
happiness; in other words, until I am so joined to him that there is
absolutely nothing between my God and me. We have got to realize the
littleness of creation and to see it for the nothing that it is before we can
love and possess God who is uncreated. This is the reason why we have
no ease of heart or soul, for we are seeking our rest in trivial things
which cannot satisfy, and not seeking to know God, almighty, all-wise,
all-good. He is true rest. It is his will that we should know him, and his
pleasure that we should rest in him. Nothing less will satisfy us. No
soul can rest until it is detached from all creation. When it is
deliberately so detached for love of him who is all, then only can it
experience spiritual rest.

God showed me too the pleasure it gives him when a simple soul
comes to him, openly, sincerely and genuinely. It seems to me as I
ponder this revelation that when the Holy Spirit touches the soul it
longs for God rather like this; "God, of your goodness give me yourself,
for you are sufficient for me. I cannot properly ask anything less, to be
worthy of you. If I were to ask less, I should always be in want. In you
alone do I have all."

Such words are dear indeed to the soul, and very close to the will and goodness of God. For his goodness enfolds every one of his creatures and all his blessed works, eternally and surpassingly. For he himself is eternity, and has made us for himself alone, has restored us by his blessed passion, and keeps us in his blessed love. And all because he is goodness.

The thirteenth revelation: God's will is that we should greatly value all his works; the noble nature of all creation; sin is known by suffering

After this our Lord brought to mind the longing I had for him earlier. I now saw that nothing hindered me but sin. And this I saw to be true in general of us all and I thought to myself that if there had been no sin we should all have been clean and like our Lord, as when we were made. In my foolish way I had often wondered why the foreseeing wisdom of God could not have prevented the beginning of sin, for then, thought I, all would have been well. This line of thought ought to have been left well alone; as it was I grieved and sorrowed over it, with neither cause nor justification. But Jesus, who in this vision informed me of all I needed, answered, "Sin was necessary—but it is all going to be all right; it is all going to be all right; everything is going to be all right." In this simple word *sin* our Lord reminded me in a general sort of way of all that is not good: the despicable shame and utter self-denial he endured for us, both in his life and in his dying. And of all the suffering and pain of his creation, both spiritual and physical. For all of us have already experienced something of this abnegation and we have to deny ourselves as we follow our master, Jesus, until we are wholly cleansed. I mean, until this body of death and our inward affections (which are not very good) are completely done away. All this I saw, together with all the suffering that ever has been or can be. And of all pain I understood that the passion of Christ was the greatest and most surpassing. All this was shown in a flash, and quickly passed over into consolation—for our good Lord would not have the soul frightened by this ugly sight.

But I did not see *sin*. I believe it has no substance or real existence. It can only be known by the pain it causes. This pain is something, as I see it, which lasts but a while. It purges us and makes us know ourselves, so that we ask for mercy. The passion of our Lord is our comfort against all this—for such is his blessed will. Because of his tender love for all those who are to be saved our good Lord comforts us at once and sweetly, as if to say, "It is true that sin is the cause of all this pain; but it is all going to be all right; it is all going to be all right; everything is going to be all right." These words were said most tenderly, with never a hint of blame either to me or to any of those to be saved. It would be most improper of me therefore to blame or criticize God for my sin, since he does not blame me for it.

In these words I saw one of God's marvellously deep secrets—a secret which he will plainly reveal to us in heaven. And when we know it we will see the reason why he allowed sin to come, and seeing, we shall rejoice in him for ever.

The heirs of salvation are shaken by sorrow; Christ rejoices in his compassion; a remedy for trouble

In this way I saw how Christ has compassion upon us because of our sin. And just as previously I had been full of sorrow and compassion at the sight of his suffering, so now I was filled with compassion for all my fellow Christians, those people greatly beloved and saved, the servants of God. For Holy Church shall be shaken at the world's sorrow, anguish, and tribulation, just as men shake a cloth in the wind. Our Lord gave me an answer about all this. "I shall make of this a great thing in heaven—a thing of everlasting worth and endless joy." I could now understand how our Lord rejoiced in the tribulations of his servants, though with pity and compassion. To bring them to bliss he lays on each one he loves some particular thing, which while it carries no blame in his sight causes them to be blamed by the world, despised, scorned, mocked, and rejected. This he does to forestall any hurt they might get from the pomps and vanities of this sinful world, to prepare their way to heaven, and to exalt them in his everlasting bliss. For he says, "I shall wholly break you of your empty affections and your pernicious pride. Then I shall gather you together, and by uniting you to myself make you humble and mild, clean and holy." Then it was that I saw that all the kind compassion and love a man may have for his fellow Christian is due to the fact that Christ is in him.

The same total abnegation shown in his passion was shown again here in this compassion. The significance is twofold: there is the bliss to which we are brought, the enjoyment that is in him; and there is the comfort we may have in our suffering. He wants us to know that all this will be changed into glory and profit through his passion; to know, moreover, that we do not suffer on our own, but with him; to see in him the ground of our being; to recognize that his suffering and self-abnegation so far surpasses anything we might experience that we shall never wholly understand it.

To see this will stop us from moaning and despairing about our own sufferings. We can see that our sin well deserves it, but that his love excuses us. In his great courtesy he overlooks the blame, and regards us with sympathy and pity, children both innocent and loved.

KARL RAHNER

Penance

Penance as a "virtue" signifies the proper moral and religious attitude of man towards sin (his own and sin in general), granted him by the grace of Christ. Its most central act is contrition. Penance essentially involves: having the courage to fear God and face the truth about one's own existence, dispensing with all repressions (the upright acknowledgment of one's past): the grace-given disposition to let God's revealing word convince one by destroying the pharisaic self-righteousness of sin; the serious and active will to amend one's life, trusting in the grace of God which triumphs through human helplessness (attested by penitential works, biblically: vigils, fasting, and almsgiving); the will to the sacrament of the forgiveness of sin; willingness humbly to endure the consequences of sin that remain even after it has been forgiven; actively helping to bear the burden of sin that assumes concrete existence in the general unhappiness and distress of the world. Precisely as a gift of God, penance is a human action and not simply a passive experience: man turns away from his past, which "pains" him (because he again accepts the unshakable validity of the divine order) and which he "abhors" (because he himself is freely renewing this order). Penance implies that what is believed and accepted in hope is not our repentance but God's deed in us. It includes recognition of man's plurality, which in turn requires a plurality of acts (external and internal works of penance, faith and charity, satisfaction, stepping into the future with the "firm purpose").

17

CONVERSION

SIMONE WEIL

from *Spiritual Autobiography*

From Marseilles, about May 15

Father,

Before leaving I want to speak to you again, it may be the last time perhaps, for over there I shall probably send you only my news from time to time just so as to have yours.

I told you that I owed you an enormous debt. I want to try to tell you exactly what it consists of. I think that if you could really understand what my spiritual state is you would not be at all sorry that you did not lead me to baptism. But I do not know if it is possible for you to understand this.

You neither brought me the Christian inspiration nor did you bring me to Christ; for when I met you there was no longer any need; it had been done without the intervention of any human being. If it had been otherwise, if I had not already been won, not only implicitly but consciously, you would have given me nothing, because I should have received nothing from you. My friendship for you would have been a reason for me to refuse your message, for I should have been afraid of the possibilities of error and illusion which human influence in the divine order is likely to involve.

I may say that never at any moment in my life have I "sought for God." For this reason, which is probably too subjective, I do not like this expression and it strikes me as false. As soon as I reached adolescence, I saw the problem of God as a problem the data of which could not be obtained here below, and I decided that the only way of being sure not to reach a wrong solution, which seemed to me the greatest possible evil, was to leave it alone. So I left it alone. I neither affirmed nor denied anything. It seemed to me useless to solve the problem, for I thought that, being in this world, our business was to adopt the best attitude with regard to the problems of this world, and that such an attitude did not depend upon the solution of the problem of God.

This held good as far as I was concerned at any rate, for I never hesitated in my choice of an attitude; I always adopted the Christian attitude as the only possible one. I might say that I was born, I grew up, and I always remained within the Christian inspiration. While the very name of God had no part in my thoughts, with regard to the problems of this world and this life I shared the Christian conception in an explicit and rigorous manner, with the most specific notions it involves. Some of these notions have been part of my outlook for as far back as I can remember. With others I know the time and manner of their coming and the form under which they imposed themselves upon me. . . .

At fourteen I fell into one of those fits of bottomless despair that come with adolescence, and I seriously thought of dying because of the mediocrity of my natural faculties. The exceptional gifts of my brother, who had a childhood and youth comparable to those of Pascal, brought my own inferiority home to me. I did not mind having no visible successes, but what did grieve me was the idea of being excluded from that transcendent kingdom to which only the truly great have access and wherein truth abides. I preferred to die rather than live without that truth. After months of inward darkness, I suddenly had the everlasting conviction that any human being, even though practically devoid of natural faculties, can penetrate to the kingdom of truth reserved for genius, if only he longs for truth and perpetually concentrates all his attention upon its attainment. He thus becomes a genius too, even though for lack of talent his genius cannot be visible from outside. Later on, when the strain of headaches caused the feeble faculties I possess to be invaded by a paralysis, which I was quick to imagine as probably incurable, the same conviction led me to persevere for ten years in an effort of concentrated attention that was practically unsupported by any hope of results.

Under the name of truth I also included beauty, virtue, and every kind of goodness, so that for me it was a question of a conception of the relationship between grace and desire. The conviction that had come to me was that when one hungers for bread one does not receive stones.

But at that time I had not read the Gospel....

As for the spirit of poverty, I do not remember any moment when it was not in me, although only to that unhappily small extent compatible with my imperfection. I fell in love with Saint Francis of Assisi as soon as I came to know about him. I always believed and hoped that one day Fate would force upon me the condition of a vagabond and a beggar which he embraced freely. Actually I felt the same way about prison.

From my earliest childhood I always had also the Christian idea of love for one's neighbor, to which I gave the name of justice—a name it bears in many passages of the Gospel and which is so beautiful. You know that on this point I have failed seriously several times.

The duty of acceptance in all that concerns the will of God, whatever it may be, was impressed upon my mind as the first and most necessary of all duties from the time when I found it set down in Marcus Aurelius under the form of the *amor fati* of the Stoics. I saw it as a duty we cannot fail in without dishonoring ourselves.

The idea of purity, with all that this word can imply for a Christian, took possession of me at the age of sixteen, after a period of several months during which I had been going through the emotional unrest natural in adolescence. This idea came to me when I was contemplating a mountain landscape and little by little it was imposed upon me in an irresistible manner.

Of course I knew quite well that my conception of life was Christian. That is why it never occurred to me that I could enter the Christian community. I had the idea that I was born inside. But to add dogma to this conception of life, without being forced to do so by indisputable evidence, would have seemed to me like a lack of honesty. I should even have thought I was lacking in honesty had I considered the question of the truth of dogma as a problem for myself or even had I simply desired to reach a conclusion on this subject. I have an extremely severe standard for intellectual honesty, so severe that I never met anyone who did not seem to fall short of it in more than one respect; and I am always afraid of failing in it myself.

Keeping away from dogma in this way, I was prevented by a sort of shame from going into churches, though all the same I like being in them. Nevertheless, I had three contacts with Catholicism that really counted.

After my year in the [Renault automobile] factory, before going back to teaching, I had been taken by my parents to Portugal, and while there I left them to go alone to a little village. I was, as it were, in pieces, soul and body. That contact with affliction had killed my youth. Until then I had not had any experience of affliction....

I knew quite well that there was a great deal of affliction in the world, I was obsessed with the idea, but I had not had prolonged and first-hand experience of it. As I worked in the factory, indistinguishable to all eyes, including my own, from the anonymous mass, the affliction of others entered into my flesh and my soul. Nothing separated me from it, for I had really forgotten my past and I looked forward to no future, finding it difficult to imagine the possibility of surviving all the fatigue. What I went through there marked me in so lasting a manner that still today when any human being, whoever he may be and in whatever circumstances, speaks to me without brutality, I cannot help having the impression that there must be a mistake and that unfortunately the mistake will in all probability disappear. There I received forever the mark of a slave, like the branding of the red-hot iron the Romans put on the foreheads of their most despised slaves. Since then I have always regarded myself as a slave.

In this state of mind then, and in a wretched condition physically, I entered the little Portuguese village, which, alas, was very wretched too, on the very day of the festival of its patron saint. I was alone. It was the evening and there was a full moon over the sea. The wives of the fishermen were, in procession, making a tour of all the ships, carrying candles and singing what must certainly be very ancient hymns of a heart-rending sadness. Nothing can give any idea of it. I have never heard anything so poignant unless it were the song of the boatmen on the Volga. There the conviction was suddenly borne in upon me that Christianity is pre-eminently the religion of slaves, that slaves cannot help belonging to it, and I among others.

In 1937 I had two marvelous days at Assisi. There, alone in the little twelfth-century Romanesque chapel of Santa Maria degli Angeli, an incomparable marvel of purity where Saint Francis often used to pray, something stronger than I was compelled me for the first time in my life to go down on my knees.

In 1938 I spent ten days at [the Benedictine abbey at] Solesmes, from Palm Sunday to Easter Tuesday, following all the liturgical services, I was suffering from splitting headaches; each sound hurt me like a blow; by an extreme effort of concentration I was able to rise above this wretched flesh, to leave it to suffer by itself, heaped up in a corner, and to find a pure and perfect joy in the unimaginable beauty of the chanting and the words. This experience enabled me by analogy to get a better understanding of the possibility of loving divine love in the midst of affliction. It goes without saying that in the course of these services the thought of the Passion of Christ entered into my being once and for all.

There was a young English Catholic there from whom I gained my first idea of the supernatural power of the sacraments because of the truly angelic radiance with which he seemed to be clothed after going to communion. Chance—for I always prefer saying chance rather than Providence—made of him a messenger to me. For he told me of the existence of those English poets of the seventeenth century who are named metaphysical. In reading them later on, I discovered the poem of which I read you what is unfortunately a very inadequate translation. It is...[George Herbert's] "Love." I learned it by heart. Often, at the culminating point of a violent headache, I make myself say it over, concentrating all my attention upon it and clinging with all my soul to the tenderness it enshrines. I used to think I was merely reciting it as a beautiful poem, but without my knowing it the recitation had the virtue of a prayer. It was during one of these recitations that, as I told you, Christ himself came down and took possession of me.

In my arguments about the insolubility of the problem of God I had never foreseen the possibility of that, of a real contact, person to person, here below, between a human being and God. I had vaguely heard tell of things of this kind, but I had never believed in them. In the *Fioretti* [Legends of Francis of Assisi] the accounts of apparitions rather put me off if anything, like the miracles in the Gospel. Moreover, in this sudden possession of me by Christ, neither my senses nor my imagination had any part; I only felt in the midst of my suffering the presence of a love, like that which one can read in the smile on a beloved face.

I had never read any mystical works because I had never felt any call to read them. In reading as in other things I have always striven to practice obedience. There is nothing more favorable to intellectual progress, for as far as possible I only read what I am hungry for at the moment when I have an appetite for it, and then I do not read, I *eat*. God in his mercy had prevented me from reading the mystics, so that it should be evident to me that I had not invented this absolutely unexpected contact.

Yet I still half refused, not my love but my intelligence. For it seemed to me certain, and I still think so, today, that one can never wrestle enough with God if one does so out of pure regard for the truth. Christ likes us to prefer truth to him because, before being Christ, he is truth. If one turns aside from him to go toward the truth, one will not go far before falling into his arms.

After this I came to feel that Plato was a mystic, that all the *Iliad* is bathed in Christian light, and that Dionysus and Osiris are in a certain sense Christ himself; and my love was thereby redoubled.

I never wondered whether Jesus was or was not the Incarnation of God; but in fact I was incapable of thinking of him without thinking of him as God.

In the spring of 1940 I read the *Bhagavad-Gita*. Strange to say it was in reading those marvelous words, words with such a Christian sound, put into the mouth of an incarnation of God, that I came to feel strongly that we owe an allegiance to religious truth which is quite different from the admiration we accord to a beautiful poem; it is something far more categorical.

Yet I did not believe it to be possible for me to consider the question of baptism. I felt that I could not honestly give up my opinions concerning the non-Christian religions and concerning Israel—and as a matter of fact time and meditation have only served to strengthen them—and I thought that this constituted an absolute obstacle. I did not imagine it as possible that a priest could even dream of granting me baptism. If I had not met you, I should never have considered the problem of baptism as a practical problem.

During all this time of spiritual progress I had never prayed. I was afraid of the power of suggestion that is in prayer—the very power for which Pascal recommends it. Pascal's method seems to me one of the worst for attaining faith.

Contact with you was not able to persuade me to pray. On the contrary I thought the danger was all the greater, since I also had to beware of the power of suggestion in my friendship with you. At the same time I found it very difficult not to pray and not to tell you so. Moreover I knew I could not tell you without completely misleading you about myself. At that time I should not have been able to make you understand.

Until last September I had never once prayed in all my life, at least not in the literal sense of the word. I had never said any words to God either out loud or mentally. I had never pronounced a liturgical prayer. I had occasionally recited the *Salve Regina*, but only as a beautiful poem.

Last summer, doing Greek with T——, I went through the Our Father word for word in Greek. We promised each other to learn it by heart. I do not think he ever did so, but some weeks later, as I was turning over the pages of the Gospel, I said to myself that since I had promised to do this thing and it was good, I ought to do it. I did it. The infinite sweetness of this Greek text so took hold of me that for several days I could not stop myself from saying it over all the time. A week afterward I began the vine harvest. I recited the Our Father in Greek every day before work, and I repeated it very often in the vineyard.

Since that time I have made a practice of saying it through once each morning with absolute attention. If during the recitation my attention wanders or goes to sleep, in the minutest degree, I begin again until I have once succeeded in going through it with absolutely pure attention. Sometimes it comes about that I say it again out of sheer pleasure, but I only do it if I really feel the impulse.

The effect of this practice is extraordinary and surprises me every time, for, although I experience it each day, it exceeds my expectation at each repetition.

At times the very first words tear my thoughts from my body and transport it to a place outside space where there is neither perspective nor point of view. The infinity of the ordinary expanses of perception is replaced by an infinity to the second or sometimes the third degree. At the same time, filling every part of this infinity of infinity, there is silence, a silence which is not an absence of sound but which is the object of a positive sensation, more positive than that of sound. Noises, if there are any, only reach me after crossing this silence.

Sometimes, also, during this recitation or at other moments, Christ is present with me in person, but his presence is infinitely more real, more moving, more clear than on that first occasion when he took possession of me.

I should never have been able to take it upon myself to tell you all this had it not been for the fact that I am going away. And as I am going more or less with the idea of probable death, I do not believe that I have the right to keep it to myself. For after all, the whole of this matter is not a question concerning me myself. It concerns God. I am really nothing in it all. If one could imagine any possibility of error in God, I should think that it had all happened to me by mistake. But perhaps God likes to use castaway objects, waste, rejects. After all, should the bread of the host be moldy, it would become the Body of Christ just the same after the priest had consecrated it. Only it cannot refuse, while we can disobey. It sometimes seems to me that when I am treated in so merciful a way, every sin on my part must be a mortal sin. And I am constantly committing them.

I have told you that you are like a father and brother at the same time to me. But these words only express an analogy. Perhaps at bottom they only correspond to a feeling of affection, of gratitude and admiration. For as to the spiritual direction of my soul, I think that God himself has taken it in hand from the start and still looks after it.

That does not prevent me from owing you the greatest debt of gratitude that I could ever have incurred toward any human being. This is exactly what it consists of.

First you once said to me at the beginning of our relationship some words that went to the bottom of my soul. You said: "Be very careful, because if you should pass over something important through your own fault it would be a pity."

That made me see intellectual honesty in a new light. Till then I had only thought of it as opposed to faith; your words made me think that perhaps, without my knowing it, there were in me obstacles to the faith, impure obstacles, such as prejudices, habits. I felt that after having said to myself for so many years simply: "Perhaps all that is not true," I ought, without ceasing to say it—I still take care to say it very often now—to join it to the opposite formula, namely: "Perhaps all that is true," and to make them alternate.

At the same time, in making the problem of baptism a practical problem for me, you have forced me to face the whole question of the faith, dogma, and the sacraments, obliging me to consider them closely and at length with the fullest possible attention, making me see them as things toward which I have obligations that I have to discern and perform. I should never have done this otherwise and it is indispensable for me to do it.

But the greatest blessing you have brought me is of another order. In gaining my friendship by your charity (which I have never met anything to equal), you have provided me with a source of the most compelling and pure inspiration that is to be found among human things. For nothing among human things has such power to keep our gaze fixed ever more intensely upon God, than friendship for the friends of God. . . .

I have not been able to avoid causing you the greatest disappointment it was in my power to cause you. But up to now, although I have often asked myself the question during prayer, during Mass, or in the light of the radiancy that remains in the soul after Mass, I have never once had, even for a moment, the feeling that God wants me to be in the Church. I have never even once had a feeling of uncertainty. I think that at the present time we can finally conclude that he does not want me in the Church. Do not have any regrets about it.

He does not want it so far at least. But unless I am mistaken I should say that it is his will that I should stay outside for the future too, except perhaps at the moment of death. Yet I am always ready to obey any order, whatever it may be. I should joyfully obey the order to go to the very center of hell and to remain there eternally. I do not mean, of course, that I have a preference for orders of this nature. I am not perverse like that.

Christianity should contain all vocations without exception since it is catholic. In consequence the Church should also. But in my eyes Christianity is catholic by right but not in fact. So many things are outside it, so many things that I love and do not want to give up, so many things that God loves, otherwise they would not be in existence. All the immense stretches of past centuries, except the last twenty are among them; all the countries inhabited by colored races; all secular life in the white peoples' countries; in the history of these countries, all the traditions banned as heretical, those of the Manicheans and Albigenses for instance; all those things resulting from the Renaissance, too often degraded but not quite without value.

Christianity being catholic by right but not in fact, I regard it as legitimate on my part to be a member of the Church by right but not in fact, not only for a time, but for my whole life if need be.

But it is not merely legitimate. So long as God does not give me the certainty that he is ordering me to do anything else, I think it is my duty.

I think, and so do you, that our obligation for the next two or three years, an obligation so strict that we can scarcely fail in it without treason, is to show the public the possibility of a truly incarnated Christianity. In all the history now known there has never been a period in which souls have been in such peril as they are today in every part of the globe....

But everything is so closely bound up together that Christianity cannot be really incarnated unless it is catholic in the sense that I have just defined. How could it circulate through the flesh of all the nations of Europe if it did not contain absolutely everything in itself? Except of course falsehood. But in everything that exists there is most of the time more truth than falsehood.

Having so intense and so painful a sense of this urgency, I should betray the truth, that is to say the aspect of truth that I see, if I left the point, where I have been since my birth, at the intersection of Christianity and everything that is not Christianity....

I think that you should understand why I have always resisted you, if in spite of being a priest you can admit that a genuine vocation might prevent anyone from entering the Church.

Otherwise a barrier of incomprehension will remain between us, whether the error is on my part or on yours. This would grieve me from the point of view of my friendship for you, because in that case the result of all these efforts and desires, called forth by your charity toward me, would be a disappointment for you. Moreover, although it is not my fault, I should not be able to help feeling guilty of ingratitude. For, I repeat, my debt to you is beyond all measure.

RAINER MARIA RILKE

An Archaic Torso of Apollo

We will not ever know his legendary head
Wherein the eyes, like apples, ripened. Yet
His torso glows like a candelabra
In which his vision, merely turned down low,

Still holds and gleams. If this were not so, the curve
Of the breast could not so blind you, nor this smile
Pass lightly through the soft turn of the loins
Into that center where procreation flared.

If this were not so, this stone would stand defaced, maimed,
Under the transparent cascade of the shoulder,
Not glimmering that way, like a wild beast's pelt,

Nor breaking out of all its contours
Like a star; for there is no place here
That does not see you. You must change your life.

18

THE GATHERING UP OF ALL THE THREADS

KARL RAHNER

Heaven

Theology uses the term "heaven" in two senses that must be distinguished from each other.

(1) As a figure of speech in the Old Testament and New Testament heaven means the upper region above the earth, in accordance with the cosmography of the ancient world with its various levels, the uppermost of which is quite figuratively conceived as God's dwelling-place. The Old Testament itself "demythologizes" this idea when it says that heaven and earth cannot contain God (1 Kg 8:27; Jer 23:24). In later Judaism heaven is also pictured as the abode of those who are saved: paradise was in heaven, the "heavenly Jerusalem" will be there. The New Testament likewise says metaphorically that Christians are to strive for the things that are "above" (Col 3:1); our true country is there (Phil 3:20; Heb 13:14). Heaven is also a circumlocution for the Name of God: the *"basileia* of heaven" therefore does not mean that the New Testament transfers God's eschatological kingdom to the next world, since that kingdom is characterized by a glorious transformation of all creation into a new heaven and a new earth.

(2) In theology heaven can be a metaphor for the fullness of salvation enjoyed by those who are finally saved in God. Whether this heaven can be called a "place" depends on the manner in which matter is likewise finally saved in God; but apart from the fact (the resurrection of the flesh) nothing on the subject has been revealed. In no circumstances may this heaven be conceived as a place existing outside time "at" or "in" which one arrives. This follows from the essentially christological structure of heaven: heaven is based on Jesus Christ's conquest of death and on his exaltation, which are the preconditions for the ability of creatures to enter the life of God himself; this abiding of personal creatures in the presence of God essentially means the gathering of mankind into the definitive Body of Jesus Christ, into the "whole Christ," to commune with God who is made (and remains) *man;* hence it is that we shall "see one another again," that the human relationships of this world continue in heaven. This union of man with God and with his fellows means no loss or absorption of individuality; rather the closer man approaches to God the more his individuality is liberated and fortified. This is clear from the language of theology, which defines the essential nature of heaven and beatitude in God as the beatific vision of God (thus the Thomists) or as utter personal love between God and his creature (thus the Scotists). Taken together, these two views show how beatitude can be differently conceived without ceasing to be beatitude: the individual who is finally saved by God's grace alone (which is what theology means by saying that man must necessarily be transformed by the "light of glory" in order to be capable of heaven) remains conditioned by what he has done and what he has become in history, and it is in this historical measure and "mould" that God wholly fills and loves him. Although heaven is based on the entry of Jesus Christ into his glory, which is the abiding validity in God of his sacred humanity and the admission to this beatitude of those who have died after him, and at the same time inaugurates a new relation between the world and Jesus and those who dwell with him, yet it must be borne in mind that "heaven" is still growing, since salvation is only complete when everything is saved (the world, history and men), so that salvation is only consummated in the consummation of all things in the *parousia,* the Judgment and the resurrection of the flesh.

Hell

The term derives from the North Germanic *hel,* "realm of the dead"; a popular expression for failure to reach the blessed society of God and the positive punitive consequences of the state of final personal alienation from God and final personal antagonism to the divine order of creation. The magisterium declares that this hell exists, that the punishment of hell begins immediately after death (without awaiting the Last Judgment) and that it lasts forever. Freely adopting the notions of later Judaism, the New Testament rather assumes than affirms the existence of a special place of punishment; what it says in this matter is to be interpreted according to the principles governing the interpretation of apocalyptic and eschatological texts of Scripture. That is, such statements are not "advance coverage," as though Scripture were reporting a future that had so to speak already arrived; rather their purpose is to shed light on the present existence of men before God. Thus the dogma of hell means that human life is threatened by the real possibility of eternal shipwreck, because man freely disposes of himself and can therefore freely refuse himself to God. Jesus directly states this possibility when he warns of the consequences of arbitrary and obstinate self-closure (lack of love, on which we shall be judged) in imagery which was current at that time. He proclaims the seriousness of one's present situation and the significance of human history, whose fruits are taken as man's own work, thus rejecting all trivializing and all superficial views of the relationship between man and God and as it were negatively stressing the utter love of God which nevertheless establishes us in individuality and freedom. Whether and how far man does in fact avail himself of his power to reject God revelation does not inform us, nor has the magisterium made any pronouncement on the question. Such information, indeed, would be inconsistent with the purpose of the doctrine of hell, which is not to provide abstract data or to satisfy our curiosity but to bring us to our senses and to conversion. Without seeing how they can be reconciled, we must confess the two doctrines: the omnipotence of God, who wills all men to be saved, and the possibility of eternal perdition, though we do not see both of these as equally powerful.

from *Resurrection of Jesus*

(1) The Easter message of the New Testament is not primarily concerned to offer apologetical proof of the historical fact that Jesus Christ, after his genuine and actual death, deposition from the cross and normal burial, rose again in his total and therefore in his physical reality to glorified perfection and immortality (see 2). But in view of the

difficulties for faith that are possible today it is important first of all to indicate the solid historicity of the fact. It is based on two experiences which fortify and illuminate one another and which even when subjected to critical exegesis and purely historical investigation defy serious contestation. The first experience is the discovery of the empty tomb (earliest evidence Mk 16:1-8), which critical exegesis proves *not* to have been used as an apologetical argument. (On the one hand the discovery was made by women, who in Jewish law were incapable of being witnesses—"idle tales," Lk 24:11; the account ends on the note of fear, Mk 16:8; but on the other hand the report could be checked in Jerusalem; and the anti-Christian controversialists there never contested the fact of the empty tomb.) The other experience is that of Jesus' repeated appearances (earliest evidence 1 Cor 15:3b-5, a traditional passage deriving from the first years of the primitive Church and originally composed in Aramaic, which according to Jewish anthropology can only refer to a bodily resurrection, and in any case cannot be an authentic "legitimating" formula) to selected witnesses. It is not primarily on the grounds of the empty tomb that these proclaim their faith, but on the grounds of a personal conviction derived from personal observation and later, in the Gospels, made credible for others also by the report of the discovery of the empty tomb, which was not and could not be disputed in Jerusalem.

(2) Like 1 Cor 15:3-5, the sermons of St. Peter, Acts 2:22-40; 3:12-16; 5:29-32; 10:34-43 and *passim* (evidence, incidentally, of the controversy between Christians and Jews over the Resurrection), the value of which has been rediscovered by critical exegesis, reveal the primitive community's paschal belief in the mighty deed of God that restored Jesus to life and made him manifest, whereby the apparitions of the risen Lord are attested as *objective* events. (Original outline of the paschal preaching: resurrection; spiritual proof; testimony of the disciples. Later outline: empty tomb; Christophany; ascension.) Another essential element in the attestation of these appearances is the demonstration that he who rose from the dead is identical with the Crucified (for example Lk 24; Jn 20); that a function of unique dignity, forseen by the Lord, vests in the Apostles and above all in Peter when they bear their witness, a function purposely fortified by the accounts of what the risen Christ said. In the New Testament, the resurrection of Jesus is always supported by the presumption (inseparable from the testimony) of an objective event, which is inadequately (even if not unjustly) represented as "resurrection into the awareness of the faithful." In view of the novelty of the resurrected body, it is understandable that some should assert that the resurrection of the flesh expected in Judaism served as an interpretament for the disciples' Easter experience; but this

experience consists not merely of an inward process of reflexion demanding interpretation, but is clearly grounded in objective events.

(3) In addition, the apostolic faith in the resurrection of Jesus and its preaching in catechesis and liturgy (especially at baptism) may be summed up as follows: Jesus' resurrection is the Father's supreme act of power—the decisive testimony of himself given by the Son; the inauguration of the last days and their salvation—the experience of salvation in the present; the full recognition of Jesus as the Messiah, the Ebed Yahweh, the Son of man, the second Adam and "inaugurator of life," the founder and model of new creation, the cosmic (Eph, Col) last Man (1 Cor 15:45), the Lord (Kyrios), present to his Church in his glorified state; hence the admonition to walk in newness of life to put on the new man, which to be sure can only be done by the grace of the risen Lord since it is ultimately his "Spirit" (see Rom 7:6; 8:9; 14:17 and *passim*) that renews the believer in the image of the second and heavenly Adam (1 Cor 15:47f.), indeed empowers him to have the risen Christ formed in him (cf. Rom 8:10; Eph 3:17; Gal 2:19).

(4) The resurrection of Jesus is acknowledged by all the creeds from the beginning. It must also form a central theme of theology today, being the consummation of God's saving activity for the world and mankind, in which he irrevocably communicates himself to the world in the Son whom the Resurrection has definitely identified, and thus with eschatological conclusiveness accepts the world to its own salvation, so that all that remains is to disclose and give effect to what has already happened in the Resurrection. The Resurrection is properly a mystery of faith because, being the consummation of Christ, it can be adequately understood only in reference to the absolute mystery of the Incarnation. Theologically, therefore, the resurrection of Christ is not one instance of resurrection in general, as though the latter were a thing already intelligible to us of itself; rather it is a unique event flowing from Christ's nature and death that first provides the foundation for the resurrection of those whom he has redeemed.

(5) From the Christological point of view the Resurrection means that Christ in his whole reality, and therefore also in his body, has risen to the glorified perfection and immortality (by contrast with raising a dead man to life) that is due to him by virtue of his passion and death, since these bring forth this concrete consummation by a intrinsic necessity of their nature. The death and resurrection of Jesus are a single process, whose phases are intrinsically and indissolubly connected (see Lk 24:26, 46; Rom 4:25; 6:4f.): the definitive being of every human being is something he dies into from within, so that this conclusiveness is the ripened fruit of an existence lived freely in time,

and not merely a temporally succeeding period which may be marked by something totally heterogeneous from what has gone before. At the same time, however, this completion is the gift of God, for to die is to place oneself in every respect at the disposition of the divine disposer. Jesus' resurrection must therefore be the perfected and perfecting end of his own personal and particular death and each element of the one process must condition and interpret the other. When Scripture and Tradition therefore regard the Resurrection as the Father's real acceptance of the sacrifice of Jesus' death and part of the nature of that sacrifice, this is not mythology but a statement of fact.

(6) Because Jesus' bodily humanity is a permanent part of one world which has one dynamism the resurrection of Christ is soteriologically and objectively the commencement of the ontologically coherent event which is the glorification of the world; in this commencement the final consummation of the world has been decided in principle and has already begun. The resurrection of Christ is also more than his private destiny because it creates Heaven and is not (together with the Ascension, which basically is an element of the Resurrection) simply an entrance into a pre-existent heaven; because here too history and saving history underlie natural history and do not simply run their course within the framework of a fixed natural order that remains unaffected by them. On the other hand these considerations must also show that because the risen Christ has been released from individuating corporeality, it is of a mere earthly kind precisely as the risen one—by his "going," then—that he has truly become he who is close to the world, and, therefore, his return is only the disclosure of this intimate and unlimited relationship of Christ with the world which the Resurrection has established....

ST. JOHN PERSE

The Anabasis
Section X

Select a wide hat with the brim seduced. The eye withdraws by a century into the provinces of the soul. Through the gate of living chalk we see the things of the plain: living things,

> excellent things!

> sacrifice of colts on the tombs of children, purification of widows among the roses and consignments of green birds in the courtyards to do honour to the old men;
> many things on the earth to hear and to see, living things among us!

celebrations of open air festivals for the name-day of great trees and public rites in honour of a pool; consecration of black stones perfectly round, water-dowsing in dead places, dedication of cloths held up on poles, at the gates of the passes, and loud acclamations under the walls for the mutilation of adults in the sun, for the publication of the bride-sheets!

many other things too at the level of our eyes: dressing the sores of animals in the suburbs, stirring of the crowds before sheep-shearers, well-sinkers and horse-gelders; speculations in the breath of harvests and turning of hay on the roofs, on the prongs of forks; building of enclosures of rose red terra cotta, of terraces for meat-drying, of galleries for priests, of quarters for captains; the vast court of the horse-doctor; the fatigue parties for upkeep of muleways, of zig-zag roads through the gorges; foundation of hospices in vacant places; the invoicing at arrival of caravans, and disbanding of escorts in the quarter of moneychangers; budding popularities under the penthouse, in front of the frying vats; protestation of bills of credit; destruction of albino animals, of white worms in the soil; fires of bramble and thorn in places defiled by death, the making of a fine bread of barley and sesame; or else of spelt; and the firesmoke of mankind everywhere...

ha! all conditions of men in their ways and manners; eaters of insects, of water fruits; those who bear poultices, those who bear riches; the husbandman, and the young noble horsed; the healer with needles, and the salter; the toll-gatherer, the smith; vendors of sugar, of cinnamon, of white metal drinking cups and of lanthorns; he who fashions a leather tunic, wooden shoes and olive-shaped buttons; he who dresses a field; and the man of no trade: the man with the falcon, the man with the flute, the man with bees; he who has his delight in the pitch of his voice, he who makes it his business to contemplate a green stone; he who burns for his pleasure a thornfire on his roof; he who makes on the ground his bed of sweet-smelling leaves, lies down there and rests; he who thinks out designs of green pottery for fountains; and he who has travelled far and dreams of departing again; he who has dwelt in a country of great rains; the dicer, the knucklebone player, the juggler; or he who has spread on the ground his reckoning tablets; he who has his opinions on the use of a gourd; he who drags a dead eagle like a faggot on his tracks (and the plumage is given, not sold, for fletching); he who gathers pollen in a wooden jar (and my delight, says he, is in this yellow colour); he who eats fritters, the maggots of the palmtree, or raspberries; he who fancies the flavour of tarragon; he who dreams of green pepper, or else he who chews fossil gum, who lifts a conch to his ear, or he who sniffs the odour of genius in the freshly cracked stone; he who thinks of the flesh of women, the lustful; he who sees his soul reflected in a blade; the man learned in sciences, in onomastic; the man well thought of in councils, he who names fountains, he who makes a public gift of seats in the shady places, of dyed wool for the wise men; and has great bronze jars, for thirst, planted at the crossways; better still, he who does nothing, such a one and such in his manners, and so many others still! those who collect quails in the wrinkled land, those who hunt among the furze for green-speckled eggs, those who dismount to pick things up, agates, a pale blue stone which they cut and fashion at the gates of the suburbs (into cases, tobacco-boxes, brooches, or into balls to be rolled between the hands of the paralysed); those who whistling paint boxes in the open air, the man with the ivory staff, the man with the rattan chair, the hermit with hands like a girl's and the disbanded warrior who has planted his spear at the threshold to tie up a monkey ... ha! all sorts of men in their ways and fashions, and of a sudden! behold in his evening robes and summarily settling in turn all questions of precedence, the Story-Teller who stations himself at the foot of the turpentine tree ...

O genealogist upon the market-place! how many chronicles of families and connexions?—and may the dead seize the quick, as is said in the tables of the law, if I have not seen each thing in its own shadow and the virtue of its age: the stores of books and annals, the astronomer's storehouses and the beauty of a place of sepulture, of very old temples under the palmtrees, frequented by a mule and three white hens—and beyond my eye's circuit, many a secret doing on the routes: striking of camps upon tidings which I know not, effronteries of the hill tribes, and passage of rivers on skin-jars; horsemen bearing letters of alliance, the ambush in the vineyard, forays of robbers in the depths of gorges and manoeuvres over field to ravish a woman, bargain-driving and plots, coupling of beasts in the forests before the eyes of children, convalescence of prophets in byres, the silent talk of two men under a tree ...

but over and above the actions of men on the earth, many omens on the way, many seeds on the way, and under unleavened fine weather, in one great breath of the earth, the whole feather of harvest! ..

until the hour of evening when the female star, pure and pledged in the sky heights ...

Plough-land of dream! Who talks of building?—I have seen the earth parcelled out in vast spaces and my thought is not heedless of the navigator.

ABOUT THE
WRITERS

The French theologian and philosopher, **PETER ABÉLARD,** was born in Pallet, France, in 1079. Because of his precocious brilliance and the independence and freshness of his views, he was often in conflict with eclesiastical authorities. He became a popular teacher at Paris, but for some years after his tragic love affair with **HELOÏSE,** the niece of a high church official, he retired to a monastery. The influence of his writings and especially his lectures was enormous. He died at St.-Marcel in 1142.

ADAM DE ST.-VICTOR was born in France, probably in Brittany, in the twelfth century. He was educated in Paris, and in 1130 became a monk in the abbey of St. Victor. A poet and writer of hymns, some of his moving Latin sequence hymns are remembered today. He is believed to have died sometime between 1177 and 1192.

ANGELUS SILESIUS was the pseudonym of the poet-priest Johannes Scheffler, who was born in Breslau, Silesia, in 1624. The son of a Polish Lutheran nobleman, he became a Roman Catholic in 1652 and, in 1661, became a priest. Many of his hymns are still sung, but he is more importantly remembered as a mystical poet of great depth, much influenced by Jakob Böhme. He died in Breslau in 1677.

The French symbolist poet, **CHARLES BAUDELAIRE,** was born in Paris on April 9, 1821. Admired for his poetry, essays, and art criticism, he also made a reputation for himself as a dandified man-about-town leading a self-indulgent and extravagant life. He devoted years to translating Edgar Allan Poe into French and wrote his own sensuous poems about the lack of spiritual values in the bourgeois civilization whose mores he flouted. His major work, *The Flowers of Evil,* ended in a court conviction for immorality. He died in 1867 in poverty and poor health.

SAMUEL BECKETT was born in Ireland on April 13, 1906. As a playwright of theater of the absurd, he has created a theatrical world of characters locked in meaningless, agonizing lives, attempting to find or save themselves. It is Beckett's belief that communication between humans is ultimately impossible, but silence is not reconcilable with human existence. He received the Nobel Prize for Literature in 1969.

SAINT BERNARD, founder and abbot of Clairvaux, was born in France in 1090. His rule inaugurated the spirit of medieval Christianity with its sentimental mysticism and politically active churchmen. He was one of the first proponents of the cult of the Virgin. A confidant of five popes and longtime opponent of Abélard, Bernard influenced political, literary, and religious life. He died in 1153.

WILLIAM BLAKE, born in London on November 28, 1757, and with no formal education, became a leading illustrator and engraver. His poetry, rising from personal visions and dreams, conjures up a world best understood in terms of magic and allegory. His political enthusiasms as a young man paralleled those of the American and French revolutionaries. In both poetry and politics, Blake strove for expression of human freedom and wholeness in contrast to the fragmenting and enslaving effects he saw in much of Western culture. In the last years of his life he espoused a private and unorthodox Christian faith, having given up hope for regenerating society. He died in 1827.

LOUISE BOGAN was born in Maine on August 11, 1897. Considered one of the finest women poets of the twentieth century, she was poetry editor at *The New Yorker* for forty-one years. She contributed to *The New Republic, The Nation, The Atlantic Monthly,* and other influential journals. Her poems, reminiscent of the seventeenth-century metaphysical poets and yet modern, explore the inevitability of physical decay. She died in 1970.

DIETRICH BONHOEFFER was born in Germany on February 4, 1906, and grew up in a suburb of Berlin. He was educated at Tübingen and, as a Protestant clergyman, heroically resisted Nazism by underground church work in the 1930s. He was captured and executed by the Nazis in 1945. Radiating happiness and joy even in prison, Bonhoeffer urged Christians to preserve the religious fellowship that could withstand a hostile world.

Born on August 24, 1902, in France, FERNAND BRAUDEL has become a leading historian and scholar of the Mediterranean world in the age of Philip II of Spain. A humanistic social scientist and a painstaking researcher, Braudel evokes the cultural wholeness of a region and an era, its geography, politics, economics, and social and intellectual life.

JOSEPH BRODSKY was born on May 24, 1940, in Leningrad. Charged with writing "gibberish" by the Soviet government, he spent eighteen months at hard labor. He was exiled and left Russia in 1972, and now lives in the United States. In spite of the political furor that sprang up around his writing, Brodsky is not so much a political poet as a lyricist of traditional human themes.

HELDER CAMARA was born in Brazil on February 7, 1909. He became a priest in 1931, was elevated to the Roman Catholic episcopate in 1952, and became archbishop of Recife in 1964. Camara has been an outspoken defender of the poor and an advocate of nonviolent revolution. In 1970 he received the Martin Luther King Memorial Award and the John XXIII Memorial Award from Pax Christi. Camara's books have been translated into a dozen languages.

CARLO CARRETTO was born in Italy in 1910. He received a degree in philosophy from the University of Turin. He lived in exile in Sardinia during the Fascist years. From 1946 to 1952 he was National President of Catholic Youth in Italy. At forty-four he heard a voice calling him to go to the desert to pray. Later he joined the Little Brothers of Charles de Foucauld in North Africa. His letters have gone through twenty-four editions and have been translated into several languages.

C.P. CAVAFY was born of Greek parents in Alexandria, Egypt, on April 17, 1863. He worked in a government office in Alexandria, wrote poetry on the side, but published little of it in his lifetime. Much of his work, at times cynical, explores the interaction of the past, including the ancient past, and the immediate present. He died in 1933.

Born in Antioch, Syria, around 347, JOHN CHRYSOSTOM studied law and theology before he took up the life of a hermit monk. He later became a priest and a popular preacher. His often humorous sermons opposing the abuse of wealth were popular in his congregations at Antioch and Constantinople. He died in 407, and was later proclaimed a Father of the Church.

Known as the "peasant poet," JOHN CLARE was the son of a farm worker and supported himself and his family by farming. He was born in England on July 13, 1793, and had little formal schooling. His farm poems are about traditional pastoral themes. From 1841 to his death in 1864, he suffered from delusions, and was institutionalized. His poems of madness are visionary and surreal somewhat like those of William Blake.

The American poet, GREGORY CORSO, was born in Greenwich Village in 1930. After an adventurous youth, with some time in jail, he became an early member of the Beat movement in the 1950s. He has been closely associated with Allen Ginsberg and Jack Kerouac. His poetry recalls the exuberance of Whitman's, but has a freshness and vision of its own.

RICHARD CRASHAW was born around 1613 in London, the son of a Puritan poet and clergyman. He was educated at Cambridge. During the English Civil War, he converted to Roman Catholicism and later served as secretary to a cardinal in Rome. He eventually became a canon at Loreto. The baroque style and metaphysical themes of his poetry establish Crashaw as a major religious writer of the seventeenth century. He died in 1649.

EMILY DICKINSON was born in Amherst, Massachusetts, on December 10, 1830. She was educated at Amherst Academy and Mount Holyoke. She lived virtually her entire life in her parents' home where she quietly wrote poems of sharp mystical visions. Her verse is noted for its terse meditative quality, revealing a deeply passionate and lively spiritual life. She was largely unpublished during her life and died in 1886.

Born to Roman Catholic parents in London in 1572, JOHN DONNE renounced Roman Catholicism to join the Anglican Church in the 1590s. He was ordained to the Anglican priesthood in 1615, and served as dean of St. Paul's Cathedral. Donne had a widespread reputation as an inspiring preacher. Out of numerous sermons and meditations, he produced a sizable body of metaphysical poetry concerned with the soul's striving to render human actions worthy of eternal merit. He died in 1631.

Born on May 25, 1803, in Boston, Massachusetts, RALPH WALDO EMERSON was descended from a long line of New England clergymen. Educated at Harvard, he held a Unitarian pastorship in Boston which he resigned because of religious doubts on several levels. He became the major spokesman for transcendental philosophy through his prolific writing and lecturing throughout most of the nineteenth century. Embodying the aspiration of his age and culture, Emerson came to symbolize for many the democratic faith and exuberance of America. He died in 1882.

Born to a Congregational minister and his wife in Lee, New Hampshire, on December 20, 1881, ABBIE HUSTON EVANS taught Edna St.

Vincent Millay as a Sunday School pupil. A social activist as well as poet and critic, Evans did social work in a Colorado mining town after World War I, and taught at the Settlement Music School in Philadelphia. She was a member of the Americans for Democratic Action and the American Civil Liberties Union. A contributor to *The Nation* and *The New Yorker*, she has won numerous literary awards and honors.

FÉNELON, archbishop of Cambrai, France, was born in 1651 of one of France's most ancient noble families. His full name was François Salignac de la Mothe. His father was Pons, comte de Fénelon. His writings on the education of young girls prefigured Rousseau and helped to promote the dignity of women. A political and social critic, Fénelon advocated constitutional monarchy at a time when the idea was considered radical, and encouraged the development of industry. He died in 1715.

Born in France in 1858, CHARLES DE FOUCAULD led the dissolute and worldly life of a French soldier. In his explorations of the Sahara, he was so impressed by the desert life and personal holiness of the Moslems, he returned to lead a contemplative life of prayer and asceticism. He was murdered by a band of marauders in 1916. The publication of his personal papers and meditations led to the formation within the Roman Catholic Church of the Little Brothers and Sisters of Jesus in the 1930's.

Born into a prosperous merchant family of Umbria, Italy, around 1181, FRANCIS OF ASSISI rejected his worldly life and hedonistic aspirations to embrace a life of poverty and ascetism. His disciples of little brothers and sisters were eventually accepted into the institutional church, their first and foremost rule being simply to follow Jesus. Francis died in 1226.

Born of American parents in Paris on September 6, 1900, JULIAN GREEN converted to Roman Catholicism at sixteen, and served at Verdun in

World War I. His novels, plays, and journals discuss the problems of violence and death and his own religious crises. After a period of religious doubt, he reconverted to Catholicism. During World War II he served in the American army and held a post with the Office of War Information, speaking every day by radio to the French. In 1972 Green became the first foreign member appointed to the Académie Francaise.

GUSTAVO GUTIERREZ was born in Lima, Peru. He is professor of pastoral theology at the Catholic University of Lima. He is identified with the development of liberation theology in Latin America, and his best known work is *A Theology of Liberation* (1973).

GEORGE HERBERT was born into a noble family in Wales on April 3, 1593. His mother was a friend of John Donne. Herbert studied at Cambridge where he became Public Orator. In 1630, he was ordained an Anglican priest and spent the remainder of his life as a rural parson. His metaphysical poems rise from his religious meditations and sermons, and develop spiritual truths by means of simple analogies drawn from his own daily experience. He died in 1633.

Born in Cooma, Australia, on July 21, 1907, A.D. HOPE has become that nation's foremost poet. His own religious consciousness was originally formed in his clergyman father's home. Although he has claimed not to have "very fixed convictions on anything," his iconoclastic, satyrical verse criticizes the shallowness of mechanical life, while his love lyrics attest to the need for human decency and devotion. Hope has taught widely in Australian colleges and universities.

GERARD MANLEY HOPKINS was born in July 28, 1844, at Stratford, Essex. He converted to Roman Catholicism in 1866 while studying at Oxford. Two years later he entered the Society of Jesus and spent his life as a Jesuit priest, working in parishes and teaching the classics. His intensely spiritual poetry treats traditional Catholic themes in the private, complex poetic style he developed over years of reflection and study. He died of typhoid fever in Dublin in 1889.

Born in Tennessee on May 6, 1914, RANDALL JARRELL attended Vanderbilt University. A well-respected poet and critic, he received many professorships and awards. Known in his earlier career for his war poetry, he presented vivid glimpses of the impersonal forces that push man into the irrational conditions of being soldier and victim. He died in 1965.

JOAN OF ARC, the Orléans farm girl who rallied the French armies during the Hundred Years War with England, was inspired by voices she attributed to the saints. Her voices told her that the English could be defeated, France would recover, and Charles VII should be crowned king. She was captured by the Burgundians, sold to the English, and tried and burned at the stake as a heretic in 1431. The church canonized her in 1920.

The Spanish poet, JOHN OF THE CROSS, was born on June 24, 1542. He studied with the Jesuits and became a Carmelite friar. Later he was ordained a priest and traveled widely to found Carmelite monasteries. His reputation as a poet rests on three mystical poems that detail the soul's torturous journey to God. He died in 1591 and was canonized in 1726. In 1926 he was made a doctor of the Roman Catholic Church.

DAVID JONES was born in England on November 1, 1895, to an English artist and a Welsh printer. His own esteemed career as a watercolorist has won him international acclaim. He converted to Roman Catholicism in 1921, profoundly impressed by the sacramental implications of the Incarnation. His own work reflects this concern, with the intermingling of matter and spirit. He has written at length about the meaning of art, religion, and tradition.

A woman of keen intellect and holiness, JULIAN OF NORWICH, an anchoress, was born in England in 1342. She had great fame as a spiritual counselor. Her revelations of divine love were inspired by visions that render her one of the leading English mystics of the late Middle Ages. Her written account of her mystical experiences—*The*

Sixteen Revelations of Divine Love—is generally thought to be the first book written in English by a woman. She died sometime after 1413.

RUDYARD KIPLING was born in Bombay, India, on December 30, 1865. He lived in England, India, and in the United States (Vermont) where he wrote travel accounts and children's books. The major themes in his writings concern the British Empire at the turn of the century. His poetry, short stories, and journalistic reporting of Britain's imperial glory made him one of the most widely read and admired writers of his day. In 1907 Kipling became the first Englishman to receive the Nobel Prize for Literature. He died in 1936.

Born in Germany, **VERA LACHMANN** was professor of classics at Brooklyn College and is now adjunct professor of classics at Hunter College and New York University. She has published two collections of poetry; a third is soon to appear.

WALTER SAVAGE LANDOR was born in Warwick, England, in 1775. Educated at Rugby and Oxford, he spent many years in Italy, where he took an active interest in her struggle for freedom from Austria's dominance. In his last years, in Florence, he became an intimate friend of the Brownings. His poetry is distinguished by a fine temper and ardor moulded by classical restraint. Dickens genially caricatured him as Lawrence Boythorn in *Bleak House.* He died in 1864.

ROBERT LOWELL was born in Boston on March 1, 1917, into a famous New England clan that included James Russell Lowell and Amy Lowell. He converted to Roman Catholicism in 1940. His early poetry is characterized by heavy religious themes and a strong Calvinist conscience. A conscientious objector in World War II because of the mass air raids upon civilian populations, Lowell served a five-month prison term. He won a Pulitzer Prize in 1947. His later poems, while less traditionally religious than his early work, continue to meditate upon the themes of chaos, turmoil, and the deterioration of man and his world.

Born in 1492, a sister of Francis I of France, **MARGUERITE D' ANGOULÊME** became duchess of Alençon by her first marriage and queen of Navarre by her second. She was grandmother of Henry IV. She wrote numerous poems, plays, and stories, many of them reflecting her sincere religious faith. *Autant en Emporte le Vent* was published two years before her death in 1549.

THOMAS MERTON was the son of an American mother and a New Zealand-born father, both artists living in France. Born in 1915, he was educated in France, England, and New York. He became a Catholic in 1938 while a student at Columbia. In 1941 he entered the Trappist monastery in Kentucky where he combined the contemplative life of a hermit with a social awareness that spoke out eloquently on war, race, and peace. He died accidentally in 1968 on a visit to Southeast Asia.

GABRIELA MISTRAL is the pseudonym of Lucila Godoy de Alcayaga, born in Chile in 1889. Her poems first won acclaim in 1915. In 1945 she received the Nobel Prize for Literature. Her lyrical poems are considered some of the finest in Spanish literature. She died in 1957.

A former literary editor of *Harper' Bazaar* and an accomplished poet, **ALICE MORRIS** is perhaps best known on the American literary scene as a discoverer and mentor of young and new writers. In 1977 she received the Lucille Medwick Memorial Award (given by the Poetry Society of America) for distinguished service to the literary community and for her "commitment to serve the young, the unrecognized, and the unpopular."

Acclaimed by many to be the greatest poet writing in Spanish in the mid-century, **PABLO NERUDA**'s works have influenced opinion throughout Latin America. Born on July 12, 1904, in Chile, Neruda spent much of his life actively engaged in politics as a member of the communist party. He enjoyed a brilliant diplomatic career as a Chilean consul and later ambassador to France. He eschewed being labeled political even though his life and poetry expressed a strong social consciousness. He was a member of the World Peace Council and won the Nobel Prize for Literature in 1971. He died in 1973.

Born in Nijkerk, the Netherlands, on January 24, 1932, **HENRI NOUWEN** is a Roman Catholic priest and a professor of pastoral theology at Yale Divinity School. Nouwen is the author of a number of reflective theological studies, blending a sure academic grasp of his subjects with a sensitive awareness of their application to the human condition.

WILFRED OWEN was born in Oswestry, England, on March 18, 1893. His family were educated, middle-class people of limited means. Although he was matriculated at the University of London in 1911, family finances were not sufficient for him to begin classes. Instead, he took a job as lay assistant to the vicar of Dunsden, in Oxfordshire, with some thought of being tutored by the vicar in studies that might lead him into the church. However, his time at Dunsden, although providing him with an awakening about the facts of life among the poor, led him away from any notion of entering religion. He went to France in 1914 and worked as an English tutor at Bordeaux. He returned to England in 1915 to join the British army. He was wounded in battle, receiving the Military Cross for Gallantry. He was sent back to the front after he recovered and was killed in action in 1918. His poetry, much of which grew from his war experiences, is considered by many critics to be the best of England's World War I poetry. He did not glorify war or battle but saw it in all its horror.

CHARLES PEGUY was born in Orléans, France, on January 7, 1873. A student of philosophy and socialism, he opened the Librairie Socialiste in Paris. His *Fortnightly Notebook,* founded in 1900, influenced French intellectual life for fifteen years. He grew disillusioned with socialism and reconverted to Catholicism before World War I. He died in action at the Battle of the Marne.

Born in Switzerland on August 9, 1896, **JEAN PIAGET** has influenced the lives of children and parents everywhere through his philosophical and psychological studies of childhood education. Using an interdisciplinary approach, Piaget spent forty years at the University of Geneva discovering the processes by which the young mind sorts out experiences and information about the world and gives some order to it. Highly acclaimed and respected for his work, Piaget died in 1980.

Born in South Africa on September 13, 1912, **f.t. prince** was educated at Oxford and Princeton and has taught in Africa and England. His fastidiousness about publishing only his best verse has given the literary world but a small sampling of his work. Prince's poems are noted for their compassionate portrayals of those who, whether in love or war, affirm the melancholy loneliness of the Son of Man.

karl rahner was born in March 5, 1904, in Germany. He entered the Society of Jesus in 1922 and received a doctorate in philosophy from the University of Innsbruck. As one of the leading Thomist scholars in the Roman Catholic Church, Rahner has attempted to create a man-centered theology to keep pace with the anthropocentrism in other modern disciplines. He was a theological expert at the Second Vatican Council.

paul ricoeur was born in France on February 27, 1913, the son of a university professor. He studied philosophy and taught at the universities of Paris and Strasbourg. A phenomenologist, Ricoeur has been praised as one of the foremost philosophers within the ambience of the Christian faith. He has received awards, honors, and visiting professorships in Europe, Canada, and America.

rainer maria rilke was born in Prague on December 4, 1875. He attended the universities of Prague, Munich, and Berlin. A highly refined and delicate sensitivity rendered him almost unfit for normal human commitments. His only passions were art and literature. He traveled extensively and was able to preserve the solitude his poetry demanded with the help of wealthy patrons. Many of his poems reflect the solitary, mystical meditations that produced them. He died in 1926.

ST. JOHN PERSE is the pseudonym of Alexis Léger, born in the French West Indies on May 31, 1889. A lawyer, he served in the French Foreign Office, distinguished himself as a professional diplomat, and wrote his poetry secretly in his spare time. He was removed from his diplomatic post in 1940 for his stand against the appeasement of Germany. He fled, and many of his manuscripts were destroyed by the Nazis. His poetry, written as a type of secret life, treats of solitude and exile and the belief that human aspirations have eternal significance. He was awarded the Nobel Prize for Literature in 1960.

E.F. SCHUMACHER, a distinguished Rhodes Scholar in economics, was an advisor to the British Control Commission in postwar Germany. He was head of planning at the British Coal Board from 1951 to 1971. A student of Gandhi, an advocate of nonviolence, and a spokesman for the Third World, Schumacher might aptly be called the ecological economist for the save-the-earth movement.

ROBERT SOUTHWELL was born in 1561 in England. He became a Jesuit priest and a missionary to his native England during Elizabeth I's anti-Catholic campaigns. He ministered underground until he was captured and imprisoned in the Tower. He was tortured for not revealing the names and whereabouts of his fellow priests. Southwell was executed in 1595. All his poetry was published posthumously.

Born in Paris on January 31, 1893, FREYA STARK was educated at the University of London and held government service jobs in Britain including a position with the Ministry of Information during World War I. Her far-flung travels to the Middle East, India, and the United States have been the sources for numerous inspirational books characterized by her sympathetic insights into nature and humanity. She has received awards from various geographical societies.

STENDHAL, whose real name was Marie Henri Beyle, was born in Grenoble, France, in 1783. The famous diarist, biographer, and novelist began his career as a French consular official in Italy. Twentieth-century readers have been especially attracted to his novels— notably *Le Rouge et le Noir* (1831) and *La Chartreuse de Parme* (1839)—because of their curiously contemporary tone, combining a spare and finely honed prose style with themes of romantic disenchantment. He died in 1842.

Born to a noble family in Spain in 1515, TERESA OF AVILA entered a convent in 1531. Her life was plagued with illness and much physical suffering. Her religious ecstasies and visions, which she recorded in poetry and autobiographical writings, establish her as one of the great mystics of the church. She traveled throughout Spain to found convents and monasteries of Discalced Carmelites. She died in 1582 and was canonized in 1622.

HENRY VAUGHAN was born in Wales on April 17, 1622. He studied at Oxford and practiced law briefly. Influenced by George Herbert, Vaughan's mystical, religious verse is typical of the metaphysical style of the seventeenth century. His poems deal with the soul's experience of God through the natural events of daily human life. He died in 1695.

Born of Jewish parents in Paris in 1909, SIMONE WEIL's brilliant career as a student of philosophy and languages found her teaching philosophy at twenty-two. She voluntarily accepted a life of deprivation, often performing low-paying farm and factory jobs. She was strongly attracted to Christianity, increasingly so as she neared the end of her short life, but she was never baptized nor was she received into the church. Because of her chronic ill health she was sent to England during the hardships of the German occupation of France. However, she steadfastly refused, although ill, to eat beyond the rations Free French troops received. She died in England in 1943.

GLENWAY WESCOTT was born in Wisconsin on April 11, 1901. As a young man he decided upon a career as a fulltime writer. His many poems, novels, stories, and essays develop the theme of the American odyssey, the search for a spiritual home.

RICHARD WILBUR was born in New York City on March 1, 1921, and was educated at Amherst and Harvard. He has achieved recognition for his scholarly work on Edgar Allan Poe as well as for his own carefully wrought poems. He won both the Pulitzer Prize for Poetry and the National Book Award in 1957. In 1961 Wilbur was the State Department's cultural representative to Russia in its cultural exchange program. He has taught at Harvard, Wellesley, and Wesleyan.

WILLIAM BUTLER YEATS, Irish poet, dramatist, and critic, was born near Dublin on June 13, 1865 into a Protestant family. He was president of the Irish National Theater Society and director of the Abbey Theater and founded Irish literary societies in London and Dublin. He was in the Irish Senate and received in 1923 the Nobel Prize for Literature. His poetry, complex, visionary, and often difficult, derives from an elaborate cosmology that includes Irish folklore, Christian themes, politics, the occult, and national aspirations for Ireland. He died in 1939.